The Charity Business

THE CHARITY
BUSINESS

The New Philanthropists

TOM LLOYD

JOHN MURRAY

© Tom Lloyd 1993

First published in 1993
by John Murray (Publishers) Ltd.,
50 Albemarle Street, London W1X 4BD

The moral right of the author has been asserted

A catalogue record for this book is available from the British Library

ISBN 0-7195-5046-7

Typeset in 11/13pt Meridien by Selwood Systems, Midsomer Norton
Printed in Great Britain by Cambridge University Press, Cambridge

*This book is dedicated to
the memory of a strong and generous spirit,
Jack Bradshaw.*

Contents

Acknowledgements

I owe a great debt of gratitude to many people for the help they gave me in writing this book. I came into the charity sector ignorant, and they did their best to enlighten me. That I remain ignorant is no fault of theirs. Some will, no doubt, wish to distance themselves from the opinions they have helped to modify and change, so I must emphasise that, except where directly attributable to named individuals, the views expressed in the pages that follow are mine, and mine alone.

I am particularly grateful to Jane Tewson, Chris Chestnutt, Seymour Fortescue, Lord Laing of Dunphail, Stephen O'Brien, Robin Guthrie, Tim Gauvain, Michael Norton, Olga Maitland, Dr Bridget Ogilvie, Michael Brophy and Lord Blakenham. I am also grateful for the help, advice and encouragement of John Murray, Caroline Knox and Kate Chenevix Trench at my publishers John Murray, to my agent Anne Dewe and to my wife and research assistant, Sheila (née Bradshaw).

I am also grateful to the charity 'industry' itself for the contribution it has made to the development of my own ideas about management and particularly to my understanding of the key role played by an organization's ethos. As a small gesture of my gratitude, both to the charity industry and to the 'clients' it does so much to assist, I have undertaken to give half of any royalties I earn from this book, over and above my advance, to a charity of my choice.

Introduction

The will to give, in its numerous manifestations, is very powerful. It has played a part, and seldom a minor one, in all the world's great religious and political movements and it shows no sign of losing its potency. In the past, it has helped turn societies upside down and it remains, today, one of the most important engines of cultural, political and economic development.

But the nature of its contribution is changing. In one way it is returning to its origins – to the time when charity was all the welfare there was. In another, it is emerging as a sophisticated adjunct of capitalism, producing a special kind of product derived from the will to give.

This book is about the future of charity; about how the twin veils of secrecy and neglect that have surrounded it are being pulled away; about how the balance of its welfare partnership with government is being transformed; about the metamorphosis of charities themselves, about how charity is ceasing to be private and personal – the preserve, if not the prerogative, of the rich – and is becoming an activity of the people, of business and, too often, of fraudsters.

Companies and ordinary people of modest means are the new stars in the charity firmament. Together, they are changing the nature of giving, and making what was previously solemn and reserved, vibrant and commercial. People are finding charity is fun and companies are discovering that charity is profitable.

As a result, giving is becoming less dignified, less self-conscious and less exclusive. In its modern settings and regalia, it has bor-

1

rowed from the theatre and showmanship, and in its collective energy, and the appetites of givers for mass involvement and communal 'happenings', it echoes the tradition of the community festival. Fund-raisers have discovered charity's power to transfigure the prosaic and turn the humdrum into the magical. A wholly new kind of experience – the doing of good together – has been invented.

I shall argue that companies are going to be transformed, in charity's new age, from soulless machines, driven by an insatiable appetite for profit, into responsible and open-handed organizations, constantly on the look out for opportunities to demonstrate their 'corporate citizenship'.

That will be how it appears, at any rate. In reality though, companies will still be pursuing profit, only in a more enlightened way. They will be buying 'reputational assets' from the charity sector. Philanthropy and the profit motive will merge and become indistinguishable from each other.

We are in an 'age of transition', as John Stuart Mill felt himself to be when he lost faith in the utilitarianism of his father and Jeremy Bentham, and laid down in *Principles of Political Economy*, the intellectual foundations of the modern welfare state. Mill put his finger on the central dilemma of the idea of a welfare state based on charity:

> Though individuals should, in general, be left to do for them-
> selves whatever it can reasonably be expected that they should
> be capable of doing, yet when they are at any rate not to be
> left to themselves, but to be helped by other people, the ques-
> tion arises whether it is better that they should receive this
> help exclusively from individuals, and therefore uncertainly
> and casually, or by systematic arrangements, in which society
> acts through its organ, the state.
>
> *Principles of Political Economy*, book V, ch. X1, # 13.

In Mill's view, the role of the state in the redistribution of wealth is a negative one. It has to impose taxes, so that it can provide guarantees against destitution. It addresses the twin problems of the uncertainty and casual nature of giving. In a world where national economic cycles are interlinked, it will often be the case that the demands on charity will be highest when the supply (the propensity to give) is lowest. According to Mill, the state is responsible for ironing out these swings between feast and famine.

In the meantime, givers should distribute their bounty as they see fit. Their role is positive. Unlike the state, which is not qualified, in Mill's view, to judge the degree of need, the charitable have the right to be selective.

But Mill's division of labour between the state and charity assumed a kind of compact, a mutual recognition, of where the former's responsibilities ended and the latter's began. That compact no longer exists, and perhaps it never did. The state is withdrawing from some areas of welfare provision, and encouraging the non-profit sector to fill the gap, but there are no clear guidelines. The waters into which charities are being asked to sail are uncharted. There is no telling where the voyage will end and what hazards lie in wait.

The reason for the loss of consensus about who should do what for whom is clear enough. It has become all too apparent to government, politicians, citizens, companies and charities that the Beveridge apportionment of welfare responsibilities between the state and the voluntary sector after World War II was an heroically splendid mistake.

Ken Young, Professor of Politics at London University argues in *Meeting the Needs of Strangers*, that the Beveridge compact has been broken on three anvils: the loss of society's homogeneity, an explosion in the number and variety of special needs and claims, and an extension of the notion of citizenship 'entitlements', or 'social rights' way beyond the basic Beveridge provisions.

Like communism, with which it has ideological kinship, the idea of an all-caring, omni-competent state has failed the test of time. The problem of welfare, because it is always changing, cannot be so simply resolved. As Professor Young has pointed out, Beveridge himself, in his report on *Voluntary Action*, recognized the need for a voluntary sector 'to do things which the State should not do . . . to do things the State is most unlikely to do . . . to pioneer ahead of the State and make experiments'.

It is this recognition that the balance of responsibilities proposed by Beveridge was wrong, and the growing awareness that no balance will be right for long – that the problem of welfare is intrinsically insoluble – which is changing the role of the voluntary sector, from junior partner to central character. Giving, and the proto-industry that promotes and deploys its proceeds, have moved centre stage. From now on it will be the voluntary sector, not government, that will shape, mould and give material substance to how we feel about meeting the needs of strangers.

But more important than this in the long run, is the leading role circumstances have assigned to companies in the charity revolution. By this I mean far more than the relatively recent emergence of companies as important donors to the voluntary sector. I shall argue that the corporate ethos, with its insatiable hunger for growth and profit, is engaged in what amounts to the wholesale takeover of the voluntary sector.

It's not a hostile takeover, although it generates hostility from time to time, and neither is it deliberate. There is no conscious, acquisitive plan on the part of companies to take on these new responsibilities. It is just that the voluntary sector, as it begins to replace the state as society's primary redistributive mechanism, has become aware of its need for new organizational and managerial paradigms, and is finding them in modern capitalism.

By a process of osmosis charities are becoming – in the way they operate, in the kind of people they hire to run them, in the emphasis they are increasingly placing on efficiency, cost control, marketing and 'good management' – more like those greedy, self-interested and brutal organizations that the charity 'old guard' (from their vantage point on the moral high ground) despised and adamantly refused to have anything to do with.

As we shall see, frictions are being generated by this coming together of the company ethos and the charity ethos, but the momentum is unstoppable. There is no going back to the time when companies were companies and charities were charities, and never the twain shall meet. Circumstances have conspired to bring them together, and their futures are now inextricably linked.

Perhaps takeover is the wrong metaphor. It is more like a merger. Companies are being changed just as much by this process of convergence. As they impart to charities their management skills and marketing imagination, they are being subtly changed by the world view of their pupils. It may be, that in the early years of the 21st century, when the 'ethos convergence' has been fully consolidated, it will be hard to distinguish the two species from one another. Maybe it will make more sense to acknowledge that, from the fusion of the charitable and corporate traditions, a hybrid species has emerged – the 'comparity' – that will eventually come to dominate the territories of both its progenitors.

Many of the seeds of such developments lie hidden in some of the issues, to do with finance and regulation, that confront the charity sector today. Money seems to be the most serious problem right now. The figures suggest that after strong growth during the mid-1980s – total voluntary income of the top 200 fund-raising charities rose from £950m in 1985/6 to not far short of £1.2bn in 1988/9 (at 1990 prices) – giving in Britain has been static or declining since, and the end of the 1980s economic boom brought an abrupt halt to the modest growth in corporate giving.

At the same time, the demands on the charities specializing in international causes soared, following an exceptional number of major disasters – in the Middle East, Bangladesh, the Horn of Africa and Eastern Europe. It seemed as if the charity sector was having to run faster and faster, just to stand still.

But these unusual financial strains are unlikely to persist. There are already signs that the multitude of disasters at the turn of the decade was exceptional; and there is a good chance that, in the foreseeable future, the UK charity industry, which handles an estimated £17bn a year through more than 165,000 charities, will be relieved of its VAT burden (increased from 15 per cent to 17.5 per cent in the 1991 budget). It is also certain that individual and corporate giving will recover as the world economy regains its momentum.

Other developments are likely to prove of greater long-term significance for the British charity sector. A new Charities Act is on the statute book, the coverage of charity and non-profit affairs in the media is growing rapidly, events like Band Aid, the telethons and Comic Relief have increased public awareness of and involvement in charities to an unprecedented level, and a whole crop of new institutions have emerged as specialist intermediaries between givers and their 'clients'.

Part of this revolution in the non-profit sector consists of the new political emphasis on self-help, exemplified by the economic philosophy of Margaret Thatcher but also reflected in recent political and economic developments throughout the world. In Britain, this change of role is formally reflected in the government's controversial policy of sub-contracting welfare provision to charitable agencies, but there is far more to it than that.

The 'privatization' of welfare is being brought about just as much by changes in the way people and companies perceive their responsibilities, and their self-interest, as it is by changes in government policy. There is a new mood abroad, consisting partly of a recognition of the limitations of state provision of welfare, and partly of a perception that need and compassion comprise a kind of product, the meeting of which can generate returns to the giver that, though not directly financial, have value. In this way, a new, secular truth has been found in the old biblical principle that 'it is more blessed to give than to receive'. All the biblical reward was to be had in heaven. In the modern, secular world the first instalment is received on earth.

Until quite recently, giving was a private and personal act because modesty forbade conspicuous generosity. The doctrine in Corinthians, that 'charity vaunteth not itself, is not puffed up' was the rule. It was felt that bragging about it detracted from the moral quality of the act of giving. But though this principle of diffidence remains influential, it is being modified by a less pious and more self-assured attitude, exemplified by the thoroughly modern prescription: 'If you've got it, flaunt it'. There is scriptural authority for this attitude too, in St Luke: 'No man, when he hath lighted a candle, putteth it in a secret place, neither under a bushel, but on a candlestick, that they which come in may see the light.'

This new dimension to charity, which is not so much boastful as contemporary and realistic, is both less and more than traditional altruism. Less, because it lacks the self-denial of pure philanthropy and more because giving inspired by an enlightened self-interest is likely to prove, in the long run, considerably more 'generous', in total, than old style giving under the diffidence principle.

As givers, particularly corporate givers, have become more open and more calculating about their charitable activities, the proto-industry which organizes the fund-raising and deploys the proceeds, has also been evolving in ways that are likely to be of considerable benefit to the recipients of charity.

Previously, the charity 'industry', if it can be called that yet, had developed in an environment free of much scrutiny and seriously lacking in the challenges and threats that are the essential goads to self-improvement. As a result, by modern company standards, the charity sector has been inefficient, uncompetitive, badly managed, and, because of the cocoon of righteousness that has surrounded it, peculiarly vulnerable to incompetence, exploitation and fraud.

In its White Paper, *Charities: A Framework For The Future*, the government pointed out that since the 1960 Charities Act (the last major piece of legislation), there has been 'an enormous increase in the number and variety of charities and a substantial increase in the funds flowing through them'. The turnover of the voluntary sector is now greater than the turnover of the agricultural sector, and new UK charities are being registered by the Charity Commission at a rate of one every thirty minutes of the working day.

The nature of the charity sector itself is, likewise, in the process of being transformed. There are a growing number of charities relying on fund-raising rather than endowments, many are becoming significantly dependent on trading income from shops and merchandizing, more and more charities are being established as companies and new fund-raising methods, some of them controversial, are constantly appearing.

These developments have inspired intense official interest in the sector. The National Audit Office investigated the role of the Charity Commissioners in 1987, the Home Office and the Treasury commissioned an 'Efficiency Scrutiny of the Supervision of Charities' by Sir Philip Woodfield and the House of Commons Public Accounts Committee got in on the act with its report on the *Monitoring and Control of Charities* in 1988. The upshot of all this was the 1992 Charities Act.

All these developments have pushed the charity sector to the brink of a new future, full of danger but also full of great opportunity. In the chapters that follow I shall look at what I call the 'democratization' of giving (the increased involvement of ordinary people in the non-profit sector) and the increasing commercialization of charity (the growing involvement of companies in giving, and in the wider area of corporate social responsibility). I shall propose a new model for corporate involvement in charity and socially responsible activities, derived from my own book *The 'nice' company*. I will then go on to discuss the industrialization of the charity sector itself (how it is learning from companies) and how the privatization of welfare is changing charity's relationship with the state. These themes will then be brought together in a speculative chapter which explores their implications, particularly for companies, and reaches some tentative conclusions about where they might be leading. Finally, in an addendum to the main argument, I will try to place British giving in an international context, based on what statistics are available.

It is impossible to write a book like this without employing figures but, partly because of the lack of regulation of the charity sector, accurate statistics are hard to come by. In the interests of readability, I have put most of the statistical information in an Appendix and merely referred to the highlights in the main text. The reader should bear in mind that although charity statistics, which have begun to improve quite rapidly, give a reasonably accurate general picture, some figures still need to be taken with a pinch or two of salt.

1

Individual Philanthropists

In the past, philanthropy has been something individuals do, its common manifestation has been the giving of money and it has usually been associated with religion. As Professor Ken Young explains in his Gresham College essay *Meeting the Needs of Strangers*, Western charity is based on the Hebrew idea of 'stewardship', developed and adapted for the Christian tradition by St Paul. This asserts that a rich man is not the owner of his land and possessions, but is their steward, and is thus obliged to use and deploy them in accordance with God's commands. Even today, the Judaeo-Christian idea of stewardship retains a strong grip on the minds of many of those involved with charity. Former Chief Charity Commissioner, Robin Guthrie, for example, talks of the inter-dependence of people and society and insists 'we are all only trustees of what we own'.

Since early Christian times, however, the concept of charity has been undergoing a continual process of secularization. One of the first milestones in this process was in Tudor times, when a rapid expansion of bequests and trusts, to meet social needs, led to the Statute of Charitable Uses of 1601. The preamble to this Elizabethan statute is still seen by modern jurists as a crucial line of legal authority in the contemporary debate about whether charity needs to be defined in some formal way and, if so, how.

Although the marks of charity's religious origins remain, in many ways, remarkably fresh and vital, it seems to me this secu-larizing process has shown that the human propensity to give is altogether more fundamental to the human psyche than a mere corollary of the will to worship a benevolent God. It is almost as if human beings have a compulsion to give to those less advantaged than themselves – as if the process of natural selection has encoded giving into humanity, because it confers some evolutionary advantage. At one time, I was planning to call this book *The Giving Gene*, to emphasise and celebrate the remarkable durability of giving. I thought better of the idea, partly because I have found that pushing the argument to the molecular level offends some people.

For it is integral to the religious view of charity that no benefit from giving should be derived by the giver. Edward Wallis, in his pamphlet *Explaining Christian Stewardship*, widened the traditional concept of the stewardship of the rich man to reflect the greater equality of wealth in modern times. But although he included, in his definition of the property of stewardship, 'everything God has entrusted to mankind – time, abilities and opportunities as well as material possessions', Wallis reiterated the traditional Christian insistence on disinterest. The Christian should give, he asserted 'in love, because he is God's child; in gratitude ... in duty, because he is God's steward' and not 'reluctantly, because pressure is put upon him; spasmodically, when he happens to feel like it; emotionally, because his more generous feelings have been stirred; [or] selfishly, to make himself feel good'.

The belief that motive somehow contributes to, and detracts from, the quality of the giving (the 'highest' motive being no motive at all) is clearly religious in origin, but it still seems to be deep-rooted, even among business leaders, although, generally speaking, they are rapidly becoming less sanctimonious about the reasons for corporate giving.

To my mind, it is a disreputable and élitist idea and there are those within the charity sector who share this view. Redmond Mullin, for example, one of the UK's most successful charity fundraisers, has sharply repudiated the implication that 'the needy benefit more from anonymous or purely altruistic than from ostentatious or self-seeking gifts'. In fact, it is easy to turn the argument on its head and say the only people who could possibly derive any benefit at all from the alleged virtues of anonymity and 'pure altruism' in giving, are the givers.

Moreover, the secularization of giving has made anonymity a less practical conceit. Corporate givers can, if they feel so inclined, be low-key, but the law now prevents them from being totally anonymous. And, as Ken Young has pointed out, volunteering and mass philanthropy (of which more later) are incorrigibly visible forms of charity. Even the royals, whose patronage must, perforce, be visible, are becoming less coy about their giving. For instance, the names of seven 'Royal donors' appear in the roll of honour published by the organizers of the Wishing Well Appeal for the Great Ormond Street Children's Hospital, though there is no indication of how much they gave.

The Royals

The most powerful argument monarchists can adduce in their increasingly vociferous debate with republicans is that without royalty, the charity sector's fund-raising ability would be seriously impaired. It is a curious feature of the charity ethos that a strong egalitarian theme is combined with a dependence on the good offices of the most privileged family in the land. It is not known how much cash the royals give, personally, to charity but their contribution to the pulling power of the causes with which they are associated is believed to be prodigious.

According to the Charities Aid Foundation's 1991 edition of *Royal Patrons*, members of the royal family were the patrons of almost 1,000 organizations, most of which had an overtly philanthropic purpose. For CAF's estimate of the distribution of the burdens of royal patronage amongst the various family members see overleaf. The number of causes an individual royal is associated with, however, gives no indication of how diligent he or she is in honouring the unwritten, *noblesse oblige* contract each of them has with the people.

The three most assiduous royal workers at the charity grindstone are Prince Charles, Princess Anne and the Hon. Sir Angus Ogilvy (whose low ranking in CAF's royal patronage league table belies an unusually heavy workload in the charity sector). Princess Anne is probably the busiest royal of them all.

But diligence is not the best measure of fund-raising power. The most important role of royals in the charity business is not necessarily to work hard at it but to make their curiously enduring magnetism available to the causes they associate themselves with.

Royal	Number of Causes	Rank
The Queen	193	1
Prince Philip	93	4
The Queen Mother	131	2
Prince Charles	99	3
Princess Diana	56	5
Prince Andrew	15	16
Duchess of York	24	14
Prince Edward	9	17
Princess Anne	51	6 =
Mark Phillips	1	20
Princess Margaret	33	12 =
Princess Alice	34	11
Duke of Gloucester	38	9
Duchess of Gloucester	33	12 =
Duke of Kent	43	8
Duchess of Kent	51	6 =
Prince Michael	18	15
Princess Michael	8	18
Princess Alexandra	37	10
Sir Angus Ogilvy	6	19
Total	973	

Source: *Royal Patrons*, 1991

Royalty has an undeniable power to induce the wealthy to give. And apart from the Queen, the most powerful money-puller of all is Princess Diana. As the *Sunday Telegraph* put it:

> When Diana is around, the virtuous aura of good causes gains an extra, ineffable glow that induces people to fall over themselves to part with their money.

Tickets for charity 'dos' attended by the Queen or Princess Diana can be sold for £200 apiece. Princess Anne is reckoned to be worth £75 a ticket, and Princess Margaret and Princess Michael are around the £50 mark.

Some fund-raising events are organized around, and formally convened by, their royal patrons. The annual Royal Children's Variety Performance at the London Palladium, for example, raises some £250,000 a year for the National Society for the Prevention of Cruelty to Children (NSPCC) and it is always attended by Princess Margaret, the NSPCC's President for the past forty years. Giles Pegram, the NSPCC's Appeals Organizer, told the *Sunday Telegraph* the charity's relationship with Princess Margaret worked on three levels: 'fund-raising, the practical business of meeting workers and visiting projects and, finally, being involved in the making of policy'.

An important event in the development of royal patronage was the decision a decade or so ago by Prince Philip, during his work for the former World Wildlife Fund, to ignore the convention that said senior royals should never rattle tins. Previously, it had been deemed unseemly for royals to ask directly for money; they could exert a passive influence on a charity's ability to raise funds, by becoming its patron, but they weren't seen to be available as active fund-raisers. Nowadays, direct royal solicitations for money on behalf of good causes are commonplace and very effective.

The charisma of royalty also has an important role to play in highlighting particular causes, through the exploitation of the obsessive preoccupation of the tabloid press with royal affairs. As Stephen Lee, the director of the Institute of Charity Fund Raising Managers, explained:

> Charities that need to broaden their base of support see members of the Royal Family as an ideal way to do it. From a vox pop point of view they capture the public's imagination on very difficult issues. There has been much more interest created around HIV and AIDS by the Princess of Wales and Liz Taylor than by government advertisements.

Little is known about how much the royals give, personally. In the summer of 1992, the Queen was reported to have sent a personal cheque to Paul McCartney to help the ex-Beatle set up a 'Fame' school for the performing arts in Liverpool, but the sum was not disclosed.

McCartney, who had himself given over £1m out of a total of £13m needed to establish the Liverpool Institute at his old school, knew that the Queen had given more than money. 'This is terrific news,' he said of the unexpected royal cheque and the good-luck letter that accompanied it. 'It is a fabulous boost for the school and for Liverpool.'

The palace line is that the Queen distributes Maundy Money each year and also makes regular contributions to various organizations, all of which are asked not to reveal amounts. It has only recently been revealed that money received by the Duchy of Lancaster from those residents who die intestate, is spent on charitable causes within the duchy.

The Lesser Nobility

The principle of *noblesse oblige*, though it is exemplified by royal involvement in charitable causes, is not confined to members of the royal family. The lesser nobility, through the good works of a regiment of 'lady bountifuls', are also important contributors, of both money and time, to charity. A *Sunday Express* report, entitled 'Ladies Most Bountiful', revealed something of the motivation of these women.

Lady Brocket, involved with the Parkinson's Disease Society of the UK and the National Society for Epilepsy, among many other charities, paid homage to the role of the royal family in setting an example for the lesser nobility: 'At the last count, I was involved with twenty-two charities, both local and national. The Royals do the greatest job of all of us. They are so well informed.' In September 1988, Lord and Lady Brocket hosted a classic car auction, run by Christie's, at their home, Brocket Hall. The event raised £500,000, in less than an hour, for the Great Ormond Street Hospital's Wishing Well Appeal.

Lady Howe, associated with the National Association for the Care and Resettlement of Offenders, stressed the importance of upbringing and of the need for personal satisfaction: 'At school we were taught to realize how lucky we were and that we should put something back into the community. Modern charities seek support from industry and the government, but each of us has a responsibility, too. Last year I joined in National Sleep Out Week. You must enjoy voluntary work so you get something out of it, too. It's pointless otherwise.'

The Duchess of Norfolk recalled how a particular event led her to dedicate her life to charity: 'Ten years ago I made a chance visit to St Joseph's Hospice in Hackney and was so amazed by what I saw that I decided that's what I wanted to do with my life. I raised £1m for a new training wing and received letters begging me to go on. In 1984 I founded Help the Hospices, a new national charity. We raise about £1m a year. I'm delighted that the number of hospices in the country has doubled from 70 to 140 and we lead the world in the care of the dying. I spend all my life doing it. I am thrilled to be part of the greatest medical breakthrough of this century and I feel extremely grateful and humble to be involved. It is a full-time job. My friends scream now when they see me coming.'

Lady Schiemann acknowledged that there are social dividends to be earned from involvement with charities, but she also emphasised the addictive nature of the work: 'Once you start doing charity work, people always ask you to do more. It grows. There is an element of glamour about some events but I run two clubs for people who have had strokes and there is nothing glamorous about that. I dread to add up the hours I do – I'd be rich if I got paid for them.'

Enjoyment is obviously part of it, and for some people no doubt, charity work can also begin as an antidote to the ennui and lack of meaning in otherwise empty lives. But there can also be a sense of the privileged paying their dues, which is entirely in tune with the idea of stewardship.

The Rich and Celebrated

The same considerations apply to the conspicuous diligence at the charity grindstone of the wives of rich commoners, and, no doubt, similar motives explain why so many celebrities become involved in charity work.

Although boredom and emptiness may be less important here, the idea that fortune is kind to some and unkind to others, and that this random apportionment of material and psychological rewards places a duty on the fortunate to do what they can to help the unfortunate, is clearly influential. It is further evidence for the view that the sense of stewardship that the Judaeo-Christian religious traditions make so much of, remains alive and vigorous in the modern, secular world. The Wishing Well Appeal's 'thank-you' list – the organizers stressed that it is far from comprehensive – included almost 200 'celebrity well-wishers'.

The campaign involved a number of charity sporting events at which sports celebrities appeared. There was the Foster's Tennis Classic, for example, featuring Boris Becker, Pat Cash, Stefan Edberg and Henri Leconte which raised £160,000, and in October 1988, Sebastian Coe and Steve Cram re-staged the Great Court Run at Trinity College, Cambridge (immortalized in the film *Chariots of Fire*), which raised over £50,000.

Other sports personalities honoured by a Wishing Well Appeal 'thank you' included track and field athletes David Bedford, Geoff Capes, Linford Christie, Daley Thompson and Fatima Whitbread, former Wimbledon tennis stars Bjorn Borg and John Lloyd, former England cricket captain Mike Brearley, boxer Frank Bruno, motor-sport stars Barry Sheen and Dr Jonathan Palmer, jockey John Francome and swimmers Duncan Goodhew and Sharron Davies (the United Biscuits' Penguin 'Swimathon', in 1988, raised nearly £690,000).

Stars of stage and screen were also well represented on the Wishing Well Appeal thank-you roster, including such names as Glynnis Barber, Stephanie Beecham, Peter Bowles, the Maxes Boyce and Bygraves, Richard Briers, Michael Caine, Cannon and Ball, George Cole, Joan Collins, Gemma Craven, Bernard Cribbins, Paul Daniels, Maureen Lipman, Martyn Lewis, Sheila Hancock, Patricia Hodge, Felicity Kendall, Ludovic Kennedy, Joanna Lumley, Juliet Mills, Bill Oddie, Christopher Reeves, Willie Rushton, Una Stubbs, Oliver Tobias, Dave Lee Travis, Dennis Waterman, Jimmy Tarbuck, Frank Windsor, Norman Wisdom, Emma Samms, Ernie Wise, John Nettles, Paul Nicholas, Moira Shearer, Derek Nimmo, Nigel Davenport, Judi Dench, Nigel Havers, Jonathan Dimbleby, Sylvester McCoy (and Dr Who himself), Noel Edmonds and David Frost.

There was a large contingent of musicians, too – Boy George, Dire Straits, Phil Collins, Eric Clapton, Michael Jackson (his concert for the appeal and the Prince's Trust raised over £100,000), Bonnie Langford, Lulu, George Harrison, Chas and Dave, Cliff Richard (his 30th Anniversary Concert raised nearly £130,000), Vera Lynn,

Paul and Linda McCartney, Hazel O'Connor, Suzie Quattro, Harry Secombe, James Taylor, Tears for Fears and Spandau Ballet.

No doubt the agents of all these celebrities approved of the Wishing Well Appeal engagements – charity 'gigs' were common items in the calendars of pop music stars long before Band Aid – but there is no denying the enormous fund-raising power of such names, and there seems little doubt that a sense of stewardship, exemplified by the extraordinary achievements of Bob Geldof, also plays a crucial part in the motivation of celebrities (and of many others – see the discussion of 'volunteering' in chapter 4), to give their talents and their time to good causes.

The Band Aid phenomenon, described in Geldof's book *Is that it?*, remains a conspicuous symbol of the power our cultural heroes and heroines have to stimulate giving. It also demonstrates how need can sometimes come to dominate the lives of individuals. Geldof was totally obsessed by his calling during the Band Aid programme (his workload while organizing it was immense) and Sir Brian Rix, of Whitehall farce fame, deserted the stage to devote his life to Mencap, the charity for mentally handicapped people.

But Mark Lattimer, writing in *Trust Monitor*, a quarterly magazine published by the Directory of Social Change, was far from overwhelmed by the conclusions of his fascinating study into the giving habits of Britain's 100 richest people. He estimated that as a group they give barely a tenth of 1 per cent of their assets to charity each year. Among the ten richest Britons and their families, only John Paul Getty II and the Sainsburys were among the ten most generous givers. Getty has given about £90m in total and the Sainsburys give about £14m a year.

Getty is an anglophile American with a passion for cricket who gives money to cricket grounds throughout the UK. He also gives generously to book restoration work and in 1985 he gave £50m to the National Gallery to endow a new fund for acquiring paintings. The £25m J. Paul Getty Charitable Trust gives £1.5m a year to small mental-health charities, conservation causes and community and self-help groups, especially those working with young people. The Getty Trust makes a point of being regionally even-handed and is one of the few foundations to give significant sums to black-run organizations.

The Sainsbury family trusts include the Gatsby Charitable Foundation and the Linbury, Headley and Monument trusts. David Sainsbury is the prime mover behind the £7m-a-year Gatsby Foundation (named after his favourite book). Most of Gatsby assets are held in the form of shares in J. Sainsbury plc.

Accurate figures are hard to come by, so Lattimer focused on personal giving through charitable foundations. He was unable to gather information on Gift Aid, which allows individuals to make donations of up to £5m without paying income tax, but he pointed out that only a few individuals and families, such as the secretive Brenninkmeyers, who own the Dutch stores group C&A, give completely anonymously.

The Brenninkmeyers used to give in the UK through the Marble Arch group of trusts, set up by family members living in the UK but, apparently in the interests of conserving anonymity, these have been wound up. In their last full year, they gave £3m for religious and charitable causes, education, youth and child welfare work, and the relief of poverty and medicine.

Garry Weston, leader of Associated British Foods plc, gives about £2.4m a year through the Garfield Weston Foundation, the assets of which consist mostly of shares in two private companies, G. Weston Holdings and Wittington Investments. In recent years the foundation has concentrated on hospitals. It gave £4m to Great Ormond Street Hospital, £1m to the Royal Marsden and made several smaller gifts to other hospitals and hospices. The Foundation also gives to social welfare charities (including some in Ireland) and to large arts organizations.

The Rayne Foundation was formed in 1962 by British property developer Max Rayne (later Lord Rayne), the founder of London Merchant Securities. It gives over £1m a year to medicine, education, social welfare, the arts and local voluntary groups. The smaller Rayne Trust supports the arts and Jewish charities.

Sir James Goldsmith, the brother of one of Britain's leading ecologists, Edward Goldsmith, publicly withdrew from his conspicuously successful business career in 1990, saying he would thenceforth concentrate his efforts on environmental causes. This was expected to mean, amongst other things, an increase in the activities of the Goldsmith Foundation, which gives £1m to £2m a year to environmental cause groups.

The Kleinwort investment banking family gives about £1.4m a

year through various trusts, the largest of which is named after the late Ernest Kleinwort, father of the contemporary patriarch, Sir Kenneth Kleinwort. It gave over £1m in 1990 to health, disability, environmental causes and local Sussex charities. The environmental emphasis reflects the personal interests of Sir Kenneth, who is associated with the World Wide Fund for Nature and the Wildfowl and Wetlands Trust. There is also the Sir Cyril Kleinwort Charitable Trust which gave £400,000 in 1989 and the Kleinwort Benson Charitable Trust, through which the giving of the Kleinwort Benson bank is channelled.

West End theatrical producer Cameron Mackintosh (thought to be worth £200m) became interested in the plight of the Vietnamese refugees while making the musical *Miss Saigon*. The Bui Doi (Dust for Life) Fund, financed largely by *Miss Saigon* spin-offs, supports refugee work in the UK and the Far East. But most of Mackintosh's philanthropic work is through the Mackintosh Foundation, which gives more than £1m a year to theatres and theatre groups, AIDS causes and children's charities.

The evangelical Christian, Robert Edmiston, gives 10 per cent of the profits of his privately-owned International Motors Group to a charity he set up, called Christian Vision, which gives about £1m a year for the relief of poverty and the support of old people.

After Paul Hamlyn sold his Octopus publishing group to Reed International in 1987, he endowed the Paul Hamlyn Foundation with £50m. In 1990 it gave £800,000 to various educational, arts and Third World causes and £1m to the Bodleian Library in Oxford.

The Moores family, which owns the Littlewoods organization, has endowed three major trusts – the Moores Family Charity Foundation, the John Moores Foundation and the Peter Moores Foundation. The former (named after the son of the patriarch Sir John Moores) supports local organizations on Merseyside and in Northern Ireland. John Moores himself is chairman of Liverpool Polytechnic, which is scheduled soon to become the Liverpool John Moores University. The Peter Moores Foundation supports the arts and youth and health charities throughout the UK. In 1991 it announced a £2m gift to Oxford University to endow a management studies chair.

The secretive twin brothers David and Frederick Barclay, who bought *The European* newspaper from the collapsed Maxwell empire in 1992, give about £800,000 a year through the David and Frederick Barclay Foundation mostly to hospitals and medical causes. The Royal Marsden, Guy's, Homerton and St Thomas's hospitals have all received donations and in 1992 the foundation gave £800,000 to St Mary's Hospital Medical School to support research into Alzheimer's disease.

Sir John Templeton, now a British citizen, endowed the US-based Templeton Foundation to award an annual prize to 'the person who has contributed most to new ideas or methods for widening or deepening man's knowledge of God or love of God.' Sir John is best known as a philanthropist in the UK for his $5m gift (recently sweetened by a further $3m) to the Oxford Centre for Management Studies, now called Templeton College.

The Westminster Foundation, endowed by Gerald Grosvenor, the Duke of Westminster, gives about £1m a year to welfare, youth and conservation charities. In 1990 it gave £200,000 to the National Society for the Prevention of Cruelty to Children, £89,000 to Business in the Community and £75,000 to the Game Conservancy Trust. The Duke also gives directly. He was among the founding funders of the 21st Century Trust.

In 1991 pop star George Michael donated all the profits of a number one hit single to AIDS research charities. He has also endowed the Platinum Trust, set up in 1990 to support charities helping people with physical or mental handicaps.

Stephen Rubin, whose investment company Pentland Industries holds a controlling stake in the Adidas footwear company, set up the Rubin Foundation in 1986. It supports the Jewish Philanthropic Association and also gives money to large arts organizations. It is thought to give about £350,000 a year.

The George A. Moore Foundation was endowed with £4m by self-made Yorkshireman George Moore. It gives about £350,000 a year to local, Yorkshire charities specializing in the relief of poverty and handicapped and young people.

The Laura Ashley Foundation, of which Sir Bernard Ashley and his son David Ashley are trustees, was set up in 1985 just before Laura Ashley's death. It gives over £300,000 a year to charities providing 'second chance' education.

Hong Kong-based Sir John and Sir Adrian Swire, whose Swire Group's interests include the Cathay Pacific airline, have recently set up the Swire Educational Trust to support educational and cultural exchange in the UK, Hong Kong and elsewhere.

Asian business brothers, Sri, Gopi and Prakash Hinduja set up the Hinduja Foundation to promote Third World development by publishing relevant research and promoting lectures and exhibitions. Its first full year of operation was 1991, when it declared its intention to support 'public health and education in the UK, especially when they are connected with India'. The foundation donates about £250,000 a year.

The JCB excavator group, run by founder Joe Bamford's son Sir Anthony Bamford, gives about £240,000 a year through the Bamford Charitable Trust to charities within a 25-mile radius of the company's headquarters at Rocester, Staffordshire.

Lattimer produced a list of Britain's top philanthropists by comparing how much they gave, through their foundations and trusts, with their estimated wealth (using wealth estimates published in the *Sunday Times*).

Giver	Annual Giving as % of Estimated Wealth
Lord Rayne	1.8
The Kleinwort family	1.6
John Paul Getty II	0.7
George Michael	0.6
The Sainsbury family	0.6
Cameron Mackintosh	0.5
Robert Edmiston	0.5
Paul Hamlyn	0.4
George Moore	0.4
Sir John Templeton	0.4

Source: *Trust Monitor*, June/July 1992

Many other foundations, like the Wellcome Trust, the Wolfson Foundation (Great Universal Stores), the Rank Foundation, the Ronson Foundation (Heron International) and the Rowntree trusts are closely linked to companies and their founders or family owners. (See tables 1.1 and 1.2 in the Appendix).

But there are other, less famous heroes and heroines of the voluntary sector – the professionals who run it and incur the costs of lower salaries than they could command in the 'for-profit sector', and the innovators like Jane Tewson, founder and director of Charity Projects (see chapter 6) and Marion Allford, the brilliant and hugely successful Director of the Wishing Well Appeal for the rebuilding of the Great Ormond Street Children's Hospital (GOSH).

The Wishing Well Appeal

I have referred frequently to the Wishing Well Appeal for two reasons: because it is widely regarded as one of the most successful fund-raising campaigns ever undertaken in the UK, and because it exemplifies so much of what is new about the charity business in Britain.

The appeal, named after a fountain that used to stand in the garden of the Victorian hospital, and into which children would throw coins and wish for good health, was initiated by Caroline Bond, chairman of the hospital's board of governors in 1985. The 140-year-old building was in a serious state of disrepair, and the government had said it could only provide £20m for rebuilding work, only 40 per cent of the funds required to cover the estimated cost of £50m. The original fund-raising target was, therefore, £30m. This soon escalated to £42m, as a result of inflation, even after the government increased its contribution to £30m.

Having decided on an appeal the GOSH Governors and Special Trustees appointed Appeal Trustees led by William Clarke. The Appeal Trustees appointed Jim (now Lord) Prior, former Cabinet Minister and Chairman of GEC, Appeal Chairman; the Prince and Princess of Wales agreed to become Royal Patrons of the appeal; and Marion Allford, a veteran of a number of successful appeals, was appointed Appeal Director in April 1985.

Allford devised a fund-raising plan of great sophistication, and executed it with military precision. An essential part of the strategy was a robust organizational structure. An Investment Committee led by Sir Kit MacMahon, chairman and chief executive of Midland Bank, was formed and an Executive Committee, supported by four specialist panels covering the City, Commerce and Industry, Special Events and Marketing, was set up.

The Marketing panel's job was to develop a high impact brand image for the appeal. A task force led by Robert Clarke, deputy chairman and chief executive of United Biscuits, and consisting of professionals from the advertising, marketing and promotion Disciplines, developed a message of great emotional and visual power that worked equally well on T-shirts as on newspaper advertisements and posters.

The 'teardrop motif', as the appeal's logo came to be known, was inundated with plaudits and awards and greatly enhanced the reputation of its creator, advertising agency Collett, Dickenson and Pearce (CDP). Some excellent copy-writing was also a feature of the CDP campaign. An early, full-page newspaper advertisement, explaining the need for the appeal, carried the message:

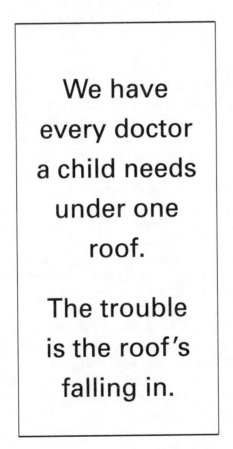

We have
every doctor
a child needs
under one
roof.

The trouble
is the roof's
falling in.

Allford was insistent that this should be a national appeal, and a total of more than ninety regional groups were formed. She also wanted to achieve a low 'cost-to-income' ratio which meant extensive use of volunteers as well as soliciting free professional services, not only from the likes of CDP, IMP (International Marketing Promotions), Alan Kilkenny and two other public relations consultancies, The Grayling Company and Dewe Rogerson, but also from accountants, Ernst & Young, head-hunters, Spencer Stuart & Associates and lawyers Turner Kenneth Brown.

Another Allford stratagem was to tap big givers – namely the government, companies and grant-giving trusts or foundations – first, before launching the public appeal. Pump-primers of this kind included the Garfield Weston Foundation (apart from the government, the largest single donor, giving £4m in all), the Variety Club of Great Britain (£3m), The Djanogly Foundation, The Clore Foundation, The Bernard Sunley Charitable Foundation, and the Wolfson Foundation, all of which gave £1m or more.

Altogether nearly a third of the original £30m target, some £9.5m, was donated or pledged by companies, trusts or people, before the public appeal was launched in October 1987. Other conspicuous early donors included Jean Sainsbury, the Grand Charity of Freemasons, Steven Spielberg and the Alan Sugar Foundation.

Companies continued to play a crucial role after the launch of the public appeal. Midland Bank funded the first wave of space buying for the advertising campaign, media owners gave as much space again, Mills & Allen donated poster sites, forty million Mars Bars carried the teardrop logo and five pence was given to the appeal for every wrapper returned (up to a total of £100,000). Hula Hoops, Skips, Comfort, Kodak, Pudgies Baby Wipes and Wendy Wools also ran on-pack promotions.

Crown Paints and other companies supported joint projects or employee initiatives, Tesco raised £2m through its stores, United Biscuits raised £1m with fundraising events, like the Penguin Swim-athon, John Laing raised over £500,000 and store groups Alders, Debenhams, Harrods and W.H. Smith mounted in-store promotions and the mail order companies GUS and Kayes sold Wishing Well T-shirts by catalogue. Between the launch date of October 1, 1986 to June 30, 1989 the Wishing Well Appeal raised a total of £46.5m and another £6m had been pledged or covenanted.

After it was all over, Marion Allford said:

> I know that the Wishing Well Appeal will prove to be one of the most exciting periods of my life... Forty per cent of our target came from people who gave or raised amounts of £1,000 or less – a staggering and unprecedented ratio in fundraising terms... None of us ever doubted that the money would be raised, but the speed of the result astounded us all. This can be explained by the important fact that we used professional marketing techniques to launch and sustain our campaign.

We will look in more detail at why and how companies involve themselves in giving in chapter 5, but before leaving this discussion of individual philanthropy, it is worth noting the unusual extent to which British business leaders are involving themselves directly in charitable causes. Stephen O'Brien, the former director of Business in the Community (see chapter 6), believes that Britain leads the world in the personal involvement of business leaders in charitable causes. A few names stand out from the pack.

Sir Mark Weinberg, founder of Allied Dunbar Insurance (among other financial services companies), was a member of the Wishing Well Appeal's City Panel, played a leading role in the formation of Business in the Community (BitC), is one of two joint chairmen of the Per Cent Club (see chapter 7), and actively promotes employee giving and volunteering, in firms with which he is associated.

Anita Roddick associates herself, as well as Body Shop, the extraordinarily successful retailing group she founded, with good causes and she is also an active promoter of employee involvement in charity work. Body Shop won the 1991 UK Award for Employee Volunteering.

Thanks partly to the evangelism of such organizations as BitC and Charity Projects (see chapter 6), it is becoming quite common these days, if not downright fashionable, for British business leaders to 'see for themselves' the needs for which the generosity of their companies is being solicited. Charity Projects, for example, arranges trips for business leaders to visit London centres for homeless people at the dead of night, and in 1990, BitC organized a series of visits for some seventy young business leaders to see community projects throughout the UK.

The ten visits were led by Martin Findlay, vice-chairman of Whitbread; John Ward, regional director of Barclays Bank; Sir Hector (now Lord) Laing (see below), Life President of United Biscuits; Ernest Hall, chairman of Dean Clough Industrial Park; Tim Melville-Ross, chief executive of Nationwide Anglia; John Raisman, deputy chairman of British Telecom; David Rowland, chairman of Sedgwick Group, Ted Merrette, managing director of AB Electronic Products, Richard Field, chairman of J. & J. Dyson and the Sheffield Training and Enterprise Council and John Neill, chief executive of Unipart.

Other names that crop up in the literature, as contributing their time as well as their companies' money, include those of Garry H. Weston of Associated British Foods, Neil Shaw of Tate & Lyle, George Turnbull formerly of Inchcape, Sam Whitbread of Whitbread, Akash Paul of Caparo, Graham Millar of Rowntree Mackintosh, Nicholas Wills of BET, Sir Lachlan Maclean of United Biscuits, Tony Cleaver of IBM (UK), John Bullock of Coopers & Lybrand Deloitte, Geoff Mulcahy of Kingfisher, Sir Brian Corby, former chief executive of the Prudential Corporation, Sir David Scholey of S.G. Warburg, Sir Allen Sheppard of Grand Metropolitan and David Quarmby of Sainsbury.

But it is probably true to say that the most illustrious of all the voluntary sector's business heroes, as much for his contribution to the development of the philosophy of company giving as for his charitable work, is the man who made biscuit-making one of the few industries in which Britain is a world leader.

Whilst playing the role of dynamic company leader (see chapter 5), devising a bold strategy of acquisition-led growth and diversification, and then implementing it with great skill, Hector Laing, now Lord Laing of Dunphail, was also thinking deeply about the role of business in modern society.

He inherited the family biscuit company with his two brothers in 1947 and likes to think that during his long tenure as leader of what later became United Biscuits, 'we were among the leaders with our "people" policies, by applying the principle of do as you would be done by'. He says making money is 'the most boring thing in the world' but that building a business is the most exciting. He is the epitome of the ethical businessman, and regards the illegal Sunday trading some companies embarked on in 1991 as unacceptable. 'Companies shouldn't drive a coach and horses through the law,' he said.

A devout Christian, Laing was invited by the Archbishop of Canterbury in 1983 to help set up and chair the Lambeth Fund which provides research support for Archbishops and helps the Church Commissioners finance restoration work on the fabric of Lambeth Palace.

Lord Laing supports his local churches, St James's at Fulmer, Buckinghamshire, and Edinkillie Kirk near Dunphail, in Morayshire, is a Visiting Professor at Stirling University, has honorary doctorates from both Stirling and Heriot Watt, and is Honorary Treasurer of the Conservative Party.

His conversion to the cause of corporate philanthropy was on the road to Minneapolis in the 1970s when he heard about the Five Per Cent Club, whose eighty members were committed to giving 5 per cent of US pre-tax profits to various charitable causes in the twin cities of Minneapolis and St Paul.

On his return, he booked a room at the Dorchester, invited a number of fellow company leaders round, and suggested they set up a One Per Cent Club. 'They didn't like the 1 per cent,' he recalls, 'and they didn't like the idea of a "club" which was thought to be élitist. However, we finally settled for Per Cent Club.' Mark Weinberg – now Sir Mark, and a tireless founder of highly successful financial services companies, such as Abbey Life and Hambro Life (now Allied Dunbar) – soon became a powerful and eloquent ally in the campaign to create a 'culture of giving' in corporate Britain.

A friend of Margaret Thatcher, Laing took the view, when the Conservatives came to power in 1979 and began cutting taxes and liberating the UK economy, that it was incumbent on companies to assume more responsibility for the health of the community and the environment.

So, being as devout a Tory as he is a Christian, Laing became a leading evangelist for greater business involvement in the community. He was instrumental in the founding of Scottish Business in the Community of which he was chairman from 1982 to 1990 and is now vice-president; he was in at the start of Business in the Community, of which he was vice-chairman from 1984 to 1987 and chairman from 1987 to 1991, and as already noted, he is the founder and joint chairman of the BitC affiliate, the Per Cent Club (see chapter 6). He recalled what it was like in the early, pioneering days as Thatcherism was changing the nature of the compact between government, business and society:

> I used to suggest to my business friends and acquaintances that they should get involved because if we have a run-down society our profits too would run down. At that time most felt that their only job was to make money for their shareholders who could decide for themselves whether to give any away.
>
> I believed that to be hopelessly out-dated and that the company chairman and board couldn't leave it entirely to the government to sort out all society's needs. Governments are too remote, the bureaucracy swallows up too much of the funds in the process of trying to help, and companies know – or ought to – what the problems are in the localities where they operate.
>
> I argued that as the government was taking a step back from involvement (or interference) in business, we had to take a step forward – and that if we didn't, we could have serious problems. Some people, like Alastair Pilkington, recognized that very early on.

But Lord Laing says that, at any one time, there is a limit to how much companies should be asked to do. He recalls that Mrs Thatcher once asked him whether he thought the government was asking the business sector to do too much in the community. 'Pendulums always swing too far,' he explained. 'We had been doing too little and now we are in danger of trying to do too much. We must work out with government what their responsibilities are on this front, and how best companies can help.'

He is convinced there would have been a shareholder revolt if companies had gone from giving 0.5 per cent of taxable profits to 5 per cent straight away. 'I met a Pakistani businessman the other day,' he told me in November 1991, 'who gives 2.5 per cent [of profits], but he owns the company.'

Lord Laing sees the development of corporate philanthropy in an historical context. 'I made a speech in the Lords on Thursday,' he smiled, 'to a packed house of fifteen. I argued that in the twenties and thirties managers had excessive power over people which was corrected by the unions and then they got too strong and that was corrected by legislation.

'In the early days, British business consisted of myriads of small firms and massive numbers of private shareholders. Now there are very large companies owned by very large institutions. The balance of power between the City and industry has changed. We have got to be very careful that shareholders don't demand too much of companies. Japanese and German companies can afford to take a longer-term view.'

He thinks that, after the reduction of the top rate of income tax from 83 per cent to 40 per cent, personal giving should have risen more than it has and says 'the next crusade is to get individuals to give more, voluntarily'. According to Lord Laing, the highest priorities, right now, are enterprise, employment and education. 'If the schools are good, that helps business,' he explained. 'The Conservatives should have tackled education sooner, in 1979, and education should have developed a partnership with industry earlier. The state cannot do it all.'

Lord Laing is retired now, and plays no part in the affairs of the company he did so much to build. He is a director of Exxon, the biggest company in the world, and chairs two Bank of England committees as well as being Treasurer of the Conservative Party and giving time and effort to other 'philanthropic things'.

He thinks there should be a pattern to an individual's life: 'adolescence, career until you're fifty-five, philanthropy until you're sixty-five and then enjoy yourself. I don't crusade any more, except about the balance of power between the providers of capital, and its users.'

2

Villains and Victims

Although official figures show that charities are far from wealthy in terms of net assets, official figures tell only a minor part of the story. The asset that really matters, both to individual charities and to charities in general, is their reputation. It is how they are perceived by those on whose generosity they depend which determines how well they are able to succeed in their aims and how fast they can grow if growth is what they require. And it is on how the charity sector at large is perceived by the giving public which will determine how well it is able to respond to the challenges and opportunities that confront it.

A charity's reputation, like that of a company, consists of a number of elements. Each charity, for instance, has a reputation for being a good or a bad place to work, and this affects its ability to recruit and keep good staff. Charities are also judged on the quality of their management and on their efficiency. This, too, affects their ability to recruit and keep good staff but, in addition, it exerts an influence on their ability to raise money, because people are less likely to give to charities that absorb an undue percentage of money raised in running inefficient and expensive operations.

Each of the 'trading' charities – those that depend for a significant proportion of their income on the sale of goods and services (see chapter 7) – has acquired, over the years, a reputation for good or bad quality. They have to compete with non-charitable suppliers and although their charitable status tends to enhance the perceived value of their products, that edge will seldom be enough in a competitive market if the other components of perceived value, such as quality and after-sales service, are poor.

People are prepared to pay a premium for china in a National Trust shop, for example, because the quality of the products is above a perceived standard. The National Trust is exemplary in this respect. Its shops are well designed, well stocked and well run and its wares are of consistently high quality. As a specialist retailer, the National Trust must rank among the best in Britain.

Charitable status thus endows an organization's products, whether goods or charity itself, with a brand value premium that is significant but is seldom conclusive. Customers or givers will respond to this premium, but it does not cause them to suspend their critical judgement.

There are two components of the charitable brand value premium: an overall premium, a kind of charity 'meta-brand' enjoyed by all charities by virtue of their being charities, and the particular brand premium, or lack of it, relating to the individual charity.

The worrying thing for the individual charity is that events at other charities, over which it has no control, can affect the value of the charity meta-brand on which it and every charity depends. When charities, in general, are perceived to be inefficient, excessively political, insensitive to the needs of their 'clients', inconsistent in their policies, or just downright crooked, the value of each individual charity's brand will be sullied. Givers are making investments when they give and if they feel organized charities are chronically inefficient or dishonest, or if they believe weak management makes them easy prey for unprincipled fraudsters and conmen, they will find other ways to satisfy their philanthropic desires.

The two kinds of charity brand value, therefore, consist of the difference between reputational assets and reputational liabilities and much the most dangerous kind of reputational liability for a charity is a reputation for unlawful and/or fraudulent behaviour. Evidence, or the suspicion, of fraud and dishonesty is even more damaging to the reputations of charities than it is to the reputations of companies, because, generally speaking, people have higher expectations of, and so demand higher standards from, charities than they do from companies. Part of the charity meta-brand consists of a belief that charity people, unlike business people, are unselfish, scrupulously honest and psychologically incapable of deceit or sharp practice. There is, in short, a high degree of instinctive public trust in charities.

This is why some believe the single most important issue for the charity sector right now is the way in which its apparent lack of regulation, its sometimes uncritical use of external fund-raisers (over whose behaviour it often exerts inadequate control), and its perceived lack of self-discipline and management competence, make it far too attractive to people bent on making a quick buck, or on perpetrating lucrative frauds.

In this chapter, we shall investigate this rottenness in the state of charity, using reported incidents and the comments of practitioners to illustrate the nature and extent of the corruption. At the end of this catalogue of villainy I shall discuss the provisions and implications of the 1992 Charities Act; the current state of the debate within the charity sector on what to do about its fraud and profiteering problems; and suggest, not solutions, but ways in which the problems might be addressed.

The Great Fund-Raising Rip-Off

The practice of employing external fund-raisers to act as agents of charities, and paying them a commission on the sums they raise, has emerged as one of the most noisome of the charity sector's cans of worms.

One company investigated by the Charity Commissioners was raising £45,000 a year in donations from small businesses but was passing less than 5 per cent of it to charity.

Following an investigation by the *Sunday Telegraph* into the exploitation of a Wheelchair Appeal by the specialist fund-raising firm, Malaglade, the newspaper was inundated with calls from worried givers about companies claiming to raise money for charity, but which callers suspected were actually lining their own pockets. Even the largest, most respectable of charities, including many with royal patrons, employ such external fund-raising organizations.

The Malaglade story was typical. The company used a team of ten self-employed telephone saleswomen to call thousands of businesses over a period of two months, asking for up to £100 each, to sponsor a balloon in a race for the Wheelchair Appeal. Sponsors were not told that Malaglade, which bought only one wheelchair, costing £2,586, did not have a venue for the balloon race or that the lease on the offices they were using ran out on the day of the race.

Such affairs inspired expressions of indignation on both sides of the House of Commons. Stuart Randall, Labour charities spokesman, advocated new legislation to combat fund-raising scams, and Tory MP Sir Teddy Taylor, an outspoken critic of the political activities of some charities (see chapter 8), described fund-raising as 'a racket, and a complete abuse of the law'.

Sir Teddy directly addressed the issue of charity's overall 'meta-brand', when he added: 'These people are providing themselves with a job and a good salary by taking advantage of people's wish to give money to charity. They're not subject to the conditions and restrictions of charities, and it's terribly wrong.' Barry Sheerman, Labour home affairs spokesman, and chairman of the International Committee for Andean Aid, said: 'Fund-raising is hard enough without people discrediting proper and reputable charities. It's appalling.'

The Charity Commissioners spoke of the undermining of public trust and of its concern 'that charities should be able to continue their fund-raising work in an atmosphere unsullied by a small number of individuals intent on appealing to the public's generosity for the sake of personal gain.' It is always a small number of people who spoil things for others, but that does not protect the others, and nor does it excuse the inadequate management controls that permit it.

But, despite such indignation, none of the Malaglade protagonists were prosecuted, because the Crown Prosecution Service felt there was insufficient evidence of wrongdoing. Chris Elliot, one of the three *Sunday Telegraph* reporters who exposed the scam, is still angry about that.

A similar scam was revealed by the *Sun* in November 1991. A Mr Barry Freeman set up a telephone appeal the previous February, to build a new dormitory for disabled children at Delrow College, Hertfordshire. But the building concerned had been completed, and paid for, ten years previously, and the college does not even cater for children.

Camphill Village Trust, which runs Delrow College, had given Freeman permission to collect money among his acquaintances. But Freeman treated this as a general fund-raising licence. From offices in Wembley, North London, a twelve-strong telesales team began asking companies in the Yellow Pages directory to sponsor a balloon in a charity balloon race. A *Sun* reporter who was working undercover at Freeman's company, Helpline Appeals, said that in five days more than £10,000 was pledged by 300 donors, and by then Helpline had been operating for eight months.

Ann Harris, the director of the Camphill Village Trust, said Helpline had given the Trust 'two or three thousand pounds' since the operation began. 'We have been completely taken in by this man,' she said. 'We never gave Helpline Appeals authority to act on our behalf like this. There's no way of us knowing how much they keep and how much is coming to us.'

The Charity Publishing Swindle

In 1983, a *Sunday Times* investigation uncovered details of a scam that revealed how easy it was for unscrupulous entrepreneurs to exploit for their own benefit the money-raising power of a good cause.

Balls, galas and royal command performances are key fund-raising events in many a charity's calendar. They need to be promoted, and a common promotional tool is a glossy brochure or programme in which companies and individuals are asked to buy advertising space.

The *Sunday Times* illustrated the conventional economics of such publications with the case of the Children's Royal Variety Performance at the Haymarket Theatre in March 1983, which was attended by Princess Margaret. The event was in aid of the National Society for the Prevention of Cruelty to Children. A souvenir programme, compiled by NSPCC volunteers, attracted £27,291 worth of advertising of which some £2,300 went to cover printing and paper costs, leaving net proceeds for the NSPCC of £25,000.

Two months earlier, a programme for a Grosvenor House 'Star Ball', in aid of a children's hospital appeal, carried a handsome 134 pages of advertising, sold by professional telesales people, at rates up to a third higher than the NSPCC's amateurs would have dared to ask. Revenue amounted to almost £80,000, but the hospital, whose urgent need for a capital injection to prevent closure had inspired the generosity of advertisers, received only 17 per cent of it.

The huge difference was because the former charity had compiled the programme and sold the advertising 'in-house', while the hospital trustees had sub-contracted the job to a specialist publishing company.

Such 'specialist publishers' have 'helped' many leading charities, sometimes without their permission. Major charities have even found themselves being named, falsely, as the destination for funds actually being raised to 'help' quite other organizations which happen to have less pulling power. There was nothing illegal about any of this before the 1992 Charities Act, which requires 'fund-raising businesses' to accompany each solicitation with a statement about the institutions it acts for and the method by which it is to be remunerated.

Invalid agreements (that do not comply with regulations laid down in the Act) are not legally enforceable and fund-raisers who enter into such invalid agreements are guilty of an offence.

But although the new Act makes it more difficult to exploit charity's pulling power, it stops short of creating a new, criminal offence of exploitation. Charities can agree to be exploited. The onus still lies on them. They must be vigilant and, if it comes to it, they must be litigious.

The Case of the Spastics Society

In May 1991, two senior officials of the Spastics Society resigned at the request of their executive council after an internal inquiry had found they had broken their contracts.

Kenneth Young, 49, the £50,000 a year chief executive, and Martyn Dunleavy, 40, the £35,000 a year director of finance and support services, left their London offices immediately following claims that they had solicited community care business for a private firm with which they were both connected.

Probably the society's chairman, Derek Ashcroft's greatest worry will have been the affect the affair would have on the way the Society is regarded by government. The Spastics Society is an

35

example of an 'agency' charity (see chapter 7) – an organization to which government has sub-contracted part of its welfare effort. According to the 14th edition of *Charity Trends*, it received almost £24m from central and local government in the year to April 1990, amounting to almost half its total income. Among Britain's top 400 fund-raising charities, only Barnardos and the Leonard Cheshire Foundation received more state support than the Spastics Society in 1990.

Clearly, if the government agencies that have supported the Spastics Society in the past, with grants and fees, come to doubt its suitability as their agent in the spastics area, it could be serious, if not fatal, for the charity even if it is to be wrongly held responsible for the activities of its officers. And it is also hard to believe the affair will not reduce the £22m of voluntary contributions the Society received in 1988/9.

The Wicked 'Lady'

The extraordinary tale of one of the most substantial and in some ways the most disturbing UK charity frauds of recent years was recounted by *The Times* in early 1992, the day after the perpetrator had been gaoled for four years at the Old Bailey.

A year previously, Richard Stevens, head of the development foundation attached to the National Hospital for Neurology and Neurosurgery in Bloomsbury, London, happened to pass the unoccupied desk of his deputy, 'Lady' Rosemary Aberdour.

He noticed a copy of a cheque for £120,000, drawn on one of the foundation's building society accounts. Next to it was a covering letter, authorizing the transfer of the money to a Barclays Bank account, controlled by Aberdour. Knowing that Aberdour was not a signatory to the account, Stevens looked more closely and was astonished to see that the names of two of the charitable foundation's trustees had been forged very crudely on the transfer document. It was only this casual glance at papers left carelessly uncovered, that led to the detection of a systematic £2.4m swindle of the charity, over a five year period.

Aberdour, described later as 'an ordinary young woman, with something of a "jolly hockey sticks" manner', joined the foundation in 1986, on a salary of £9,000 a year. With several GCE passes, including a distinction in book-keeping, to her credit, she seemed well qualified. Within two years, she was running the foundation's annual charity ball, known as the Queen Square Ball.

She was an accomplished fund-raiser. During the period she was in charge of the ball, income rose from a few thousand pounds to £40,000 a year. But from Aberdour's point of view, the beauty of the ball was that its accounts were never audited. She used them to collect money stolen, with forged authorizations, from the foundation's other accounts.

During the five years between Aberdour's appointment and her arrest in 1991, the foundation raised nearly £8m, of which a little over £5m was spent legitimately. The rest was stolen by Aberdour, to finance her progressively more extravagant life style. She started in a small way but gained confidence and was soon transferring six-figure sums into her own bank accounts, via the unaudited ball accounts.

It became all too easy when her book-keeping skills led to her being asked to prepare the foundation's main accounts for 1990 and she was able to dupe the auditors, Coopers & Lybrand, that all was well. She was preparing for the 1991 audit, when her fraud was discovered.

This extraordinary story has a happy ending because it looks as if the charity will get most of the money back. At the time of writing, three building societies had already repaid £1.7m, after claims that they should have spotted the crude signature forgeries on transfer authorizations, and Barclays Bank was in negotiations over the return of a further £1m.

But the worrying thing is that it should have got so far, in the first place, and in the second place, that it was luck, not systematic regulation, that uncovered the fraud.

There was no lack of signals. Explaining to friends and colleagues that she had inherited a title and a £20m fortune on her 25th birthday, Aberdour embarked on a spending spree of conspicuous profligacy. She spent over £750,000 on extravagant parties, bought a Bentley and a Mercedes for herself, and five cars for her personal staff, ran up credit card debts of over £250,000, bought £200,000 worth of jewellery and spent a further £450,000 on furnishing and renting her home and a luxury Docklands flat.

The fabrication and abuse of noble and royal connections are common themes in the annals of charity fraud. Veteran fraudster Peter Kersey demonstrated how easy it was. He wrote to the Princess of Wales describing a charity he had set up, called the Cranberry Trust, which was to build homes and holiday centres for people who were mentally and physically disabled.

The Princess wrote two letters of encouragement which Kersey used to persuade banks and building societies to lend him money. The fraud started less than a fortnight after Kersey was released from jail for earlier frauds. He was convicted again and sentenced to twenty-one months imprisonment, suspended for two years.

Charity frauds, because of the stark affront they present to normal standards of human decency, are meat and drink to newspaper editors. In this area at least the public interest has been well served by the fourth estate.

The London *Evening Standard* exposed a grubby little fraud at the end of 1990. An organization called the Association for the Disadvantaged was closed and investigated by the Charity Commission and the police after the *Standard* revealed it had been using 'hard sell' telesales methods to raise money from companies, while not a registered charity.

The scripts which telesales people were told to use when calling companies stressed the organization's work with children but gave no details about how money raised would be spent. The purpose of one appeal was said to be to help 'kiddies terminally ill with cancer'. Every sentence of the script encouraged the respondent to say yes. For instance, 'You would like to help the children, wouldn't you?' and 'Helping people must be an ongoing thing, don't you agree?' If anyone said no, the salesperson was told to say 'We're not talking about a large amount of money here and the children you are helping are much worse off than you will ever be, isn't that true?'

The *Standard* reported that one former employee said, 'It was surprisingly easy to get people to agree to giving money. As soon as they had offered a donation, waiting motorcycle despatch riders were sent around to the company to collect it. I was very uneasy about what was going on. I am just seventeen yet I managed to earn as much as £360 a week with commission. We all wondered how much was actually going to charity.' He was on a basic salary of £3 an hour, plus ten per cent commission.

In January 1992, the Charity Commission announced that over £16,000 given by Londoners to the Association for the Disadvantaged had been 'in danger of going astray' but had now reached the purposes for which it was originally given. The Commission's inquiry found that only 0.5 per cent of the money raised by the Association was being spent on charitable purposes. Its bank accounts were frozen, various individuals were restrained from acting in its administration and new trustees were appointed.

Official Concern

Since most charity frauds go undetected, it is very hard to assess the scale of the problem. The Charity Commission, in its 1990 annual report, revealed that of the 455 cases of irregularity it decided to investigate that year, more than a quarter involved suspicions of deliberate fraud and a third related to maladministration of one kind or another. The Commission removed charitable status from a record 749 organizations in 1990 as a result of its investigations and of a census launched the previous year to identify inactive charities.

Cause for concern was established by the Commission in eighty-one of the 303 completed investigations. One trustee was removed, twenty-four cases were referred to the police and, as a result of the inquiries, further fund-raising was forbidden in another eight cases. The report also reiterated a refrain that has become familiar in recent years: that trustees often failed to maintain adequate financial and management controls.

The persistence of fraud, and of the inadequate controls that permit it, has been a cause of deep official concern for many years, but the anxiety was not fully articulated until the publication of a report on the Charity Commission by the House of Commons Public Accounts Committee (PAC) in 1988.

The PAC pulled no punches. Noting that total tax exemptions for charities were by then costing non-exempt taxpayers some £2.5bn a year, the PAC took the Commissioners to task on most of the key aspects of their work, and dismissed their plea that their resources were inadequate. 'Why is it', PAC chairman Robert Sheldon asked, 'that because they could not do everything, they did nothing?'

Dale Campbell-Savours, a Labour PAC member, said the Charity Commission had got by on trust and a low profile for too long and claimed the committee's report would 'blow the lid off its activities and lead to the most searching questions being asked by the giving public'. The PAC demanded urgent government legislation to strengthen the Commission's powers and immediate 'vigorous' action by the Commission to improve its performance under its existing powers.

The PAC expressed its belief that failure to act would lead to a disastrous loss of public confidence in charities. It said it was 'gravely concerned' by the risk of fraud and abuse, particularly in the field of fund-raising, and it accused the Commission of complacency. Even the Metropolitan Police had become sufficiently concerned by the issue to set up a dedicated charity fraud unit.

The PAC was disturbed by the wide range in the proportion of charity revenues consumed by overheads, and pointed out that administrative costs accounted for over 60 per cent of gross income at nearly a quarter of all charities. Members saw this as an 'extremely worrying situation', were dismayed that only fourteen of the Commission's 330 staff were employed on investigative work, and were astonished that the Commission did not employ a qualified accountant and saw no need for one.

The Commission's register of charities was described by the PAC as being 'seriously out of date and unreliable' and was criticized for giving no indication of a charity's trustworthiness. The Commission was also criticized for not enforcing the statutory duty of charities to submit annual accounts. Less than a quarter had submitted any accounts in the previous five years.

Shortly before this withering PAC broadside, Robin Guthrie, formerly director of the Joseph Rowntree Memorial Trust, had been appointed Chief Charity Commissioner. In retrospect, the PAC report, an equally critical report on charities by Sir Philip Woodfield a year earlier, and Guthrie's appointment, together marked a turning point for the Charity Commission that was to lead to the passage, four years later, of the 1992 Charities Act.

In July 1992, Richard Fries, Robin Guthrie's newly appointed successor as Chief Charity Commissioner, pledged that the Commission would 'work as hard and effectively as we can' to root out fund-raising abuse and he called on all professional fund-raisers to join with the Commissioners in their fight to curtail the activities of those whose motives and methods damaged charity.

Fries was speaking at the annual convention of the Institute of Charity Fund-raising Managers, and was at pains to stress the threat that fraud and abuse posed to all charities. 'Charity promises integrity,' the new chief Commissioner declared. 'The Commission's role is to underwrite that assurance. But we cannot do this sin-glehanded. Charities and their fund-raisers have the most import-ant contribution to make towards preserving and improving standards ... The damage which just one well publicized fraudulent fund-raiser can do is immeasurable ... Abuse catches the attention whilst the efforts of reputable fund-raisers go unrecognized.'

The 1992 Act

The new act, the first major piece of charities legislation since 1960, extends and strengthens the power of the Charity Commission, and tightens the law relating to fund-raising. The Commission may now require a charity to change its name, if it is too similar to that of another charity; if it sees fit, it can waive the new, automatic disqualification from trusteeship of those convicted for theft, fraud, forgery or financial mismanagement; it has more scope for co-operating with government departments and statutory bodies, like local authorities; it has the right to appoint receivers, managers or additional trustees; it can restrain debtors from parting with money which they owe to a charity; and, with the consent of the Attorney General, it can issue legal proceedings with respect to charities.

Although some, including the Chief Charity Commissioner, are fearful of an excessive codification of the law, there are a number of important new definitions in the act:

A **charitable institution** is a voluntary organization formed for charitable, benevolent or philanthropic purposes.

A **fund-raising business** is 'any business carried on for gain and wholly or primarily engaged in soliciting or otherwise procuring money or other property for charitable, benevolent or philanthropic purposes'. This illuminates the grey area that

41

exists between charitable institutions and organizations making money out of charity.

Commercial participators are involved in business other than a 'fund-raising business' which are engaged 'in a promotional venture in the course of which it is represented that charitable contributions are to be given to or applied for the benefit of the (charitable) institution'. This covers firms with whom charities and other voluntary organizations undertake joint commercial ventures.

A **promotional venture** is 'any advertising or sales campaign or any other venture undertaken for promotional purposes'.

Professional fund-raisers are any people who carry on a fund-raising business or solicit charity funds for reward. These do not include: charities and voluntary organizations and their connected trading companies, charities' staff and trustees, volunteer fund-raisers paid less than £5 a day or £500 a year (excluding expenses), collectors who volunteer or are employed to collect for charities or celebrities who solicit for charities on radio or TV (though celebrities may be professional fund-raisers if they are paid a fee).

To **represent** and **solicit** includes spoken, written, fax and phone communications.

Following expressions of concern from charities and the National Council for Voluntary Organizations, it was made clear by Earl Ferrers, government minister in charge of the bill, that

> it is not intended to catch as a professional fund-raiser the market consultant who gives advice to a charity on how it should prepare its fund-raising pamphlet or indeed a direct mailing firm which might simply send out appeal letters on behalf of a charity or another firm which might put the appeal notices into envelopes ... Those people such as the ones who print the document, put it in the envelope and mail it are acting as contractors. It is not intended that those people should be caught.

It is unlawful for professional fund-raisers and commercial participators to solicit money or property on behalf of a charity, or to represent that the charity will benefit from the proceeds of a promotional venture, unless there is a written agreement, satisfying requirements laid down by the Secretary of State. Charities may injunct those who do not comply with this stipulation. As the NCVO has pointed out, this is an important change because it gives charities much more power to protect their reputations from the predations of unauthorized fund-raisers.

Professional fund-raisers or commercial participators are not entitled to remuneration or expenses unless they are entitled to them under a valid agreement. Invalid agreements (that do not comply with the regulations) are not legally enforceable and professional fund-raisers or commercial participators who enter into such agreements are guilty of an offence. As the NCVO has pointed out,

> this places the burden on the professional fund-raisers and commercial participators to comply with the law but it is clearly in charities and voluntary organizations interest to help them to do this.

The act also places professional fund-raisers and commercial participators under a legal obligation to disclose much more information to prospective donors. Each charitable solicitation must be accompanied by a clear and accurate statement about:

1. The name or names of the institutions concerned.
2. If more than one is concerned, the proportions in which they will respectively benefit.
3. The method by which the fund-raisers remuneration is to be determined and, with commercial participators, the proportion of the price of goods and services sold that is to be given to the charity.

The act makes it a criminal offence for trustees and in some cases, staff, to fail to include the charity's registration details on documents, to fail to submit accounts and to fail to comply with the more important provisions on fund-raising.

Though the charity sector has generally welcomed the amended legislation, it is clear that charities themselves, although better protected, now, by the law, are obliged to behave in ways that will ensure the greater protection is effective.

What the Charities Must Do

Although the scams described above would be harder to work under the new law, the cases raise a number of key issues for the charity sector, the importance of which has not lessened appreciably since the *Sunday Times* revelations a decade ago, or since the passage of the 1992 Act. Let us consider two of them:

To what extent should particular charities, and charities in general, use sub-contractors for fund-raising?

There is a strong business case for employing sub-contractors to do work you have no expertise in. This is particularly true of small organizations but, as the contemporary debate in business circles about the balance of the so-called 'make or buy' decision shows, there is an argument applicable to all organizations that says you should only 'make' the goods and services you're good at making, and you should 'buy' the rest from organizations that specialize in making them.

The emphasis the Tories have placed on the sub-contracting of local authority services, such as refuse collection, exemplifies this principle. 'Stick to the knitting' is the cry of the management theorists; focus all your energies on exploiting your particular expertise.

But the use of sub-contractors will only generate additional value for the contracting organization if the profitability of the sub-contractor is under some kind of control. If it is not, then the added value of specialization, proclaimed long ago by Adam Smith in *The Wealth of Nations,* can quite easily end up in the sub-contractor's pocket.

Charities using sub-contractors should follow three, simple rules:

1. Shop around. Find out who the best sub-contractors are, using your network, and put the job out to tender.

2. Draft the sub-contract in ways that comply with the new regulations and which also guarantee you full access to the books and the selling techniques.
3. Monitor contract performance in terms of contributions, costs and perceptions of ultimate donors or users.

Sometimes easier said than done, of course, but the evidence suggests that some charities were not even trying.

The essence of good sub-contractor management is control. It should never be forgotten that, insofar as the rewards of charity sub-contractors are linked to performance, the sub-contractors are deriving benefit from the reputation of the charity they work for and from the reputation of the charity sector at large. Both these reputations are of great fund-raising value and both are undermined when sub-contractors abuse them.

An aspect of sub-contractor control that is of considerable significance for the reputations of charity in general, and of particular charities, is the selling 'style' used by the marketing professionals employed by sub-contractors. This raises the question:

To what extent should charities allow themselves and their reputations to be associated with 'hard sell' techniques?

Leaving aside, for the moment, the fact that certain charity publishing companies appear to have made substantial profits from the brochures and programmes they compiled for their charity clients, there is no doubt that with their professional sales teams they could sell more advertising pages, at higher page rates, than could charity 'amateurs'.

Suppose sub-contractors play fair and hand over all the cash they raise, less production costs, modest commissions and a reasonable profit. The question still arises whether the cost, in terms of the reputational damage caused by the use of such 'hard sell' methods, is worth the extra revenue in the long term.

The sub-contractor may be tempted to take a short-term view of the project, and may not care much about the reputational damage it inflicts, but the charity usually has to consider whether maximizing revenue today will damage its ability to raise more funds tomorrow.

There are plenty of well-documented cases where charity sub-contractors were found to be using methods of a 'hardness' that would do credit to the most aggressive of the financial services marketing companies. An example is the well-known selling technique of always asking questions that beg the answer, 'yes'. The patter goes something like this:

'Don't you agree the plight of disabled kiddies is awful?'
'Wouldn't you say that the government is doing too little to help them?'
'Don't you think it's the responsibility of all of us to do what we can to help?'
'Surely you could afford £50?'

It may be effective but is it appropriate for a charity? The irony is that the charity 'sell' is perfect for these heavy-handed techniques, because it engages the emotions of prospective donors, while at the same time subduing their normal, critical faculties. Charities should, therefore, be very careful about how their subcontractors act on their behalf, and the precise nature of the relationship should always be clear to both parties.

In July 1991 a dispute arose between a Manchester company, Rocket Sportswear, and the Great Ormond Street Children's Hospital over allegations that the final destination of the £5 entry fee for an exotic 'Win-a-Ferrari' competition was unclear.

Rocket claimed it had never pretended that its competition, featuring bright red Ferraris in the concourses of major railway stations and airports, was anything other than a commercial venture. The company insisted that it had been agreed, right at the start, that Great Ormond Street would get £1,000 a month for the use of its name, plus a share of the entry money and of profits.

The competition was abandoned (before it reached break-even, according to Rocket) when Great Ormond Street withdrew. It is far from clear, however, whether the problem was one of exploitation of reputation, over-zealous salespeople, or a simple misunderstanding about the true nature of the financial relationship between the company and Great Ormond Street.

Unless strict selling guidelines are laid down to protect a charity's reputation, and unless they are effectively policed with 'spot-checks' and the like, professional salespeople will always be tempted to exploit the 'easy' sell of charity.

It may be right for a charity to sub-contract fund-raising, and other charity functions, to professionals, but a balance needs to be struck between the ethos of professionalism, on the one hand, and the ethos of altruism on the other. This balance, and the conflicts it must resolve, is the most important of all the questions now confronting charities. It lies at the heart of both the charity 'meta-brand' issue and the danger zone that straddles the frontier between business and charity.

To marketing professionals charity is an 'easy sell', but if the managers of charitable 'brands' (including the charity 'meta-brand') allow the techniques of professional marketing to be used too vigorously or indiscriminately, public trust and confidence will be undermined, and the value of the brands, and hence the 'easi-ness' of the charity 'sell', will be eroded.

The same considerations apply to the issues of internal mis-behaviour highlighted by the Aberdour and Spastics Society cases. A strict, *dirigiste* style of management, in which all executive action is closely monitored and controlled, is not consistent with certain aspects of the charitable ethos, such as being trusted to get on with one's job without interference, on the grounds that those who work in the sector have a calling which makes them psychologically incapable of fraud and deception.

This atmosphere of trust is very valuable but it is also very attractive to those bent on exploitation. Charities should recognize that the more trusting they are, the more vulnerable they are to that trust being betrayed.

3

An Age of Compassion

Greater equality of income, higher living standards and the advent of the era of mass communication have, over the past two decades or so, brought about a philanthropic revolution. The traditional idea of philanthropy as something a few rich people did for the poor masses is dead and buried, and with it has gone much of charity's religious association.

As charity has become more popular and more secular, its horizons have been both widened and deepened. To the new age of compassion, mass communication, particularly television, has brought a high-fidelity sensor system that can convey, in equally vivid detail, the calamity of mass starvation and the tragedy of one small child with a rare disease.

Some of the consequences of these changes are quite obvious – ordinary people are giving to charity more money and more time (see the discussion of 'volunteering' below), they've become less parochial (21 per cent of donations to Britain's top ten fund-raising charities in 1990 were for international causes) and there has been an extraordinary explosion in the number and variety of causes for which people rattle tins. Less obvious are the changes being brought about by the age of compassion in the ways in which society is grappling with the problem of welfare.

The collapse of communism, and the damage this has inflicted on the reputation of its Western variant, socialism, have generated confusion and doubt about the role of the state in modern societies, and about who should do what and for whom. As the state with-draws from the direct provision of welfare, and begins to sub-contract more of the responsibilities it retains to the voluntary sector, the decisions about how the proceeds of the human urge to give should be deployed are being left, more and more, to givers. Instead of voting for political parties with particular welfare policies, people are revealing their preferences by the causes to which they give.

And because vast numbers of people are involved in this new decision-making process, the decisions reached are better – in the sense that they are more accurate reflections of what society wants. An economist would say this 'democratization' of giving is improving the 'efficiency of the need market'. In this way these mass demonstrations of generosity, whether they involve gifts of time or of money, have become important indicators of the public mood that both politicians and companies can learn from and can exploit, in their constant efforts to increase votes and sales.

In this chapter we shall look at how the patterns of giving have changed over the past few years, at how a new and much more colourful style of mass giving has emerged (and at where it might lead), at how ordinary people are involving themselves more in the 'charity work' that was previously the preserve of the rich, the privileged and the retired, and at the intriguing role companies are playing, in stimulating these developments.

The Changing Pattern of Giving

Although total 'real' giving, after inflation, has probably risen only modestly in the past five years, there have been some interesting changes in the patterns of giving (see table 3.1 in the Appendix).

There was a sharp increase in the percentage of giving going to international aid in 1985, which was largely attributable to Bob Geldof's extraordinary Band Aid campaign. The Live Aid concert in July 1985, accompanied by a television appeal, raised £50m directly and contributed far more than that, in terms of the publicity it gave to famines in Africa, to the fund-raising efforts of the international aid agencies.

There was also a less dramatic but still significant jump in the percentage going to medicine and health in 1988. This, too, was attributable to a particular campaign, namely the Wishing Well

Appeal for the Great Ormond Street Children's Hospital (see chapter 1).

A cynic might interpret these shifts in giving patterns as indications of how susceptible public giving is to the news-values of the media. No doubt hard-pressed charities in the health and welfare sectors saw it that way when their shares of the charity cake slumped in 1985.

But for those who believe the press and the broadcast media reflect public attitudes more than they lead them, the same patterns can be interpreted as evidence of a remarkable responsiveness among the giving public. They are regular givers to long-term causes (if they were not, where would the established health and welfare charities be?), but they are also flexible, responding quickly to disasters and other urgent needs.

It is simply not true that campaigns and appeals that win heavy media support generate bucketfuls of extra money. If that were the case, total charitable income – going up and down according to public whim – would be too changeable for anything but the most opportunist fund-raising.

Broadcast Appeals

Peter Halfpenny, of the Centre for Applied Social Research at the University of Manchester, suggests individual giving has probably been falling since 1987. In his commentary on the Charities Aid Foundation's 1989/90 Charity Household Survey, he acknowledges that this may be surprising to those who have interpreted the highly visible charity media events of recent years as evidence of an upsurge in giving.

'But it is worth remembering' he says, 'that although Comic Relief raised £27m in 1989, the 1989 Children in Need Appeal raised almost £22m, and the ITV Telethon 1990 raised £24m, these three events generated less than 2 per cent of the overall amount that individuals donate to charities each year.'

Diana Leat, the leading chronicler of UK Telethons and other broadcast appeals, has pointed out that extended broadcast appeals (as opposed to regular advertising slots), like the BBC's annual Children in Need Appeal, ITV's Telethons, Live Aid and Comic Relief, have an importance that extends beyond the money they raise. 'Some of those responsible for the organization of extended broadcast appeals', Leat wrote in 1990, 'have at worst actively encouraged and at best not actively discouraged the notion that the measure of an appeal's success is the amount of money raised. Alternative measures of success – how well the money was spent, what the money raised enabled to happen, affects on public attitudes and awareness, effects of public involvement in fund-raising – have not been widely discussed.' Leat suggests that by concentrating on the 'scoreboard', the organizers of such appeals 'have created a rod for their own backs – each successive appeal must raise more than the last otherwise it will be deemed a failure.'

But whether or not an extended broadcast appeal does 'fail' in this way, and in so doing breaks the spell that has been cast by the hitherto constantly rising totals, there is no doubt the broadcast media have won their fund-raising spurs, and will continue to play an important role.

In her booklet *Fund-raising & Grant Making: A Case Study of ITV Telethon '88*, Diana Leat described the complexity of the structure and the enormity of the effort that went into the project. The aim was to raise money from corporations, community and voluntary organizations and the viewing public. Each of the fifteen regional TV companies appointed full-time fund-raisers several months before the twenty-seven hour broadcast (from 7pm on Sunday, 29 May to 10pm on Monday, 30 May). Their job was to encourage corporate donations and stimulate fund-raising events run by community and voluntary organizations and individuals.

In addition to the regional fund-raisers there was a team of network/national fund-raisers based at Thames Television in London, headed by the executive producer and fund-raising organizer. Their job was to co-ordinate and support company and community fund-raising events which involved all or most of the regional companies. A network programme team based at London Weekend Television, liaised with the national corporate fund-raisers, the national community fund-raising co-ordinator, and producers at each of the regional companies.

Since a key principle of the ITV Telethon '88 was that money raised locally should be spent locally, a network of trusts was attached to each regional company (except Scotland, where the three companies co-operated in one trust). Money raised nationally was to be spent nationally, by a central grant-making body, the Independent Broadcasting Telethon Trust (IBTT). The IBTT was charged with the task of achieving some re-distribution from rich to poor regions.

The IBTT and each of the regional trusts were serviced by a trust administrator and/or a trust secretary. In some cases this job was undertaken by a member of the company staff; in other cases, full-time outsiders were recruited. The trusts were supported and co-ordinated, nationally, by the Regional Trust Liaison Officer. The project also employed a financial co-ordinator, with a team of assistants, a press and publicity team, a sales and merchandizing team, numerous technical staff and, of course, hundreds of tele-phonists.

The relationship between television and the voluntary sector has developed, since then, in subsequent 'extended broadcast appeals' and perhaps more significantly, in the emergence of the charities as buyers of TV airtime. The larger charities have already clubbed together, with the help of companies and media owners, to buy discounted airtime in bulk, and the willingness of TV per-sonalities and other celebrities to help ensure charity airtime attracts good viewer ratings, continues to be amply demonstrated.

Although it is hard to be sure, it seems probable that the greater media exposure given to the idea of charity, and to the idea that charity can be fun, even glamorous, has contributed significantly to the recent growth of what has come to be known as 'vol-unteering' – the giving, by ordinary people, not just the rich and famous – of their time.

Volunteering

'Volunteering' – the gift of time, skill and experience – differs from the gift of money in a number of ways. It seems both less and more than 'charity' – less because the monetary cost of volunteering is usually negligible and more, because voluntary action is a personal gift that requires the giver to enter into a much more intimate relationship with his or her charity 'clients' (as charities call their beneficiaries these days). Professor Ken Young, in his Gresham College essay, *Meeting the Needs of Strangers*, suggests that the term 'charity' is inappropriate for this kind of giving, because 'its neo-

Victorian connotations of coldness seem to be at odds with the usually cheerful and mutually sustaining experience of volunteering'.

In this respect volunteering is similar to (and its growth has probably been inspired by) the mass fund-raising events associated with Band Aid, Comic Relief and the Children in Need and Telethon appeals. There is a social dimension to it. Charity has the power to transfigure what would otherwise be prosaic experiences. The difference with volunteering lies in the transparency of the experience. In the case of mass fund-raising events, the organizers are the immediate client, not the beneficiaries of the various charities who receive funding from it. Volunteering usually involves a much more direct link with the ultimate clients.

This is why Young prefers the word 'friendship' to 'charity' to describe volunteering, and why he regards it as 'entirely appropriate that Michael de-la-Noy should have entitled his intimate profile of the Samaritans, *Acting as Friends*, just as it is appropriate that this quintessential volunteer service to distressed strangers should have taken the title of Samaritans'.

There are many kinds of volunteering ranging from acting as unpaid trustees or governors to caring for relatives, but the term is usually applied to volunteer labour of the kind employed by charities like the Samaritans or *ad hoc* charitable projects. The 1991 *National Survey of Voluntary Activity*, published by the Volunteer Centre UK, shows that fund-raising is the most common activity (involving over two-thirds of volunteers), that half had organized or run events and that a quarter had served on committees.

An average of about three hours a week per person is spent on voluntary work which indicates a national total of sixty-two million hours a year. The 35–44 year olds are most likely to volunteer, and there is a close link to social position. Some three-quarters of those in managerial or professional positions say they do voluntary work compared with 58 per cent in skilled manual jobs and 37 per cent in unskilled occupations. Retired people are least likely to volunteer. This suggests a large untapped pool of expertise that, if it could be organized, would be of great value to smaller charities lacking the resources to employ professional people. Efforts are being made by the Confederation of British Industry and the Institute of Directors to encourage members to include information on volunteering opportunities in pre-retirement courses.

The motivations for volunteering are, doubtless, legion. Martin Knapp in *Time is Money: the Costs of Volunteering in Britain Today*, suggests volunteers may be trying

> to fit some normative expectation of behaviour, to gain prestige or social approval for participation, or to expand their social circle. There may be therapeutic or rehabilitative reasons for volunteering: to help cope with inner anxieties and uncertainties about personal competence and worth; to feel needed.

Although there is little evidence that religious beliefs are important inspirations for volunteering, research indicates that those with a religious commitment are more likely to be volunteers.

There have been two significant developments in volunteering in recent years: an increase in 'employee volunteering' and a more vigorous exploration of the possibilities of matching the skills, talents and abilities of the volunteers to the voluntary labour. An advertising copy-writer, for example, can be a passably competent stuffer of envelopes for a fund-raising mailing campaign, but could create much more value, with the same amount of time, by using his or her skills to draft the mailing material.

A story is told about David Ogilvy, founder of the Ogilvy & Mather advertising agency. He was in the habit of walking to his Madison Avenue office each morning across Central Park. Each day he passed a beggar with a sign round his neck which informed passers-by he was

Blind

Ogilvy did not believe in giving money to beggars but on one fine April morning his conscience pricked him. He took the sign from the beggar's neck and edited the message with his felt-tip pen, so that it read

It is spring and I am
Blind

... and replaced it. Legend has it that by noon the beggar's cup was overflowing.

Charity Projects (see chapter 6) has gone further than most in the recruiting of talent, skill and knowhow – in addition to money – to charity's cause. In so doing, it has tapped what appears to be a rich and under-exploited seam of volunteer effort. The involvement of thousands of ordinary people in the fund-raising events associated with extended broadcast appeals, including the Charity Projects 'Red Nose Day' Comic Relief appeals, is an example of a kind of volunteering where specialist skills are not needed.

But Charity Projects has helped to show that whether one is exploiting specialist skills, from show-business, the media, advertising and the professions, or whether one is just seeking help with fund-raising legwork, volunteering needs to be properly organized if its full charitable potential is to be realized. This is why the growth of employee volunteering – actively encouraged, supported and sometimes inspired by companies – is seen by some to be such an important development.

Employee Volunteering

The idea of employee volunteering is that employees donate time, skills and resources to the local community with the support and the active encouragement of their employers. Examples include supporting the environment, by planting trees and clearing river banks, caring for children and disabled and elderly people, fund-raising for charities and manning ambulances with St John Ambulance.

Sam Whitbread, chairman of the Whitbread brewing group, says in his foreword to the Whitbread-commissioned *A Guide to Employee Volunteering* that 'successful and forward-looking businesses have an important role to play in creating a climate where the giving of time and talent to the community is seen as something to be actively encouraged.'

By all accounts, there is plenty of enthusiasm for this idea amongst employees. A MORI survey in 1990, commissioned by the Volunteer Centre UK, found that nearly 40 per cent of adults had been engaged in voluntary activity of some kind during the previous twelve months and that almost a quarter had been active volunteers in the week prior to the survey. However, only a fifth of the volunteers felt they had the support of their employers, and 25 per cent said they would be more inclined to volunteer if such support were forthcoming. The same proportion of those who had already volunteered said they would do more volunteering if their employers supported them. (A 1989 Employee Attitude Survey at Whitbread found that over half those questioned 'would be interested in volunteering, given help and support from the company'.)

All of which suggests that employee volunteering is still in its infancy in the UK. If the majority of companies begin to feel it is in their interest to encourage it, the corporate sector could soon emerge as a substantial sponsor, and even a major organizer of voluntary work. There is no lack of trail-blazers for them to follow.

Shell UK, the oil company, established its Community Service Fund in 1980 to enable existing and retired employees and their spouses to give financial support to voluntary groups with which they were actively involved as volunteers. Awards of up to £350 can be applied for, and the scheme is actively promoted within the group. It is a hands-off scheme, as Chris Bullock, Shell UK's community affairs manager explains:

> We see the Community Service Fund as an excellent way of signalling our firm support for the voluntary efforts of Shell people, without in any way invading their privacy or putting pressure on them.

Two hands-on volunteering schemes are Shell's use of retired staff as Campaign Officers for the Shell Better Britain Campaign, and the involvement of more than 500 existing and retired staff acting as business advisers in the company's Livewire initiative aimed at fostering enterprise in young people.

IBM UK's LEAT programme (it stands for Local Environment Action Team) was launched in 1990 as part of a $1m world-wide IBM programme to stimulate employee involvement in projects meeting community need in the fields of education or the environment. The LEAT programme operates with selected environmental agencies, and workshops are held to inform interested staff of local opportunities. Staff actively engaged in relevant projects can apply for a cash grant for their project of up to £15,000. The programme is run by a full-time co-ordinator, seconded from the Action Resource Centre.

IBM has been encouraging employee volunteering for years. It operates a 'ten per cent scheme' allowing employees, if managers can spare them, half a day off a week to engage in approved community activities.

Another computer group, Honeywell, runs an annual Community Service Awards scheme for employees who make substantial contributions to organizations that help people or otherwise enrich the community. A 1989 award winner was communications manager Allen Sparks who had for many years organized an annual Christmas food parcel programme in conjunction with Age Concern.

A neat example of using employee volunteers for fund-raising are ScotRail's Paybill Volunteers whose task is to recruit new members for the company's pay-roll deduction scheme for the benefit of Barnardos.

Lawyers in the Community, a pilot project run by the Action Resource Centre in furtherance of its aims to develop ways for business to support community organizations, matches volunteers from London law firms with charities operating in selected, inner-city boroughs.

In 1984 the board of the civil engineering group John Laing challenged their employees to raise £100,000 for the NSPCC Centenary Appeal and promised to double the contribution if they hit the target. In the event, employees raised £365,000 and the company contributed a further £250,000.

A similar scheme was launched four years later but this time each of the group's twenty-five business units linked up with a local children's hospital. The Laing Children's Hospital Appeal raised £625,000, the company contributed a further £200,000, and successful efforts were made to encourage business units to sustain the links established during the appeal, after it had ended. John Farrow, group director of community affairs, seemed tickled pink by the whole thing: 'I'm delighted to say this is still going on all over the company, and it is very rewarding for everyone involved.'

But perhaps the most impressive UK exponent of the employee-volunteering concept is the financial services group, Allied Dunbar

Assurance. The company is now part of BAT Industries but was founded by Sir Mark Weinberg who has done more than almost any other UK company leader – not counting his friend Lord Laing (see chapter 1), of whom he has been a staunch ally for many years – to promote the idea of the socially responsible company.

Sir Mark is also the most conspicuously successful financial services entrepreneur of recent times. He has left the firm now, to form another company (his third), but the imprint of his ideas and of his business philosophy remains embedded in the Allied Dunbar culture.

Allied Dunbar's 'Volunteers at Work' scheme was launched in 1987. It offers a package of information, support and advice on volunteering opportunities in the Thamesdown area around the company's Swindon headquarters. By 1990 more than 800 volunteers (over 25 per cent of total staff) had been recruited by the scheme and in 1989 a group of them formed the Dunbar Conservation Group to concentrate on environmental matters.

In addition, the Allied Professional Help and Advice (ALPHA) scheme offers company skills to local voluntary organizations to complete specific tasks. The manner of delivery varies – Weinberg is very keen on flexibility – but a typical arrangement is for an ALPHA volunteer to receive paid time off for half the number of hours needed to complete the task.

Employees also run a Staff Charity Fund which was set up in 1975. It generates £150,000 worth of income a year and made sixty-five grants in 1989. It is managed by a committee of thirty-five and there is a system of paid leave for key committee members.

Apart from flexibility, Weinberg believes a number of other principles are crucial to successful employee volunteering:

1. Communication – community activity should be a routine item on regular business meeting agendas.
2. Recognition – volunteering efforts should be acknowledged by the company. When the firm won the Lord Mayor of London's 'Dragon Award' in the employee involvement category in 1989 every active volunteer received a letter of thanks from the managing director.

3. Ownership – initiatives should always be in the hands of the staff themselves.
4. Monitoring and evaluation – the company's Community Affairs team regularly seeks the views of both the participants and the beneficiaries of volunteering.
5. Professional resources – in 1988 the firm broke new ground by appointing a Staff Charity Co-ordinator within Community Affairs, specifically to look after volunteering.

Allied Dunbar is not just a trail-blazer in the general area of employee volunteering. It is also a very generous company by UK standards. According to the 14th edition of *Charity Trends*, it gave £1.5m to charity in 1990, equivalent to £500 per employee and way in excess of the standard required for membership of the Per Cent Club, of which Sir Mark is one of the joint chairmen. In a 1990 interview in *Management Today* Sir Mark said: 'I think the amount of money we've put into charities has been more than made up by the increase in the morale and the number of people who stay with us.'

It is to this idea, that corporate philanthropy and corporate social responsibility, whether they take the form of giving or volunteering, are not so much gestures as investments in a strong corporate culture, that we shall now turn.

4

Why Companies Give

Because the power of mass compassion comes from people, it is inevitable that it should reach into every nook and cranny of society, and exert an influence on the behaviour of every social institution. But although companies are no exception, and are fast becoming major suppliers of funds and of assistance in kind, to the non-profit sector, it is important to recognize how different they are from human beings. Companies are driven by instincts, hungers and appetites that are primitive by human standards, so it is unreasonable to expect them to understand the meaning of words like compassion, generosity, unselfishness, or pity, still less to exhibit those qualities spontaneously, out of the goodness of their hearts, in their day-to-day behaviour.

The failure to recognize that the corporate species, unlike the human, is not philanthropic by nature has provoked, in the age of mass compassion, a modern debate about corporate generosity and ethics that is as misguided as it is passionate. Many people, including most of those involved in one way or another in the 'charity industry', take an anthropomorphic view of the company – they assume the behaviour patterns of companies reflect the attitudes of the human beings who lead them.

These self-righteous guardians of the purity of giving tend to regard with distaste the way in which modern companies are taking up the challenges, and responding to the demands and provocations of the age of compassion. Because they value £1 given out of the goodness of a human heart more highly than £1 given out of self-interest, be it ever so enlightened, they see in the new style of corporate giving a deviousness bordering on the cynical.

To understand why companies give, and to be in a position to speculate sensibly about how corporate giving is likely to develop, it is first necessary to recognize how surprising it is that companies give at all. It is not corporate selfishness that is aberrant and in need of an explanation – it is its opposite.

In this chapter we shall look at some aspects of the history of the corporate species that have contributed to its modern character, at the present state of corporate development and at why and how companies have started to simulate peculiarly human qualities, like compassion, for non-human reasons.

The Origin of Companies

The first companies were created by Royal Charter to exploit crown monopolies and began appearing in Britain in the early 17th century. The English East India Company, for example, was established in 1600 by a charter from Queen Elizabeth 1. The underlying intent of the company legislation passed from the eighteenth century onwards, was that monopoly privileges of the kind granted to such chartered companies should carry with them certain obligations.

The 'joint-stock' company, in which capital was divided into small units (shares) so that a number of investors could contribute, was invoked to satisfy the insatiable demand for capital provoked by the rapid development of world trade. Mines and the overseas trading companies were the leading practitioners of this new art of financial engineering. The notorious South Sea Company raised astronomical sums in this way. At the peak, its capital amounted to almost £34m, three times the capital of the Bank of England at that time.

These joint-stock companies attracted such a large share of available funds that governments were obliged to borrow from them (and so become associated with their fates). The South Sea Company lent £9m to the government in 1711, the largest loan ever made at that time.

By the early 18th century, abuse of joint-stock arrangements – exemplified by the notorious South Sea Bubble crisis – and the epidemics of personal bankruptcies that always followed in the wake of corporate collapses, led to the Act of 1720 which created the statutory company with limited liability. This development unleashed such a proliferation of business activity that by the early 19th century the creation of new companies by separate Acts of Parliament was threatening to overwhelm the legislature. In 1825 a new act allowed company formation by registration.

A third feature of the modern corporate species was fixed in 1862, when the principle of limited liability was extended to all registered companies, not just statutory companies.

These three acts of Parliament indelibly marked the company and have exerted a profound influence on its evolution over the subsequent century. The 1720 Act, by introducing the statutory company with limited liability, freed it from royal patronage and from its human constituents, giving it independent life. The 1825 Act, by making the company formation process easier and less expensive greatly increased the fecundity of the species leading to its dominance of the productive process. The 1862 Act, by making limited liability a right available to all companies, rather than a privilege conferred on a few statutory companies, gave new coherence to the species. The forced convergence of the evolution of public and private (non-statutory) companies rendered still-born the embryo of what might have been a quite separate managerial tradition among private companies, vestiges of which survive today in professional partnerships.

Limited liability, the company's insatiable hunger for more capital and the rapid geographical spread of its activities, have all combined to produce a progressive alienation of the corporate from the human species. The price of the company's liberation was the loss of moral constraints on its behaviour. Had the old tradition of individual corporate ownership survived, a more ethical managerial tradition might have evolved. There was no lack of introspection and philosophizing during the early days of Western capitalism. The idea that people matter, for example, inspired a number of experiments on the common ownership theme dating back to well before such 19th-century evangelists as Robert Owen and Charles Fourier.

Modern UK companies such as the John Lewis Partnership, the Scott Bader specialist chemicals company, the quoted office equipment supplier Kalamazoo, the transport group NFC, the computer software company, FI Group, the Baxi Partnership, as well as the much-studied Mondragon movement in Spain, show the tradition of the producer cooperative is still far from extinct. The consumer cooperative tradition also survives in building societies, 'mutual' insurance companies and the Co-Operative Wholesale Society. Even today, such organizations tend to achieve significantly higher scores than their conventional competitors in surveys of consumer trust and confidence.

Another vestige of a more socially responsible corporate past survives in Quaker economics, originally inspired by the teachings of the 17th-century mystic, George Fox, and developed subsequently by the economist Kenneth Boulding. The distinctive Quaker economic philosophy, which I believe will enjoy something of a revival in the 1990s, holds that 'harmony' is desirable as an end as well as merely a means.

That Quaker companies, like the Lloyds and Barclays banking groups, the Price Waterhouse accountancy firm, the Cadbury and Rowntree confectionery groups and the J. Walter Thompson advertising agency, have proved remarkably robust on both sides of the Atlantic suggests this approach to business has a lot going for it.

The story of Cadbury, the hugely successful sweets and soft drinks group, shows how the founding family's membership of the Society of Friends led to the formation of the company in the first place, dictated its style of management and how Quaker principles not only survive at Cadbury today (alongside more modern business ideas) but are, if anything, becoming more important.

The Case of Cadbury

When Richard Tapper Cadbury, great-great-great-grandfather of Dominic Cadbury, present chief executive of the Cadbury Schweppes group, moved to Birmingham in 1794, the family had been members of the Society of Friends for four generations. Three Cadburys had been imprisoned during the early days of the Quaker movement.

Richard Tapper was a silk mercer and had a shop at 92 Bull Street in the centre of Birmingham. In 1824 his third son, John, then twenty-three, set up in business next door, at number 93, selling tea, coffee and cocoa. In the local paper he advertised his cocoa, called Nibs, as 'a most nutritious beverage for breakfast'.

In 1831 he took a warehouse in Crooked Lane and began making cocoa and chocolate, so founding the Cadbury business and beginning another chapter in the extraordinary story of the contribution of the Quakers to Britain's economic and social development.

Sir Adrian Cadbury points out that Richard Tapper Cadbury was a Birmingham Street Commissioner for fifty years (he was chairman of the Commissioners for the last twenty-five years of the Commission's existence), and that his son John was also a Commissioner and was deeply involved with the change from rule by the Commissioners to an elected City Council in 1851. John was also Chairman of the Steam Engine Committee which, in 1828, was charged with reducing smoke from factory chimneys in the industrial area of Birmingham. He installed a device, known as Beddington's Patent, in his boiler house, and showed that efficient smoke control saved fuel as well as reduced pollution.

George and Richard Cadbury's response to the Quaker injunction to understand and remove social evils was to rebuild the Cadbury factory in the country on a site called Bournville. It was a controversial decision. The view of the Birmingham business establishment was that the brothers were embarking on a wild adventure that would end in disaster. But George and Richard understood that the injunction made business sense; that the increased contentment of their employees in the fresh air and rural surroundings would make a greater contribution to the efficiency of their operations than machinery or method. 'We consider' they said, 'that our people spend the greater part of their lives at their work, and we wish to make it less irksome by environing them with pleasant and wholesome sights, sounds and conditions.' (A.G. Gardiner, *Life of George Cadbury*).

Fearful of the city's inexorable expansion towards their rural enclave, the Cadburys started buying land around the Bournville factory in 1895, with the twin aims of preserving the rural amenities they had won and of showing how decent houses, with large gardens, could be self-financing at rents that working people could afford. The industrial village the Cadburys created attracted the interest of social reformers throughout the world.

Another Cadbury response to the injunctions of the Quaker

creed was the company's generosity in giving employees time off, with pay, for public service, an early example of 'employee volunteering'.

Today, Cadbury Schweppes gives to charity through the Cadbury Schweppes Charitable Trust and, directly, through its operating units. Community involvement ranges from donations of cash, management time and site facilities to local activities, as well as secondment of employees to community projects.

The company is a member of the Per Cent Club and specializes in job creation and youth unemployment, the environment, the promotion of education and industry links, health and welfare, clubs and societies in local communities and industry related matters.

In a booklet entitled *The Character of the Company*, Sir Adrian said: 'I find no conflict between the values and characteristics we have inherited from the past and the actions we have to take to ensure a successful and independent future for Cadbury Schweppes.' He stressed the importance of keeping a balance between the company's responsibilities to its 'shareholders, employees, customers, suppliers, government and society' and the need to maintain the company's reputation 'for meeting society's legitimate expectations of the business and for contributing to the life of the communities of which we are part'. Sir Adrian also showed how well he understands how corporate reputations are made by emphasising that 'Cadbury Schweppes' concern for the values I have described will not be judged by this statement, but by our actions.'

According to the 14th edition of *Charity Trends* published in November 1991, Cadbury Schweppes gave total support to the non-profit sector of £731,000 in 1990, including £246,000 in cash donations. Total support amounted to 0.57 per cent of group pre-tax profits and £45.63 per employee.

Though Quaker principles provided a set of clear operating principles for 18th- and 19th-century companies, uncannily congruent with modern management thinking, it should not be supposed that the notion that companies are integral parts of the communities in which they live, was confined to the Quakers in particular, or even to the non-conformists in general. The principle was applied with more rigour, and more conviction by the Quakers, but it was just as much to do with patterns of ownership, during the early days of capitalism, as with religious affiliation.

As wealth was accumulated by the entrepreneurs of England's industrial revolution, it was natural that a variation of the *noblesse oblige* principle (*richesse oblige*, perhaps) should develop. The early companies played central roles in the lives of their communities, and their patriarchs were soon vying with local landowners for the front pews in church.

When individuals and families owned companies, there was little distinction between human and corporate social responsibility – the latter was merely an extension of the former. It was unimportant in those days that companies, because of changes in their legal status, were becoming intrinsically amoral. Their owners, most of them anyway, retained their human morality and this was reflected in the behaviour of their companies.

The turning point – the cusp of change that drove the wedge between human and corporate morality, and revealed the intrinsic amorality of the corporate species – came in the 20th century, with the so-called 'divorce of ownership and control' (first identified by Berle and Means in 1932). This separation of ownership from an executive role was both a reflection and a consequence of two crucial developments: the rise of the financial institutions (pension funds and life insurance companies) as the new owners of companies and the emergence of professional managers as the holders of all executive power. In this way, the basic ethical orientation of companies was reset. Two new, overriding duties emerged: the fiduciary responsibilities of company managers to shareholders (the former are, legally, the agents of the latter), and of fund managers to the beneficiaries of the funds in their care.

It was then that it became reasonable to wonder why managers should spend shareholders' money on giving, and on socially responsible projects, when shareholders, as human beings, were willing and able to make their own decisions about how socially responsible they wished to be and in what ways.

An article about the Bata shoe company in the November 1990 edition of *International Management* suggests that the 'descent' of the company this century from the morality associated with family ownership to the amorality associated with ownership by institutions (whether pensions funds, insurance companies or the state) is not peculiar to capitalist economics.

The Bata company was founded by the Czech Tomas Bata in 1894 in the Moravian town of Zlin. Following its nationalization in 1945 (it became part if the Czech state-owned shoemaker, Svit), the founder's son Thomas moved to Toronto, Canada, and set up a new Bata company, which is now the world's largest footwear group. The Canadian Bata manufactures in forty countries, owns 6,200 retail outlets and is still privately owned.

Meanwhile the old Bata factories now run by the state-owned Czech shoemakers, Svit, went the way of many communist manufacturers, so much so that the author of the article, Tammi Gutner, reported plans afoot (no pun intended) to reunite Bata and Svit in the hope that the former's capitalist-bred qualities can redeem the down-at-heel reputation of the Czech company. Embarrassingly for the Party apparatchiks in Prague, Gutner reported, '... the people of Zlin still harboured happy memories of the former owners. Tomas Bata had introduced profit-sharing for his workers, paid them above the national average wage, and built them houses, schools, a hospital, a hotel and cinema.' Such corporate social responsibility had become quite unknown in Czechoslovakia since.

Ethics, Greed and Generosity

Corporate generosity, or the lack of it, is best seen as an aspect of the wider issue of corporate ethics, or the lack of them. A company's ethics and the generosity they inspire, are rough measures of the extent to which the firm is aware of, and responsive to, the wider communities of which it is part.

The legal status of companies demands that firms seek profit above all other goals. In the past, this intrinsic greed has meant that, since their 'liberation' from personal or family ownership, firms have frequently behaved in ways that are in conflict with society's ethics and moral codes. The laws and regulations with which society has constrained corporate behaviour in this century reflect a deep mistrust of companies and a belief that, left to their own devices, the corporate species will behave badly. There is plenty of evidence for this view.

Companies have sold unsafe products, run hazardous plants and other operations negligently, traded with unacceptable regimes, peddled powdered milk to the Third World, launched untested drugs, poisoned the atmosphere, tried to subvert national governments, perpetrated frauds on consumers, lied to and cheated governments and regulatory authorities, victimized their critics, exploited employees and bullied suppliers and competitors.

A 1988 survey of opinion about occupations by the UK Market Research Society found most people think business people are a pretty dishonest lot, with national newspapers rather worse and MPs only a little better (see Appendix, table 4.1). In a 1989 Harris Poll of American adults, the question: 'If you had to say, which of the following things do you think business would do to obtain greater profit?' elicited the answers: 'harm the environment' (47 per cent), 'knowingly sell inferior goods' (44 per cent), 'deliberately charge inflated prices' (42 per cent) and 'put its workers' health and safety at risk' (42 per cent). (See Appendix, table 4.2 for full results.) This widespread belief that business people are incorrigibly unethical has inspired numerous initiatives aimed at putting pressure on companies to improve themselves. The US has been the pioneer in this area.

According to the Ethics Resource Centre (ERC) in Washington DC, by 1988, 92 per cent of America's largest 2,000 companies had ethical codes of practice for their employees, compared with less than half of European firms. More than a third of US companies had 'ethics education' programmes.

The idea of the 'ethical business' is deeply embedded in the American establishment. In addition to the ERC, whose chief executive Gary Edwards is one of America's leading ethics gurus, there is the Centre for Business Ethics at Bentley College, the Olsson Centre for Applied Ethics at Virginia University, and the Trinity Centre for Ethics and Corporate Policy, sponsored by Trinity Church in Wall Street. Harvard was running classes on 'social factors' in business as long ago as 1915 and expanded its ethics effort after the 1929 Wall Street crash. Today, there are ethical aspects to all Harvard Business School courses (see below).

More recently, Europe has also been invaded by a new breed of business 'ethicists'. Since 1983 four chairs of business ethics have been founded in the Netherlands, a similar post exists at the Hochschule in Switzerland, there is another at the Ecole Superieure in Lyon (France), and Jack Mahoney founded the Business Ethics Research Centre at King's College, London in 1987. Non-academic institutions include the Centrum voor Economie en Ethiek in Belgium, the Seminario Permanente Empresa y Humanismo in Spain, the Gesellschaft fur Ethik, Bildung und Management in Germany and the Institute of Business Ethics in the UK, set up by the Christian Association of Business Executives in 1986. The pan-continental European Business Ethics Network was founded in 1987.

But although Europe appears to be catching up, it still lags far behind America in the development of business ethics in general and in business generosity in particular. One of the most striking facts in *Companies & Communities* by Michael Fogarty and Ian Christie is that whereas the median for declared charitable donations by UK firms in recent years has ranged from about 0.1 per cent to 0.2 per cent of taxable profits, average tax deductible contributions by US companies were around 1.8 per cent or between 2–2.5 per cent, when other 'corporate assistance' is included. Part of the reason for this surprisingly wide discrepancy is that US companies are more assiduous than European firms in recording their generosity and ethical standards, but there is more to it than that.

Professor Henk van Luijk, of the University of Groningen in the Netherlands suggested in the *Journal of Business Strategy*, that business ethics are culture specific. He points out that it is America's liberal business culture, which stresses personal morality and responsibility, that has led to the higher level of US interest in business ethics, and a higher level of corporate giving.

He argues that this cultural difference is reflected in and is also a reflection of, the differing political traditions on the two sides of the Atlantic; that, whereas in liberal America, business ethics have been seen as the business of companies themselves, in the social democratic traditions of Europe they are seen more as the business of government. In other words, within Europe's social democratic tradition, people have sought to ensure minimum standards of business ethics through laws and regulations, whereas in America it has been left to corporate commitments to voluntary ethical codes.

The same applies to company giving. In America the welfare state has never been as all-encompassing a provider as it has in

European countries like Sweden, Holland and the UK. There has hence been more need for American companies to give, merely to maintain minimum standards of welfare provision. High levels of US corporate giving, therefore, may be more a reflection of a political judgement about the balance between state and private sector welfare provision, than of an inherently more generous breed of companies in America.

Models of Business Ethics

At a conference in 1991, chaired by HRH the Prince of Wales, Business in the Community (BitC) launched its 'Directions for the Nineties. An Action Strategy for Companies and their Partners in Community Involvement'. The document includes a SWOT analysis (Strengths, Weaknesses, Opportunities and Threats) of the general field of community involvement.

One of the weaknesses that BitC identified was that, as yet, there is 'no coherent management theory or vocabulary of business involvement in the community' or of company giving. Though most companies are aware of the need to do something, there is no methodology, no standard way for them to decide how much to give, and where and in what ways to deploy their largesse.

BitC was echoing a point made more forcefully by Peter Whates, formerly of the Volunteer Centre UK. In the final issue of the Centre's journal *EC Eye*, which he edited, he said 'as far as I am aware, there is no real coherent intellectually based management theory of the business-based case for an active involvement strategy, and as a result little or no academically grounded literature that would underpin such a belief system... there is not even a unifying vocabulary that could help to popularize the idea espoused by supporters of the 'active business' strategy...'.

This lack of a theory and a methodology of company giving and community involvement is serious because it provides too many excuses for companies to do nothing, or to do too little. And, ironically, it is the evangelists themselves – those who urge companies to do more – who have in part created the problem by confusing two fundamentally different arguments: that firms should give more because it is *in their interest* to do so and that firms should give more because it is *right* that they should do so.

Delivering the keynote address at the Per Cent Club's annual meeting in November 1991 the Archbishop of Canterbury, Dr George Carey, said that 'enlightened self-interest is a good and healthy starting point. Yet it is not enough. We need to explore where we go from there and what scope there possibly might be for taking further the arguments in favour of corporate community involvement'.

John Swanda, Professor of Management at Indiana University, argued that 'accepting ethical standards of behaviour simply for economic advantage alone, may have a chilling effect on decision-makers in the firm. The economic reasoning-only approach lends itself to mercenary motives. As humans who are members of a social order, business decision makers need to behave according to the edicts of ethical standards because it is the *right* behaviour' (my emphasis). He spoke of 'psychological benefits' as well as economic 'dividends' and of 'psychic' as well as 'financial' income.

But it is far from clear how one could distinguish a company that behaves ethically because it is right, from one which appears to behave ethically because it believes that is the best way to maximize long-term profits. It is also far from clear that socially responsible corporate behaviour inspired purely by self-interest, will be less generous than socially responsible corporate behaviour inspired purely by ethical conviction. And, in the end, as Sir Adrian Cadbury says, it is what companies do for their communities that matters, not why they do it.

I call the two approaches to improving the general standards of corporate behaviour the 'exhortatory approach', on the one hand, and the 'Groucho approach' on the other. The first takes the view that business is unethical right now, but can be persuaded to become ethical. The second takes the view that business is an intrinsically non-ethical undertaking, can never become ethical, but that companies can be expected to behave in ways that appear to be more ethical as they come to realize such behaviour is in their interests.

The Exhortatory Model

A US ethical 'exhortationist' is the Woodstock Theological Centre, at Georgetown University in Washington, which has proposed an

71

ethical checklist that executives, bankers and lawyers should strive to honour in takeovers. In a report on the controversy aroused by the high level of takeovers in the 1980s, the centre called for tax changes and a change in voting rights to disenfranchise speculators.

The UK's Institute of Business Ethics (IBE) was established in 1986 to 'provide a forum for responsible study, research and opinion formation in the field of business ethics'. Patrons include the Archbishop of Canterbury, the Cardinal Archbishop of Westminster, the Moderator of the Free Church Federal Council, the Chief Rabbi and the Imam of the London Central Mosque. The IBE's council includes business people, business commentators from varying backgrounds, and a cleric.

The official IBE view, as expressed by its chairman Neville Cooper, was that 'industry and commerce are highly ethical undertakings' and that business ethics are merely personal ethics writ large. Council member Sir John Hoskyns, the then director general of the Institute of Directors, argued that 'there is no real difference between business ethics and individual ethics. It is a matter of personal behaviour and individual moral responsibility'.

Barbara Mills, the UK's new Director of Public Prosecutions, came in for some criticism from an ethical exhortationist in early 1992 because of her assertion, in an interview with the *Financial Times*, that low ethical standards in business do not generate long-term business advantage. By apparently seeking to promote ethical corporate behaviour through the fear of commercial retribution, the new DPP was accused by a reader of confusing the ethical with the self-interested.

But it was her accuser who was confused, not Ms Mills. He had failed to recognize a fundamental difference between the moral status of the individual, on the one hand, and of the company, on the other. As I and others have pointed out, the company is not an ethical or moral creature, and no theory of the firm can accommodate the idea that companies have a moral sense. But I believe that in my book *The 'nice' company* I have laid out the ground plan of a 'real coherent intellectually based management theory of the business-based case for an active involvement strategy' that BitC and Peter Whates deplore the lack of.

The Groucho Model

Groucho Marx provided the basis for an alternative theory of corporate giving, that recognizes the intrinsic amorality of business, when he said:

> The secret of life is honesty and fair dealing. If you can fake that, you've got it made.

Ethical corporate behaviour, or behaviour that appears, to individuals, to be ethical, is good for business, just as its opposite is bad for business. This is an idea the theory of the firm can readily accept. Having accepted it, the same theory will urge firms, out of enlightened self-interest, to behave in ways that appear, to individuals, to be ethical.

Why do people find this idea so objectionable? Why do they regard corporate behaviour consistent with the possession of a moral sense, but motivated by enlightened self-interest, as more desirable or more admirable than the same behaviour, *really* motivated by a moral sense? It is the behaviour that matters, not what inspires it.

There are at least three reasons why the assignment of some kind of moral sense to companies is, actually, a rather bad guarantor of ethical corporate behaviour.

The first is that, since companies are not inherently moral, the deliberate assignment to them of a moral sense will not act as a reliable discipline. Conflicts of duty and interest will constantly arise and, at times of crisis, survival will have to take precedence over moral duty.

The second is that if ethical corporate behaviour is treated as separate from commercial behaviour, it needs a separate budget, and that budget may be small. There will be a moral compliance cost, requiring firms to incur opportunity costs, and those costs cannot be too high, without compromising the firm's competitive position.

The third reason why higher standards of corporate behaviour are unlikely to result from some kind of moral rearmament in the corporate world – which is what some people appear to be advocating – is that the espousal of an ethical code will remove the motivation to seek an ethical reputation out of enlightened self-interest.

It is my belief that, in the future, much more good will be done by companies, in general, because of enlightened self-interest, than will be done as a consequence of the adoption of an ethical code.

Plato revealed himself to be a 'short-termist' when he said: 'honesty is, for the most part, less profitable than dishonesty'. The Greek poet Hesiod, writing two and a half centuries earlier, was much nearer the mark: 'Do not seek dishonest gains; dishonest gains are losses.'

The problems caused by this persistent confusion of ethical exhortation with business pragmatism are evident in the difficulties Harvard Business School is experiencing in the teaching of business ethics. Despite the enthusiasm for the subject of business ethics, and the handsome $15m gift by John Shad, former chairman of the Securities and Exchange Commission, to advance the cause, ethics have yet to find a comfortable place for themselves in the HBS curriculum.

There is a compulsory Decision Making & Ethical Values course at HBS, there are three elective courses in ethics, of which Moral Dilemmas of Management is the most popular, and ethics are supposed to be integrated in all other Harvard courses. But students and faculty alike, whilst applauding the idea of business ethics teaching, still seem very unclear about what it is and should be doing.

I have a proposal for Thomas R. Piper, leader of the Harvard ethics initiative. Introduce a new, compulsory course called 'Making money out of ethics', and allow students to give the John Shad gift away to charities of their choice.

Business is a non-moral endeavour and therefore, the hope that business ethics can ever be persuaded to match human ethical standards is a vain one. But despite my scepticism about the idea of the ethical, unselfish company, I remain optimistic about the chances for long-term improvements in the general standards of corporate behaviour.

Companies have an 'invisible' balance sheet, consisting of such assets as the knowhow of their staff, their brands and their various reputations, the value of which good managers are obliged to maximize. Companies *will* come to be seen as behaving in a more ethical and socially responsible way, not because they are becoming more ethical but because their managers will realize that to remain competitive, they must modify their behaviour in ways that attract the employees and customers they need.

Companies will endeavour to appear to be socially responsible in order to maximize the value of their reputational assets. The best way for companies to appear to be socially responsible is for them to adopt codes of behaviour (values) that are indistinguishable from human ethical codes.

As companies begin to compete on the basis of reputations – what I call 'culture-based competition' – they will see that it is in their interest to invest more and more in their reputational assets. There is no need for a purely ethical element of giving, over and above what is prescribed by enlightened self-interest. The argument for such an ethical premium not only confuses the issue; it also undermines the security of companies that acknowledge it, by making them less competitive.

The Stakeholder Model

How and to whom companies do or should give is a somewhat less controversial matter than why they should give, though no less actively debated.

The most influential model for the manner of company giving is based on the idea of the 'extended company', with a number of 'stakeholder' groups in addition to its shareholders. These include society at large and existing and potential bankers, local communities (or 'neighbours'), employees, customers, suppliers, collaborators and competitors. Let us look at a few of them:

A theme of this chapter is that a reputation for behaving in a socially responsible way can be a considerable competitive advantage for a company. Thus, social responsibility and self-interest can be different sides of the same coin.

It follows that companies should consider doing better than average, and more than the law requires of them, to protect the interests of existing and former employees because by so doing they will gain competitive advantage. This is not just because it is important to keep good employees, but also because companies must do all they can to make themselves attractive to school leavers and graduates, their future employees.

A reputation for paying well, having a good health and safety record, operating a consultative management style and being a caring employer, all help in recruiting as well as keeping good staff. A reputation for being socially responsible in other ways, like caring for the environment, refusing to trade in arms or with repressive regimes, giving to charities and other worthy causes and contributing to the local community, can also improve a company's attractiveness as an employer. Recent research by KPH Marketing at the University of Surrey showed that 74 per cent of students regarded a socially responsible corporate image to be important, when considering potential employers.

Corporate neighbours are individuals and organizations which live or operate close to the company. They include residents of nearby housing estates, farmers and other water users downstream of a company's riverside sites, and anyone else occupying areas close enough to the site for their material, mental or financial environment to be affected by it.

A reputation for being a good neighbour confers on a company valuable competitive advantage. It makes it easier for it to recruit people locally, to win planning consents from local authorities, to minimize company-community strife and to maximize opportunities for collaboration and joint ventures with like-minded local companies. And, of course, a reputation for 'corporate neighbourliness' earns rewards in other constituencies too, such as employees (existing and potential), customers, suppliers, the media and government.

It is a small and logical step for a firm conscious of its need to be a 'good neighbour', to acknowledge that it also has a responsibility to society at large. There are after all no practical limits to the extended neighbourhoods of international companies.

The main demand of society as corporate stakeholder is that companies should minimize the impact their operations have on the environment. Just as it is important for good neighbour companies to look after their local environments, so it is important for them to look after their extended environments. They will get a bad press, and their general reputation will suffer, if they are implicated in serious environmental disasters, for instance, or if they are regularly hauled over the coals by environmental protection agencies and the many environmental pressure groups that are constantly chastising companies for diminishing air and water quality, or contributing to global warming by using excessive amounts of energy.

UK chemicals giant Imperial Chemical Industries (ICI), which had been a favourite target for environmentalists for many years, launched new policy guidelines for the environment in November 1990. In a letter to employees, ICI chairman Sir Denys Henderson outlined four objectives 'over and above what we have to do to comply with law and regulation':

1. All new plants will be built to standards that will meet the regulations we can reasonably anticipate in the most environmentally demanding country in which we operate that process. There will be no double standards.
2. We will reduce wastes by 50 per cent by 1995. We will pay special attention to those which are hazardous and we will try to eliminate all off-site disposal of environmentally harmful wastes. Because it may take a long time to meet that last target fully – and in a few cases it may not be feasible to do so – we will ensure that all the off-site disposal facilities which we use will conform to regulatory requirements. We will conduct audits to ensure that this is the case.
3. We will . . . establish an even more rigorous energy and resource conservation programme, giving special attention to environmental impact. I expect this to achieve significant benefits by 1995.
4. We will set up during 1991 waste recycling programmes, not only in-house, but also in collaboration with our customers to assist their efforts in recycling product and packaging materials.

He concluded the letter: 'Good environmental performance is no longer optional. It is essential if ICI is to continue as a leading international chemical company into the next century'.

ICI has introduced free recovery and recycling services for industrial users of CFCs in Europe and a recycling scheme for refrigerant recovered from domestic fridges in the UK. Recent environment-friendly ICI product launches include waterborne resins, CFC replacements and new technology for producing chlorine without using mercury.

ICI's Group Environmental Laboratory in Devon investigates water toxicology and designs systems for the safe treatment and disposal of industrial waste and its Central Toxicology Laboratory in Manchester develops new testing methods that avoid the use of animals. The company has also set up an Environmental Affairs Group at its London headquarters, responsible for promoting good practice throughout ICI in support of environmental policy.

Thorn EMI, the TV rental and music group, is another large UK company that has recognized the importance of achieving and maintaining a reputation for caring for the environment. In the technical section of the group *Policies Manual* dated January 1991, the following environmental policy was spelled out:

1. Use, wherever possible, and commercially sound, earth resources which can be replaced in a lifetime.
2. Prevent pollution at source whenever and wherever possible.
3. Conserve natural resources by the use of energy management, recycling and other appropriate means.
4. Ensure that the company's facilities and products meet and sustain the regulations of all Governmental environmental agencies.

All Thorn EMI Companies are required to:

1. Formulate and publish a statement of their own environmental policy.
2. Carry out independent environmental audits – the frequency varying according to the product process of the business concerned.

Individual policies will need to have regard to the above corporate policy but they will identify more closely with the workplace operations and management structure of the companies concerned. This should include consideration of the following issues:

1. energy consumption
2. recycling
3. packaging
4. environmental impact of products and services
5. product/service promotion in an era of increasing environmental concern
6. chemical discharges (into air, sewers)
7. transport

History shows that a tradition of corporate social responsibility existed from the earliest beginnings of companies but was progressively eroded by successive changes in the company's legal status during the eighteenth and nineteenth centuries.

The contemporary pressure on companies to behave in a more socially responsible way can be seen as an acknowledgement of this loss of intrinsic responsibility and of the failure of governments, of all colours and creeds, to compensate for it adequately.

The challenge for the modern company is to respond to public demand for greater corporate social responsibility in ways that are consistent with the new responsibilities it has incurred as a result of its alienation from the human value system.

Companies should not be tempted to feel that they are under any ethical obligation to give, over and above what self-interest dictates, because this will weaken them, and reduce their ability to give in the future. Of the models of business ethics mentioned here only the Groucho is sufficient to meet this challenge.

5

Corporate Philanthropists

Corporate giving is much more than just giving cash. There are also secondments of employees and companies make other donations 'in kind', of products, office space, equipment and knowhow.

The repertoire of corporate giving has expanded rapidly in recent years, as companies have sought to differentiate the styles of their generosity, and tailor it more precisely to their needs and to the needs of their 'clients'.

Several examples of non-monetary giving were included, under a number of headings, in *Directions for the Nineties* (BitC 1991).

Full- and part-time secondments: Guardian Royal Exchange, the insurance group, seconds staff to the charity, Disability Care and Enterprise; Marks & Spencer seconds up to thirty people at any one time on two-year assignments with the Council for Environmental Education, the Careers National Association and other groups; Nationwide Building Society seconds staff on 100-hour assignments to community projects in partnership with the Action Resource Centre.

Provision of surplus premises: British Gas has provided a headquarters, and small business workspace to be managed by Hackney Business Venture; British Rail's 'urban renaissance' scheme converts redundant and derelict rail buildings in depressed areas into workspace for community projects; Grand Metropolitan provides space for a wide range of charities including Business in the Community, Cities in Schools, the

Prince's Youth Business Trust and the Employers' Forum on Disability.

Provision of retail premises: Body Shop has promoted Amnesty International and Friends of the Earth through in-store campaigns; Burton Group raised over £1.5m on behalf of Comic Relief in 1989 through sales of branded goods and in-store events; Tesco sponsors the Gateshead Shopping and Information Service enabling 1,000 housebound consumers to shop, using new technology.

Provision of facilities and equipment: IBM has established a creative management skills course which has been completed by 400 senior managers of not-for-profit organizations; the Securicor Group provides free security vehicles for cash-raising campaigns such as Comic Relief and Children in Need.

Product donations: Boots gives a wide variety of its goods to the voluntary sector, schools and areas of need such as Romania and Africa; since 1980 ICI, through its Dulux Community Project scheme, has run an annual competition to provide paint for voluntary groups and charities; Unisys gave computer equipment worth £90,000 to Chapeltown and Harehills Action Learning Centre, an out-of-hours school project, that provides educational opportunities for ethnic minorities in Leeds.

Marketing support: Carlton Communications made a video for the Prince's Youth Business Trust; Daily Mail Ideal Home Exhibition provides free space for new businesses started by young people; Thames Television pioneered the Telethon and has developed initiatives to make it easier for charities to advertise on television. (It will be interesting to see if this precedent will be respected by the new holders of the Thames region franchise, including Carlton Communications.)

Professional knowhow: British Telecom has worked with the Royal National Institute for the Deaf to develop a new telephone relay service for deaf and speech-impaired people; the Law Society encourages solicitors to give free legal assistance to small firms through Lawyers for Enterprise and community organizations; Sedgwicks provided expertise and industry contacts to establish the Apex Trust Fidelity Bonding insurance scheme, on behalf of ex-offenders seeking employment.

Directions for the Nineties also cites cases of companies making use of a new concept in corporate giving which some predict will account for a substantial portion of the total in years to come. It is known as cause-related marketing and exemplifies not only the current confusion between, but also the prospective integration of, marketing and giving.

Like most of the innovations in this area, it started in the US in the mid-1980s. A pioneer was Johnson & Johnson, which launched its Shelter Aid Programme in 1986. It included a $1m campaign to educate the public about domestic violence, funded a toll-free domestic violence 'hotline' and set up a number of domestic shelters.

In 1988 Reebok International, the sports shoe group, spent $10m on underwriting the 'Human Rights Now!' concert tour which included appearances by rock stars like Sting, Tracey Chapman and Bruce Springsteen.

The 'Pepsi Challenge', launched by the Pepsi-Cola Company in 1989, was designed to give inner-city youths an incentive to stay in school. The school drop-out rate is a cause of great concern in the US, so the campaign was well targeted. The scheme increases the incentive to stay in school by giving graduates the opportunity to earn $500 for each year of high school completed, to be used for post-secondary education.

UK examples of cause-related marketing include the donation by Mercury Communications of a proportion of its revenues from phone card sales to the Prince's Trust, the raising by Girobank of £150,000 for Oxfam through its Visa 'affinity card', a similar arrangement between Visa, Leeds Permanent building society and the Imperial Cancer Research Fund, the sale, at cost, of Mates condoms in Virgin Megastores and Texaco's impressive 'Children should be seen and not hurt' campaign, where petrol customers are given glow-in-the-dark stickers and bracelets to make children more visible on the roads at night.

Cause-related marketing is an extremely powerful idea, for

two reasons. First, it gives companies a way of revealing to their customers, and other 'stakeholders', deeper aspects of their corporate personalities that cannot be conveyed through ordinary marketing. Secondly, it offers an opportunity to attribute the reputational value derived from giving, directly to products, rather than indirectly, through the corporate reputation in general.

The American Model

In considering the likely development of corporate giving in the UK, it is reasonable to regard the US pattern as somewhat in advance of ours and, therefore, a kind of model on which UK corporate giving may converge. For reasons we have already discussed, giving in general is very culture specific, so it is unlikely, given our very different economic and political traditions, that overall patterns of giving, here and in the US, will become indistinguishable.

But the UK and US corporate cultures are very close to each other, much closer than the UK corporate culture is to any of its continental counterparts, for example. Insofar as the relationship of companies to the charity sector is concerned, therefore, the American model may be instructive.

As already noted (see chapter 4), American companies are much more generous than British or European companies but, because their circumstances, interests and giving potential differ, there is no standard pattern of giving, even in the US. The 1989 edition of the US Conference Board's annual *Survey of Corporate Contributions*, based on a questionnaire filled in by 328 of America's 1,200 'top' firms, revealed a median for corporate giving of 1.05 per cent of US taxable income, a lower quartile of 0.56 per cent and an upper quartile 2.03 per cent, and this wide spread has been steady since 1978.

Some companies give 6–10 per cent of taxable income but, according to Michael Fogarty and Ian Christie, 'the typical American company does not give at all' because it is still struggling for growth. The typical company only starts giving when its earnings achieve a plateau of stability.

In other words, young, high-growth companies tend to be such rigorous conservers of cash that they regard giving which, as we have seen, is an investment in reputational assets, as a luxury they cannot afford. One could say that firms in 'hunting' mode tend to be less generous than firms in 'farming' mode.

But the evidence, such as it is, also suggests the smallest companies tend to give the most. So although high growth is a constraint on giving, small size is not. It probably has a lot to do with the ownership relationship. As I suggested in the previous chapter, the wedge that has been driven between corporate and individual giving by the divorce of ownership and control is less deeply embedded in some cultures than in others. It is also less deeply embedded in the small company sector where the founder, chief executive and controlling shareholder are often one and the same.

I came across a small consultancy firm a couple of years ago where the policy was to give 30 per cent of taxable profits, and the anecdotal evidence suggests that there are scores of family-owned firms which routinely give much more than the Per Cent Club's putative standard of 1 per cent of taxable profits. As we saw in chapter 1, International Motors Group, wholly owned by Robert Edmiston, covenants 10 per cent of its profits to the charity Christian Vision.

US evidence also shows corporate giving varies considerably from sector to sector. Manufacturing and insurance groups, for example, give on average about three times as much as utilities and telecommunications companies. There are wide variations within sectors, too, and there are sharp, year to year fluctuations which bear only a general relationship to changes in taxable profits.

In a US giving intentions survey in 1989, firms in 'business services' said they expected to increase contributions by a third, while electrical machinery and equipment makers intended to reduce theirs by a quarter, so cancelling out an increase of a third in the previous years.

We must be clear what Americans mean by company giving. Tax-deductible contributions, for example, include the costs of certain types of giving in kind, such as securities, company products, property, equipment, and this mix also varies very widely. For instance, in the US Conference Board's 1989 *Survey of Corporate Contributions*, thirty-one of the seventy-five largest US corporate donors gave only cash and eleven gave half or more in kind. For obvious reasons there is far less of the latter sort of giving in banking, finance, distribution, utilities and oil and gas than in manufacturing. Companies making electrical machinery and equipment, for example, gave two-fifths in kind.

Americans also include, in their corporate giving figures, non-tax deductible corporate assistance, like grants to colleges and universities for basic research, support for public radio and TV stations, and other 'non-profits' through subscriptions, secondments, gifts of product and property, 'soft' loans, free use of office space or services and also the costs of administering the company's contributions function. These non-deductible items accounted for about 20 per cent of total giving between 1983 and 1987.

The lack of a standard pattern is also evident in the causes American companies patronize. According to the Taft Group's 1990 review of US corporate giving, education has been the greatest beneficiary of corporate philanthropy for more than a decade, and remains so. By and large US companies appear more education-minded than their UK counterparts, but British employers are taking a greater interest in literacy and numeracy standards in schools because this has a direct bearing on the quality of their recruits. The UK government is encouraging the process by involving companies in Training and Enterprise Councils.

British Gas makes its greatest social policy effort through schools and universities. Tony Wyatt, the group's head of social policy, explained the rationale to *Management Today* (June 1990): 'these are not only tomorrow's consumers but potential recruits as well. Regular contact with teachers has a lasting effect too – they're likely to be around for several years after the students have gone'.

In the US, where the school drop-out rate is a worrying 29 per cent, employers are estimated to be spending some $25bn a year on teaching their employees basic skills, so they have an obvious interest in helping to reduce the drop-out rate.

'Compacts', pioneered in Boston, are agreements between firms and schools that include job guarantees for graduates who come up to scratch. Resources for the schools involved are supplied by business groups and individual companies provide tutors and management assistance. Compacts have been set up in several British cities, too. An early sponsor was Grand Metropolitan which is also introducing to the UK another American idea, Cities in Schools (CIS), pioneered by Burger King, its fast-food subsidiary, many of whose 250,000 employees are teenagers.

The CIS scheme, aimed at lowering the school drop-out rate, involves school officials, government, volunteer groups and companies. It provides support for school children at risk to work alongside teachers. Companies also use the scheme to involve employees.

At Rich's store in Atlanta, employees get time off to teach at Rich's Academy, which gives school drop-outs a second chance, and students can take part-time work in the store.

Recent changes in the pattern of US corporate giving include a fall in the percentage going to health and welfare, and a related fall in 'federated giving', through fund-raising organizations like United Way (see chapter 7). Transport and utility groups give a particularly high proportion to health and welfare, and give a correspondingly high proportion through federated giving.

Non-manufacturing companies passed twice as many dollars per employee through federated giving as manufacturing firms, while chemical, oil and gas and electrical machinery groups gave over 40 per cent to education, compared to a range in most non-manufacturing of between 18 per cent and 28 per cent.

Most large American firms have a structured, professionally staffed giving programme. Some see it as an advantage for the contributions officers to have other duties and many large firms set up their own foundations alongside direct giving. In most industries most of the giving is deployed by the corporate centre, but proportions spent in the field by operating units vary from 0–90 per cent and there are also wide variations in the types and degree of 'volunteering'.

One family-owned American company insists that US practice should be adopted world-wide and its UK subsidiary is therefore very generous by UK standards. Other US firms distinguish between markets. One UK division has a high consumer profile and is a large giver, while another produces basic materials and is considerably less generous.

According to Fogarty and Christie, the US experience shows that the development of what they call a 'culture of giving' in the corporate sector is a slow process and takes several decades. They suggest the process can be accelerated in the right conditions, including the setting of a proper balance of roles between public and private sectors, appropriate law and the right tax and other incentives, but that it is mostly driven by personal initiatives and networking. They also emphasise how important it is for charities to do their homework before they approach companies, so they know each firm's individual circumstances and interests.

Investing in Reputations

Another feature of American corporate philanthropists that has been evident in the UK for some time is the extent to which giving is regarded as one aspect of an overall policy of investing in reputational assets, that also includes what might be called 'quasi-charitable' spending.

This is consistent with the existence of an implicit system of reputation management of the Groucho kind (described in the previous chapter). Companies are beginning to realize that if they want to be seen by their 'stakeholders' and by other key audiences such as potential employees, as charitable, ethical and socially responsible, giving is not enough. The 'whole' corporate personality, and all the ways in which it interacts with society, are now seen as legitimate objects of deliberate grooming.

The perception was evident, in the 1980s, in the decision by numerous companies, British and American, to cease trading with South Africa, and is also manifest, in a more parochial way, in the efforts companies are making to forge links with local political systems, and to co-operate with government agencies as part of their community relations programmes. UK food and drinks group Allied-Lyons, for example, supports local training and enterprise schemes, encourages executives to stand for local council membership, and makes a point of co-operating with state-sponsored education initiatives.

By the same token, corporate reputations can be enhanced by positive policies towards less developed countries. Body Shop International, for example, explains in its corporate literature how it uses materials sourcing to generate jobs and business in the Third World.

We will look more closely at the way companies are becoming involved in local communities in the next chapter. For the moment, let us consider by way of example a particular aspect of socially responsible corporate behaviour: how the desire of companies to appear responsive to human needs is changing the shape of the working life.

Retiring and Returning

The number of people aged seventy-five or over is projected to rise by 40 per cent between 1981 and 2001, and the Tories made it clear, in their White Paper *Caring for people – community care in the next decade and beyond*, that they intend to rely more on private and voluntary care. Some predict that increases in longevity and changes in worker-retiree ratios will put such pressure on social security programmes that the retirement age will have to be raised for financial reasons. But a survey by the Institute of Personnel Management, based on a sample of 500 UK companies, showed special arrangements to help employees care for the old are still rare.

Pilkington, the glass group, is a UK pioneer in the area of retiree support. Its charitable trust runs post-retirement seminars to help ex-employees adjust to retirement, and operates a welfare programme that includes goodwill gifts, a 'keeping in touch' service, contact, visiting and community care. The scheme cares for 20,000 people in the UK, 11,000 of whom live in the area around the company's original headquarters in St Helen's, Lancashire. The trust funds 90 per cent of the welfare programme and the company contributes the rest.

In the US, companies like IBM, Pitney Bowes and Levi Strauss provide funds for retirees to take courses that could lead to new careers. In 1985, 9,000 IBM employees took advantage of the company's Retiree Education Assistance Programme, which provided $5,000 in tuition aid to employees and their spouses in the three years before, and the two years after retirement. California's New Career Opportunities Inc, which gives older people hands-on professional training to help them to start their own businesses, is supported by Grumman, Rockwell and other local high-tech aerospace and computer companies.

The Polaroid company in the US offers leaves of absence to older employees which it calls 'retirement rehearsals'. If an employee dislikes retirement he/she can return. About half choose to return. Rehearsers can cut either hours per day or days per week. Aerospace Corporation in California offers a number of retirement rehearsal options in the form of less work, part-time work or unpaid leave. At Varian Associates, in Palo Alto, soon-to-retire employees can work a four-day week for a year, and then a three-day week for another year before leaving. Known as phased retirement planning this is becoming quite fashionable in the US. The International Society of Pre-Retirement Planners, founded in 1976, had only 150 members in 1985 but three years later the figure was over 800 members, most of whom are employed by major companies to help older employees with retirement-related concerns.

Quite apart from the reputational assets to be acquired from such programmes, changes in the mix of ages, and the increased bargaining power they give to employees are likely to force companies to become more accommodating towards the circumstances of individuals.

So-called 'age discrimination' (still legal on both sides of the Atlantic), a lack of flexibility on the part of firms and the physical demands of ordinary work have previously prevented most people from continuing to work after official retirement. But in areas like law, medicine, architecture, writing, the Church and small business, people keep working long after the official retirement age. This will become more common throughout the company sector.

Fifty and sixty year olds, partly because of greater health consciousness, are seen (and see themselves) as much more vigorous and productive than a decade or so ago. A study by the Industrial Society found job challenges remain very important to three-quarters of all working people over fifty-five. But as the then IS director Alistair Graham says: 'older people often have other agendas; they must be given the space and time to accommodate them'. US research by Public Agenda showed most Americans want to work, in one way or another, after sixty-five, even if they have no need to, because they 'like working'.

US hamburger chain McDonalds advertises for new recruits at senior citizens' clubs, offers older recruits the choice of days, hours and jobs and runs a special 'McMasters' training programme. According to a 1986 US Department of Commerce report, fast-food restaurants were becoming major employers of what it called 'gold-collar workers'.

American companies are experimenting with all sorts of ideas in this area, including hour banks, retirement rehearsals, flexitime, flexiyear contracts, sabbaticals, job-retraining, project-orientated work, job-sharing and telecommuting. In addition to generating corporate reputations for sensitivity to the needs of employees, including so-called 'returners' as well as retirees, these schemes are starting to undermine the old idea of the full-time, workplace-based nine-to-five job. The Institute of Gerontology, at the University of Michigan, has identified no less than 369 variations of such ideas, operated by US companies.

Retired employees at Kentucky Fried Chicken, for example, can return as part-time managers, on a regular or an occasional basis, working twenty to thirty hours a week with full benefits. The Toro lawnmower group in the US also offers pro-rated benefits, including healthcare, disability insurance, profit-sharing and holiday pay to part-time employees.

At the Aerospace Corporation, employees only lose pension benefits if they work less than 1,000 hours a year (about half-time). At the Travellers insurance group, Connecticut, where a 'job bank' schedules part-time work, the minimum is 960 hours a year without losing pension and health benefits.

The qualities of older people – useful employees at a time of skills shortages but with their own agendas – are shared by 'returners' (usually mothers returning to work after their children have grown up) and others not wishing to work full-time. Travellers, for example, was also a US pioneer of job sharing which is now widespread in the US, both between companies and within them. At Pittsburgh's Mellon Bank, for example, two people share the $30,000 a year position of 'corporate identity coordinator'.

Not far short of half US employers use part-timers and some companies have become very dependent on them. Intertek of California employs 12,000, 9,000 of whom are retiree part-timers working as independent contractors. (This practice, when applied to employees of all ages, is sometimes known as intrapreneurship). Almost two-thirds of employees of Sterile Design, in Florida, are senior citizens working four-hour mini-shifts to supplement Social Security.

Telecommuting, working part of the time from home, and often associated with intrapreneur programmes, is also becoming a fashionable employment practice in the US. AT&T, one of America's largest companies, has been experimenting with it, and the practice has its guru Gil Gordon, whose *Telecommuting Review: The Gordon Report* is the leading newsletter on the subject. The definitive book in the UK is *The Telecommuters* by Francis Kinsman. Pioneers of the practice include Xerox, Pacific Bell, Mellon Bank and Mutual Life Insurance in the US and FI Group in the UK.

A 1986 study by the US firm Challenger, Gray & Christmas found over half those asked expected more and more white-collar workers to work from home computer terminals part of the time. One estimate is that by the year 2000 over 20 per cent of US workers will work from home.

By 1988 over a quarter of US companies operated so-called flextime arrangements, where employees schedule their own work, and they are becoming increasingly popular in Germany. Mutual Life Insurance, for example, allows managers to start work any time between 7 and 9am and to earn a three-day weekend by squeezing ten days' work into nine. Corning Glass allows R&D employees to design their own work schedules, subject to approval, and GM allows some employees to work a thirty-two-hour compressed work week called 'flexible service'.

An increasingly popular variation on the flexitime theme is the hour bank advocated by Dr Max Kaplan of the Center for Leisure Studies at the University of South Florida. Total hours of work needed over a week, a month or a year are calculated and are saved in an hour bank as they are worked. In a yearly arrangement, for example, an employee might negotiate ten days of leisure for every twenty days work. He/she might work twenty days and then have a ten day holiday or might work every other weekend for six years and then take a six-month holiday. Or you might wish to retire for a year at the end of each decade.

(I mention these experiments to demonstrate how much effort some companies are putting into re-designing the working life. I know such schemes have often been tried and abandoned, because of a lack of interest or the inherent inflexibilities in many types of work.)

Much of the corporate response to the changing nature of the working life is a matter of a shift in attitudes, and much of it can be interpreted as a self-interested anticipation of the human resources problems posed by ageing populations. But considerable sums are being spent on these initiatives, and a significant proportion of this expenditure should be construed as quasi-charitable. The new responsiveness companies are showing to employees is an example of how, through various kinds of giving, they are trying to differentiate themselves.

In the case studies we will look at the charity and social responsibility policies of a handful of major UK companies. The strategies underlying all of these policies can be seen as variations on the theme of what I have called the 'nice' strategy (see chapter 4). It looks like charity but it can, just as easily, be seen as enlightened self-interest. For the moment, we will investigate how this new kind of competition could develop in the UK retail banking sector.

BANK ROBS MAN

Some time over the last decade or so Britain's banks began to lose something. Quite what it was, and precisely when it began to slip away, is hard to say, but the signs are clear, in survey after survey.

The enthusiasm with which the banks embraced the 'financial services revolution' in the 1980s is partly to blame for the vertiginous decline in banking's favourability ratings. The idea of a bank as an un-exploited distribution system, through which more product could be sold, came with the new 'marketing people' who joined the sector in the 1980s, during the run up to the City of London's deregulation 'Big Bang' in 1986.

Banking, as a fast-moving consumer services industry, is a far and raucous cry from old style, relationship-banking, where customers were clients and bankers were professionals. Which is not to say the trade was a bad one. Some people find horses more attractive than cars but they still drive. Maybe it was time the banks swapped the trappings of an antiquated professionalism for a more contemporary, commercial style. Something is lost and something is gained as the pattern of corporate evolution unfolds.

The first question to be addressed therefore, is not whether banks can retrieve what they have lost but whether, taking everything into account, they are better off than they were. In other words, is the modern 'commercial' bank better, or worse, for share-holders, when all is said and done, than its precursor?

The short answer is that it is too early to tell and that the intervention of a deep and prolonged recession makes it very hard to compare the two models on equal terms. But one can say that reputation and 'corporate personality' are critical and that the recession has been a bruising time for the reputation of banks. The opportunity they perceived in mortgage business has become a poisoned chalice that has dragged relationships with personal customers into the agony of repossessions.

At the same time the recession has exposed the mortality of the army of small businesses spawned by the last recession and nourished in the hothouse of the Thatcher boom. This winnowing, too, has reaped a grim harvest of personal enmity between banks and the thousands of bitter entrepreneurs who regale friends and business acquaintances with tales of their banks' perfidy.

The collapse of BCCI, National Westminster's involvement in the Blue Arrow affair, and the prominent role of the banks in the Maxwell scandal have all contributed to the growing perception that the big banks have ceased to be the pillars of society they once were. The same people who would previously have described banks as courteous, secure, efficient and reliable, are more likely to see them nowadays as irresponsible, ignorant, importunate, uncaring, and selfish.

The evidence, such as it is therefore, is that the exchange of the old professional ethos for the new commercial one has reaped considerable 'reputational liabilities'. There is good cause to suspect, if not reliable means to demonstrate, that the change has produced more losses than gains. And one cannot blame it all on recession. It is an axiom of the approach to the management of 'reputational assets', outlined below, that the value of reputation, within a sector, depends more on relativities than absolutes. If all players are losing reputation, the winner is the one who is losing the least. Recessions are great opportunities for 'bottom fishing' in the pool of reputation.

So assuming something of value has been lost in banking, and there have been insufficient offsetting gains, what can the banks do about it? In my view, turning the clock back is not an option. The commercial model of banking is here to stay. The question is how to adapt it, so it is more user-friendly. I recommend a four step process:

Step 1. Analyse the reputational loss, and identify the elements worst affected.
Step 2. Design a programme for the piecemeal restoration of the loss, including the appropriate alignment of the corporate culture.
Step 3. Organize communications so that the company is both sensitive to changes in reputation, and equipped to maximize returns on reputational assets.
Step 4. Establish measurement and monitoring procedures, to keep track of changes in reputational assets.

We are concerned here with the first two strategic steps.

It seems to me that the two areas most in need of treatment are reputations among small businesses and personal customers. The two are linked, of course, but it is convenient to treat them separately.

In their relationships with small businesses, banks have the reputation for being ignorant and unimaginative lenders, and indecisive and irresponsible creditors. Though head office will swear blind that lending decisions are based on ability to repay, not security, everyone knows it is still routine for bank managers to insist on personal guarantees for small business loans. Research suggests that about 46 per cent of people believe banks do not lend as readily to small businesses as they should.

According to a study by the Financial Services Department at the Birmingham Polytechnic, published in January 1992, bank managers pay too much attention to narrow financial criteria when assessing business proposals, and too little to factors such as management skill and technical knowledge. But more important, right now, than their reluctance to lend on 'borrower-friendly' terms, is the way the banks play the business end-game.

Banks have enormous power in liquidations. They can protect themselves with covenants, demand financial information not available to trade creditors, take security over a firm's assets without shareholders or other creditors even being aware of it, let alone being consulted, and can veto the appointment of administrators.

The security usually takes six months to 'crystalize', but even so, the twin rights of UK banks to take security first and then to pull the plug at their convenience endows them with a power over the life and death of small firms that is unmatched elsewhere in the world. If they do not exercise that power in ways that are seen to be responsible, banks will acquire reputational liabilities and, moreover, will bring about a misallocation of resources from which the economy as a whole will suffer.

The appointment of a receiver is usually the end of a firm's life. It also marks the end of many jobs and may put at risk the continuing viability of ordinary creditors. In every liquidation there is the potential for a domino effect which may lead to an accelerating sequence of failures that can be very hard to stop.

It is not, of course, in the interests of the banks that this should occur, because many of their own borrowers are among the dominoes waiting to fall, but banks do not appear to take these second-order effects into account. They behave as if they are compelled to treat every case in isolation. 'It is not for us to be concerned with the full consequences of our actions,' they seem to be saying. 'We've lent money on certain terms, which give us certain rights in certain circumstances. We have depositors and shareholders to worry about. It would be a breach of our duty to them not to exercise those rights.'

But they are not seen to exercise their rights responsibly. 'Clearing bankers are not very bright,' said a former finance director of a failed company. 'They don't understand balance sheets, so it is unrealistic to expect them to understand a borrower's problems. And yet they sit in judgement on firms when they are at their most vulnerable. It's terrifying.'

To make matters worse, UK bankers, under strict instructions from their lawyers, have become extremely reluctant to give anything resembling constructive advice during tough times, or even to express opinions, in case they are deemed 'shadow directors' under the 1986 Insolvency Act. This legislation, introduced when the reforming zeal of the Tory government was at its peak, was designed to reduce the corporate mortality rate and provide better protection for unsecured creditors. If its first real test, namely the grim crop of company failures harvested by the current recession, is anything to go by, it has done neither of these things.

The new concepts introduced by the Act, including 'wrongful' (as opposed to fraudulent) trading, 'shadow' directors and licensed insolvency practitioners have either made no difference or have made matters worse.

Administration, designed to emulate the American Chapter 11 'protection from creditors' system, has been an embarrassing failure. Debenture holders – usually banks – have to approve the appointment of administrators, and they have rarely felt inclined to do so. In the four years following the passage of the Insolvency Act there were 46,273 company liquidations and only 675 administrator appointments (less than 1.5 per cent) and the percentage has fallen further since.

There is no pressure on them to ponder their responsibilities for corporate failures. They can continue to lend to firms in the good times, and to call in loans in the bad. There is no sanction on them because there is no offence of 'negligent lending'. In short, banks have power without responsibility which, as Kipling said of the press, has been 'the prerogative of the harlot throughout the ages'. When a bank abuses this power, companies that could have been saved, fail and the unsecured creditors have to pick up the tab. It may be legal, but it does not seem fair.

The reputation of banks among their personal customers is also being eroded. Recent research shows although banks are still well regarded by most people, in the past four years their 'favourability' score has fallen sharply – from 73 per cent to 61 per cent. At that rate it will not be long before most people see banks in the same way as they see estate agents.

Banks are associated with long queues, with the loss of the 'personal touch', and with irresponsible lending. Two out of three people believe banks make too much profit, and one in two dislike the way they sell new products and services.

The draft voluntary Code of Practice, produced by the banks and building societies in December 1991, has done little to redeem the sector's reputation. It was roundly rejected for not going far enough, not only by the Consumers' Association and other consumer groups but also by the Banking Ombudsman.

Specific accusations levelled against banks in the personal area are that they do not explain their charges, they charge too much, they raise charges without warning, they routinely breach their duty of confidentiality, they take far longer to clear cheques than necessary, and managers are very slow to reply to letters and phone calls. There is particular disquiet, following the BCCI affair, about the adequacy of the Deposit Protection Fund, and about the fact that compensation levels are not index-linked.

A recent study by the consultancy firm Prospektus found that so-called 'high net-worth individuals' believe that despite strenuous efforts by the big banks to promote a customer service ethos, they have lost the 'personal touch' completely. There is a feeling that staff are moved round too fast these days for there to be time for good banking relationships to develop, and there is a deep distaste, particularly among older customers, for the practice of rewarding managers with commissions and sales-linked bonuses.

More disquieting still is that banking knowhow is perceived to have deserted the branches, making managers 'glorified clerks' who are obliged to refer all but the most trivial of decisions further up the organization.

Research by Janet Levin Associates indicates that banks are no longer perceived as sources of objective advice, and have acquired a 'hard sell, profiteering image'. People talk of a loss of 'professional respectability' aggravated by 'tacky' marketing gimmicks. And research by 'telebanking' pioneer, First Direct, shows only 51 per cent of 'big five' customers are 'very' satisfied with their banks and barely a third would recommend their banks.

So what to do? What kinds of programme for image improvement should the banks design and execute? I believe the reputation difficulties of UK banks (Scottish banks do not seem so plagued by the problem) should be attacked on three fronts: through culture, structure, and the systematic, and opportunist, management of reputational assets.

The problem with the contemporary banking culture is that it is confused. Rapid commercialization has been lain over the old professional ethos, rather than integrated with it. In the mid-1980s, employees were urged to sharpen up and get 'commercial'. Managers seemed not to realize how hard it was for a culture based on relationships to shift its focus on to 'transactions'. When they belatedly recognized this, their response was not to reach back and re-incorporate the old culture, but to overlay 'customer service' and 'quality' systems on a culture already suffering from schizophrenia.

Overlays are no good. They create conflict, and they obscure the organization's purpose. The whole culture must be moved and tuned so that desirable qualities like friendliness, efficiency and empathy (the acceptable face of marketing in relationship banking) are automatic rather than contrived. It is tricky to do, because cultures are fragile, and bruise easily, but the rewards of well-tuned and accurately aligned cultures are prodigious.

For example, a culture that recognized the need to acquire, and then maintain, the bank's reputational assets would not encourage the 'macho' approach to liquidations in the small business area. It would be more inclined to adopt a German approach to corporate banking, which is not unlike the attitude of UK equity investors. They involve themselves in their clients' affairs, and are less inclined to pull the plug. They have a reputation for contributing positively in fluid situations, and for trying harder than their UK counterparts to avoid the ultimate catastrophe.

For many UK companies, particularly those led by people with first-hand experience of how UK banks conduct themselves in insolvent liquidations, the sooner German banks enter the UK corporate finance market, the better.

Cultures and corporate structures are intimately linked, but structural changes can transform cultures, as well as assist in tuning them. I think the best way to address the problem of the 'alienation' of personal and small business customers is to turn branches into self-standing business units, in which managers and senior staff have a 'virtual', if not an 'actual' equity interest.

The idea of a full federal structure, where the centre is no more than a keeper of a common culture, a holder of a common pool of liquidity and a provider of administrative services, is probably too radical, but that is the way corporate evolution is going, and there are reputational assets to be gained from moving in that direction at a faster rate than one's rivals.

Managers who are part-owners of their branches, and who are, therefore, highly motivated to make a success of their own business units, will see their futures, not so much in terms of moving up the organization, as in maximizing the number of profitable local relationships, in both the personal and business areas.

Reputation is created by the perception, in the minds of the two most important audiences (customers and employees), of a wide variety of attributes and qualities, the importance of which change over time, as the focus of public attention shifts. It seems fair to say the most fertile ground for cultivating reputational assets right now, is 'soft' ground.

In recent years, public opinion has become more sensitive to a number of issues that are not overtly 'commercial' and which are hard to accommodate within traditional strategic models. There is a great public interest in the environment, for example, and in 'corporate social responsibility'.

The strategic idea suggested by these shifting patterns of public concern is that there are reputational assets (of considerable commercial value) to be gained from corporate behaviour that, though ostensibly uncommercial, reflects the moral and ethical prejudices of a company's customers and employees. In other words, if banks began to behave more like socially responsible human beings and less like commercial organisms, driven by an insatiable appetite for profit, they might make more profit.

They need look no further than their own history to see the merits of such strategies. Two of the 'big five' clearers, Lloyds and Barclays, have Quaker origins and Quaker business principles constitute an excellent model for good corporate citizenship. The banking sector once exemplified the breed (the donations committee of the Committee of London Clearing Banks was formed over sixty years ago), before the intensity of competition caused the old principle of *richesse oblige* to fall into disuse.

The ethos needs to be revived, not reinvented. It is still alive – witness the large sums the banks give to charity and sponsorship of the arts – but it is not contemporary. Vestiges of good corporate citizenship survive despite the exigencies of public listing and competition, not because of them. If banks were to see giving as an investment in reputational assets, which attracts new customers and makes it easier for them to recruit and keep good people, they would be minded to give more and to give more systematically.

The 1991 edition of *Charity Trends* shows how Britain's eight major retail banks compare in charitable giving per head of staff (see Appendix, table 5.1). TSB came top with £159, followed by National Westminster, Barclays and the Royal Bank of Scotland.

Lloyds, Midland, Bank of Scotland and Abbey National came some way behind.

A similar analysis of arts sponsorship by the major banks is summarized in the Appendix (table 5.2). It ranks the eight banks by the number of their involvements (not the monetary value) in sponsorship (opera, music, dance, education, drama, visual arts, festivals and literature), adjusted for differences in the number of employees.

The systematic management of reputational assets requires a bank to be profoundly interested in such statistics. Giving and sponsorship should not be hived off to specialist units who bid for funding each year and have learned to expect less at times of low profitability. They should be seen as integral parts of corporate strategy. The Maxwell scandal illustrates how an opportunist approach to the acquisition of reputational assets might work.

In March 1992 the House of Commons social security select committee claimed firms which had bank-rolled Maxwell had a 'moral duty' to help defrauded pensioners. The suggestion was made more out of frustration than out of any hope that the banks would acknowledge such an obligation. 'Pontius Pilate would have blushed', the select committee fumed, 'at the spectacle of so many witnesses washing their hands in public before the committee of their responsibilities in this affair.'

The theory of moral sense holds that perceptions of certain events or actions arouse distinctive feelings of pleasure or pain in spectators, enabling them to distinguish right from wrong. The theory says, in other words, that embedded in the normal human psyche there is a faculty for the detection of moral properties.

There is, on the face of it, no way to impute the same faculty to companies. Those who run companies may have it – no doubt many bankers who washed their hands before the committee secretly harboured a private sense of regret and sympathy, and even a feeling of personal responsibility, for the defrauded pensioners – but the companies themselves are incapable of acting accordingly. They have responsibilities to shareholders, depositors and staff which take precedence over the indulgence of the management's moral sense.

But though companies may lack the faculty to perceive moral properties, they possess the faculty to detect what is in the long-term interests of their shareholders, and should recognize that violations of the moral sense of customers and staff damage their reputation. It therefore seemed to me that there was an opportunity in the Maxwell affair for a bank to enhance its reputation and its profile.

Despite heavy advertising – 'the action bank', 'the listening bank' etc. – retail banks have found it hard to differentiate themselves from each other. The first bank to announce that it will be making *ex-gratia* payments to Maxwell pensioners, equivalent to ex-pension fund assets it holds as security, will have every right and, what is much more important, will be seen by its customers and its employees to have every right, to style itself 'the moral bank'.

The opportunity was greatest for the bank with the least to lose. Indeed, the chance to acquire substantial competitive advantage in this way, at relatively low cost, was so great for one particular bank that its directors could be said to be failing in their responsibility to their shareholders if they did not exploit it. Returning the money without being required to by the courts would have been a conspicuously charitable act and it would have been interesting to see what effect such an initiative would have had on other banks which were holding more of the tainted money.

*   *   *

CASE STUDIES

There are 3,000 quoted British companies and several times that number of private firms, so a small group of case studies like this could hardly be a representative sample. The purpose of this section is to convey something of the thinking, about the kind of things with which this book is concerned, that is going on in the board-rooms of a few of our largest companies.

I shall look at four companies, NFC plc, Pearson plc, Tate & Lyle plc and United Biscuits plc, and shall conclude with a brief discussion of what seem to me to be a few of the more interesting points arising.

NFC

The National Freight Consortium (now NFC plc) was bought by its employees from the government in 1982 for £53.5m. It is now the largest transport and distribution company in the UK and, at the time of writing, its market value is £1.5 billion.

In 1986 the capital was restructured as a prelude to the company's flotation on the stock market in 1989. The main inspiration of the restructuring was the limited liquidity of the internal market for NFC shares, but there was more to the 1986 reorganization than a new financial deal.

A new tradition and a new culture, as well as a new balance sheet, was being put together. A booklet, *The Way Ahead*, was issued to employees and pensioners. It included a report on discussions within the company, and on market research conducted by MORI, about the kind of company NFC people wanted.

As well as employee ownership and control and profit sharing NFC people said they wanted their company 'to have a high regard for its social responsibilities to NFC pensioners and the community'. The eventual package included a savings and bonus scheme to encourage share purchase by employees, an earnings related profit sharing scheme and a new charter for pensioners.

The caring way in which NFC, and other companies like glass-maker Pilkingtons, look after their pensioners is properly seen as part of their charitable activity. Ex-employees are an 'outside' constituency for a company. Any efforts the company makes to care for pensioners, over and above what is required by law, are of an overtly altruistic nature.

At NFC all employees approaching retirement can attend a two-to-three-day course, accompanied by their spouses, to assist them in making the transition from employment to retirement. There is a Pensioners' Association run centrally by the NFC Pensions Department and linked with local associations that are run by the pensioners themselves. The network arranges meetings, social events and outings to maintain contact with all former employees and efforts are made to identify those pensioners needing special help. A special newspaper is sent regularly to all pensioners, and for particular cases, NFC arranges sheltered accommodation and helps with the special requirements of the very old, and chronically ill, where existing social services are reckoned to be inadequate.

The Pensioners' Charter is financed by the NFC which pays for the organization of the Pensioners' Association and the newspaper by an initial NFC endowment that pump-primed the sheltered accommodation and by income from a foundation that was issued with 1 per cent of NFC's equity capital. Dividends from this are available as a foundation fund to meet the cost of help to specially deserving cases.

After its establishment was unanimously approved at the 1986 annual general meeting, the fund was worth less than £1m. By 1990 it was worth nearly £9m and dividend income was running at £300,000 a year.

Sir Peter Thompson, chief architect and leader of the modern NFC until he retired at the end of 1990, says in his book *Sharing the Success*:

> Good businesses have been doing these sorts of things for years. As a nationalized industry, which in concept was supposed to have a caring face, it didn't happen. It is yet another example of how a political solution does not necessarily create the right culture in which the needs of the individual are paramount.

Sir Peter recalls that he suggested, after the buy-out, that the NFC board should, 'in recognition of the good fortune we were all experiencing', give half their final dividend to charity and let it be known they expected others to do the same. There was no support for the idea. The view was that 'charity was a personal matter and that the board should not seek to influence an individual's charitable activities'.

But Sir Peter was unrepentant. His own view was that 'as the Thatcher government withdraws state-funding to the arts, sports and charity, the void has to be filled. Business must play its part if the quality of life of the country is not to sink to unacceptable levels'.

Sir Peter believes that it is significant that although the Marks & Spencer store in Brixton was at the centre of the rioting in that borough a few years ago, it was neither attacked or looted. 'Perhaps it had something to do with the fact', he suggested, 'that the directors had, over many years, developed a policy of community and charitable activity.'

He thinks directors of public firms should seek a mandate from shareholders for charitable activities. At NFC's 1986 annual meeting, shareholders agreed that the board should aim to allocate up to 0.5 per cent of taxable profits to charity and community work. That figure was reached in 1988. Another resolution, at the 1989 AGM, to raise the allocation to 1 per cent, was exceeded in 1990 when total corporate support for charities accounted for 1.68 per cent of pre-tax profits (equivalent to £35.20 per employee). As Sir Peter pointed out, 'We more than qualify for the Per Cent Club, so well promoted by Sir Hector Laing (now Lord Laing), the chairman of United Biscuits.'

But the NFC board were not content with giving a well above average proportion of profits to charity. They thought the company's employee shareholders should also have a say in how the money was spent, so they sought their views through another MORI survey. This revealed that the highest priority was the well-being of NFC pensioners, and there was a demand for an even higher level of pensioner care. NFC people expressed themselves willing to give to medical, children's and old peoples' charities, but they were not happy giving to the arts, education, sport and culture, and would have no truck at all with political donations.

A Social Responsibilities Council (SRC) was set up to organize the NFC's charitable donations. It has supported many charities, and likes to top up the fund-raising activities of employees and their communities. Causes have ranged from the Lockerbie air crash – 'because we had an old-established depot in the town', Sir Peter explained – to support for the starving in East Africa, 'including sending out one of our managers to help with the transport problems of delivering the relief food to the remote regions of the Sudan'.

Recent SRC interests have included help in the community to the underprivileged and handicapped. There has been emphasis on helping them start their own businesses and acquiring skills to make them more independent and reduce the need for social security help.

Sir Peter regards NFC's unusual generosity as an investment. 'It is hard to find a causal relationship, but it cannot be coincidence that the majority of the really successful companies see the need to play a full role in community support projects. I guess it is one of the values in a business that makes the better people want to work for it.

'As I have repeatedly said, in a service industry it is the quality of the workforce that gives the marketing edge. We must therefore have values which appeal to the best.

'We do not want NFC's employee ownership to be measured solely by profitability, the value of the shares and the number of millionaires it has created, but by whether a company is emerging that has a culture and values that are respected by its own employees and in the wider community in which it does its business. That is a higher hurdle to jump, but we believe we are on the way.'

The constitution, and the terms of reference of NFC's Social Responsibilities Council (SRC), exemplify the company's open and democratic approach to giving. The jobs of the SRC are:

1. To be the keeper of the firm's social conscience and to recommend forward looking and appropriate social responsibility policies to the Board of NFC that will ensure that NFC carries out its responsibilities to society in an appropriate manner, taking into account NFC's size and financial strength.
2. To recommend to the Board how these policies will be financed.
3. To allocate available funds to the various committees it controls and to ensure that the committees that it oversees are well and efficiently run.

The SRC reports to the NFC board twice a year. Members are also trustees of the NFC Foundation and act as the reporting body for the NFC Foundation, the Pensioners' Foundation, the Charities Committee, the Sheltered Housing Committee and the NFC in the Community Committee. Four of the SRC's members are elected by shareholders, and the chairman and four other members are nominated by the NFC board. The SRC may also co-opt up to two additional members, if it so wishes.

Pearson

Lord Blakenham, chief executive of Pearson, the company that owns the *Financial Times*, half the *Economist*, Royal Doulton China, Madame Tussauds, Penguin, and other prestigious book publishing firms, including Addison-Wesley in America, says companies 'have social obligations beyond the profit motive' and interprets the term 'corporate social responsibility' to mean that companies should be 'good neighbours', and should acknowledge obligations to the local community and to their employees.

Blakenham is also one of those business leaders who feel his company, and British companies in general, are obliged to give more, and do more than they have in the past, because of the great improvements in the climate for business during the 1980s.

'When the Conservative government came in,' he explained, 'it sensibly made it clear that part of the philosophy behind its tax cuts, and indeed the other side of the coin, was that companies and individuals should take on more responsibility for the community and the environment – since the state would do less.'

According to *Charity Trends* (14th edition), Pearson donated £1.13m in 1990, equivalent to fractionally under 1 per cent of pre-tax profits, and £61 per employee. Normally, about half the donations go to charities and half to sponsorship. Pearson is a member of the Per Cent Club, in manifestly better than average standing, because a company qualifies when it gives more than 0.5 per cent of taxable profits.

Blakenham thinks it is important to keep everyone in Pearson informed of the group's charitable activities, and details of socially responsible spending and behaviour are given in the annual report and in the house journal, *Panorama*. The company also encourages employee initiatives by matching any donations by individuals.

Of the £600,000 given directly to charity in 1990, about a third was spent by the operating companies, and the rest was spent by the group. The deployment of group support is determined by the Pearson Charitable Committee, of which Blakenham is the chairman. The committee sits at the beginning of each year, reviews existing arrangements and lays down the plan for the current year. Existing giving arrangements may or may not be changed.

'We avoid committing the whole budget at the start of the year,' Blakenham explained. 'That can happen if you have nothing but covenants, stretching for years ahead. For the smaller donations we tend to concentrate on one-off help and to target specific areas of activity such as the environment or job creation. In some situations, long-term commitments also make sense, so there are exceptions.'

For its more substantial donations Pearson's giving policy, in common with the policies of many other large companies, has more or less half a long-term eye on business relevance. It is a gesture towards shareholders – a recognition that it is important to give but that it is hard to persuade shareholders of that, so it helps to develop a connecting theme.

The company, for instance, is giving £150,000 a year, over three years, to the British Dyslexia Association. 'The connection is with reading and we publish a lot of books,' says Blakenham. 'There are so many good causes. We try to find ones with some link with our businesses.'

Because of the group's newspaper interests Blakenham became the 1990 Festival Chairman (effectively chief fund-raiser) of 'Old Ben', the Newsvendors' Benevolent Institution, which provides homes and help for hard-up pensioners of the print distributing trade. The group contributed £50,000 to 'Old Ben' in 1990 and held fund-raising events at Chessington World of Adventure, part of the group's Madame Tussauds leisure division.

Closer to home and part of its good neighbour policy, the group has recently committed £100,000 to the Cardinal Hume Centre in Westminster. The centre is close by Pearson's headquarters office at Millbank and provides temporary accommodation and rehabilitation services to young homeless people in the area.

Education is also a central theme in the Pearson view of its social responsibilities. There are scholarship schemes for employees' children going into higher education, Pearson has made an endowment of £1m, spread over ten years, to establish the post of New Media Librarian at the Bodleian Library in Oxford and the group is a supporter of other educational causes.

All major sponsorship is handled by the centre. Pearson was a pioneer of arts sponsorship in Britain. It has sponsored three exhibitions at the Tate Gallery (next door to group head office), the Armada exhibition at Greenwich, the Raj exhibition at the National Portrait Gallery, the Toulouse-Lautrec exhibition at the Hayward Gallery and it helped, as did a number of other companies, in the move of the Courtauld Galleries to Somerset House. This policy also reflects, in a less direct way, the principle of enlightened self-interest. Such up-market cultural activities have pedagogic qualities and Pearson companies publish a lot of educational books.

In common with many other companies today, a concern for the environment is associated with Pearson's and Lord Blakenham's sense of social responsibility. 'The consciousness of the fragility of the world environment has burst upon a large number of people with some surprise,' he says. 'Five years ago, responsible politicians would say "yes, the environment's important but there are no votes in it." People are more aware now.'

He has personally been conscious of the environment for many years because of his interest in birds. His association with the Royal Society for the Protection of Birds (RSPB) dates back to the '50s. He was on the RSPB Council for twelve years and was chairman for five. He was also on the Nature Conservancy Council for three years and is currently President of the Sussex Wildlife Trust. 'The environment is becoming increasingly important, and you shouldn't be too cynical about it,' Blakenham opines. 'Some companies just do it because they think they should, but it also helps companies by making them more conscious of things like energy saving.'

There is as yet no group-wide policy statement on the environment or on wider social responsibility. 'We tend to avoid great group statements,' Blakenham said. But he points out that the *Financial Times* has an environment page on Monday, that it is a sponsor of the RSA's 'Better Environment' awards and that Pearson itself is a launch member of the Confederation of British Industry's initiative for improving company action on the environment which is likely to involve a written code.

On the subject of corporate ethics, too, Blakenham suggests that you cannot rely totally on a written ethical code. 'In fact, if you have to start writing down codes of ethics, that says something about your company that's not necessarily very good. Ethics are very important, from the board downwards and from the bottom upwards. It's extremely important to encourage high ethical standards. I wouldn't criticize a company for writing down its code of ethics, but even if you write them down, it doesn't necessarily mean they'll be followed.'

Blakenham says company law makes it clear that the company's primary duty is to shareholders but he believes 'other interests are not irreconcilable. If you behave responsibly, that is in the long-term interests of shareholders. But you have to be aware of the short term too.'

Tate & Lyle

David Tate, director of corporate affairs at the sugar group Tate & Lyle, says that since its formation, the company has had a social awareness policy 'in line with the philosophy of our two founders, Henry Tate and Abram Lyle'. The Tate public library in Brixton and the Tate Gallery itself were both founded by Sir Henry Tate in the late 19th century.

The group employs 15,304 people (3,600 UK-based, 7,000 in North America). The present chairman Neil Shaw is a Canadian and a leading light in the corporate philanthropy movement. He is chairman of Business in the Community's East London Partnership which covers Newham, Tower Hamlets and Hackney, and is joint chairman of the Per Cent Club.

Tate & Lyle's annual reports show the group gave £247,919 to UK charities during the year to September 1989 and £244,636 in the year to September 1990; 0.48 per cent and 0.49 per cent respectively of profit before interest and tax. The company says that in 1989/90 qualifying donations for Per Cent Club targets were £390,000, 0.8 per cent of UK pre-tax profits.

Giving by overseas subsidiaries amounted to £540,000, making a total of £930,000, or 0.43 per cent of total pre-tax profits. This suggests Tate & Lyle's UK operations are giving almost twice as much, relative to their profit contribution, as the group is giving as a whole. This may reflect the fact that the UK operations, selling strongly branded sugar products, are in closer contact with consumers.

More than eighty different causes were supported by Tate & Lyle in 1989. Important beneficiaries were health and welfare charities, including 'significant contributions' to the Leukaemia Appeal and to the Wishing Well Appeal for Great Ormond Street Children's Hospital. There were also federated company-employee contributions by North American offshoots, Staley, Amstar, Western Sugar, Pacific Molasses and Redpath, through the United Way charities.

A 'starter' gift went to a new Save the Children initiative in London, enabling the organizers to raise nearly £50,000; Tate & Lyle Sugars gave twenty tonnes of sugar to the Save the Children Special Appeal for Uganda, one of several similar donations over the last three years; and the parent became a founder member of the corporate council of CARE Britain.

The board said that, through the London Enterprise Agency (LENTA), and involvement with Business in the Community, 'we are reinforcing our links with the communities around our headquarters at Sugar Quay and the group's four manufacturing plants in East London, particularly in Newham which has the unfortunate distinction of being one of the most deprived boroughs in the United Kingdom'. Specific support is given to, amongst others, Project Fullemploy and the Mansfield Settlement.

In 1989 the company's Sixth Form Scholarship in the London Borough of Newham, the site of T&L's largest refinery, was revised and re-launched. Thirty local pupils, who would not otherwise have been financially able to do so, are studying for 'A' levels and have access to T&L managers for further career guidance and counselling.

The Tate & Lyle Cambridge Commonwealth Scholarship Scheme awarded six scholarships in 1989 to graduate and post-graduate students from developing ACP (African, Caribbean and Pacific) countries with which the company has trading links, and sixteen

T&L scholars were in residence at Cambridge University. Other education initiatives included:

> Redpath, in Canada, awarded twenty-four scholarships in 1989 and contributes to the Ontario Junior Achievement Programme.
>
> Rumenco in the UK offers a bursary for children who are to study science or agriculture.
>
> Staley awarded twenty scholarships at national and local level in 1989, and in 1990 it introduced National Merit Scholarships for children of employees as well as supporting academically-talented minorities at Illinois State University.
>
> Zimbabwe Sugar Refineries awarded ten scholarships to local schoolchildren.
>
> Western Sugar, in the US, gives Outward Bound Scholarships to children in communities where it has factories and awarded eight Safety Scholarships, of up to four years, to children of employees who proposed good ideas for improvements in the company's safety programmes.
>
> In 1989, ninety-two Youth Training Schemes and apprenticeships were provided, mostly by Richards (Shipbuilders) and Tate & Lyle Sugars. In 1990, sixty-two YTS students were employed, mostly at Richards.

Most group companies have close links with local schools and colleges, offering, where appropriate, work shadowing and work experience, and involving employees in a range of activities from school governorships to careers conventions and programmes on understanding industry.

The company's links with Reading University continue with a direct grant and a gift of laboratory equipment to a total value of £250,000. Most went to the University's Innovation Centre where T&L's research labs used to be and which has been renamed the Philip Lyle Building.

T&L also works with the Industrial Society on its Challenge of

Industry conferences and employees give their time to the Young Enterprise programme.

Tate & Lyle is also an active sponsor. With its Redpath subsidiary, the parent company supported the 1988 tour of Canada by the BBC Scottish Symphony Orchestra, and the Portuguese companies sponsored a series of concerts by the New Portuguese Philharmonia Orchestra.

Because of the links between T&L products and human energy, the company has long supported sporting activities. For fourteen years it has encouraged young UK tennis players through sponsorship of a five-day tournament, in conjunction with the British Women's Tennis Association. In 1989 it launched its 'Treasure Island' promotion which raised over £30,000 for the Sports Aid Foundation, and support was also given to the England Gymnastics Team, managed by a Rumenco employee, for the 1990 Commonwealth Games.

SORES, a Portuguese subsidiary, sponsor their local football team, Santa Iria, and Staley has long supported local sport – the Chicago Bears American football team began life as Decatur Staleys.

The group pledged £50,000 for the establishment and running of the Food and Nutrition Gallery at the National Science Museum, and supported the 'Tall Ships' visit to the Pool of London to mark the 800th anniversary of the Lord Mayoralty of the City.

In common with many other large companies these days, Tate & Lyle regards the environment as a key source of reputational assets and, for the unwary, of reputational liabilities. In October 1990 it agreed an environmental policy statement to be disseminated throughout the group. It reads as follows:

> The Group will conduct its operations in full recognition of its responsibilities towards the natural environment within which we live and work. In order to achieve this, all Group units will take every necessary step to comply with relevant laws, regulations and Codes of Practice.
>
> It is the responsibility of managers at each operating site to ensure that procedures are in place and are regularly reviewed and updated, and that employees are appropriately trained in order to implement this Policy.

Adding substance to the rhetoric the group converted all its UK company vehicles to run on lead-free fuel and was a sponsor for the UK launch of the 'Programme for Belize'. It matched employee contributions to help buy 160,000 acres of tropical rain forest in Belize, as a conservation area for Central American wild-life, insects and plant species.

United Biscuits

United Biscuits is a jewel in British industry's crown. It is the world's largest and most efficient biscuit producer and biscuit making was one of the very few UK industries mentioned by Harvard management guru Michael Porter in his monumental book, *The Competitive Advantage of Nations*, as enjoying a position of world leadership. Annual sales in 1990 were over £2.72bn, pre-tax profits were nearly £200m, and the company employed 40,000 people world-wide.

At the same time, UB has a reputation for caring deeply for its employees and acknowledging its responsibilities to the various societies and communities in which it operates. The company gave £1.47m to charity in 1990; over 0.7 per cent of taxable profits world-wide, and probably slightly over 1 per cent of UK pre-tax profits, although it is hard to be sure from the figures (see Appendix, table 5.3).

To a significant extent its persona is the creature of one remarkable man, Hector Laing, later Sir Hector and now Lord Laing of Dunphail (see chapter 1) who became UB's managing director in 1964 and then its chairman in 1972, until his retirement in 1990. He is now Life President of the group.

The company was formed in 1947 with the merger of two long-established, family-owned biscuit makers McVitie & Price – young Hector Laing's family company, of which he became a director in 1945 – and Macfarlane Lang. The enlarged group went public in 1948 and in 1965 it integrated two more acquisitions, William Crawford & Sons and William MacDonald & Sons, and began trading as United Biscuits. Meredith & Drew joined the group in 1967, and the following year UB bought Kenyon Son and Craven, Europe's largest nut processor, to form KP Foods.

The 1970s, under Hector Laing, was a decade of hectic growth at home and overseas. By 1980 Westimex of Belgium, Carr's of Carlisle, Productos Ortiz of Spain and Keebler and Shaffer Clarke of the US had all been added to the portfolio; UB Restaurants had been formed with the acquisitions of Wimpy, Pizzaland and Perfect Pizza (sold to Grand Metropolitan in 1989) and UB Frozen Foods was being put together.

In 1982 the company diversified into confectionery with the acquisition of Terry's. In 1988 Callard & Bowser arrived to strengthen the confectionery business, and Ross Young's was bought from Hanson, as part of the latter's dismemberment of Imperial Group.

The 1990s is witnessing a major push into continental Europe with confectionery acquisitions in the Netherlands, France and Italy, snacks purchases in Spain and Belgium and biscuit buys in Denmark, Finland and Hungary.

For an ordinary company leader such fast-paced and ambitious expansion and diversification would have left no time for anything else, but Hector Laing is no ordinary businessman. He retired as chairman, and from the UB board, in May 1990, becoming Life President. The company remains infused with his values and beliefs.

The new chairman, Robert Clarke, said in his annual statement in March 1991: 'I am conscious that the new team is building on the achievements of the remarkable Laing era, and the legacy of those years – the drive, the integrity, the social responsibility, and the commitment to all stakeholders in our business – will continue as cornerstones of the UB enterprise.'

In the 1991 annual report and accounts, the directors refer to close company links with schools and colleges, to the encouragement given to site managers to 'give a lead in local community affairs', to the group's local job creation and community-based training schemes and to the fact that a dozen or so UB managers are seconded to such schemes in the UK.

The report also reiterates the group's commitment to give 1 per cent of UK taxable profits each year to community affairs and charitable giving, and points out that UB businesses apply the principle of pound for pound matching of employee giving. The company and staff raised over £350,000, in this way, for Save the Children.

American subsidiary, Keebler, gave over $600,000 to a number of community initiatives, including a Drug Awareness scheme, which concentrates on preventing addiction among children. Dollar for dollar matching of employee giving also continued in the US, through the charity umbrella organization, United Way (see chapter 7).

In Hungary, via UB's interest in biscuit maker Gyori Keksz, the company is committed to the creation of an Enterprise Agency, to assist in the regeneration of commercial activity in the local economy.

The uncompromising UB approach to the 'nice' company ideal is apparent in the company's booklet, *Ethics and Operating Principles*, issued to employees in 1987. Notable passages include:

> No employee may give money or any gift of significant value to a customer if it could reasonably be viewed as being done to gain a business advantage.

> No employee or any member of his or her immediate family, will accept from or give to anyone in a business relationship, gratuities or gifts of money or any consideration of significant value which could be perceived as having been offered because of the business relationship or to gain a business advantage.

> Suppliers will be paid on time, in accordance with agreed terms of trade.

(The last seems rather prosaic but is actually a significant undertaking at a time when the deliberate and callous late payment of business debts by large companies is forcing many small firms out of business.)

These four case studies, of UK companies of comparable size, each with an above-average record in corporate philanthropy and social responsibility, demonstrate the wide variety of personality types that can be projected by the style and the practice of giving.

NFC is an employee-orientated company that takes great pains to ensure the image projected by its activities and spending in these areas is consistent with the wishes of its employee shareholders.

This has led to an emphasis on pensioners and to quite elaborate administration and consultation systems.

Pearson is a less integrated group, and the centre tends to keep a low profile. Largesse is distributed carefully, and in line with the preoccupations of the company's market. It is quiet about its giving, even though it is more generous than most companies. Though operating companies do their own thing, most giving is deployed from the centre, with little or no consultation.

Tate & Lyle is proud of its record in these areas, and is in the habit of reporting its contributions more fully than most. The openness may reflect the strong influence its North American acquisitions have come to exert on the style of its management, notably through the person of its Canadian chief executive. The company's approach to giving seems relatively sophisticated, compared to the less deliberate and systematic approaches of most UK firms.

United Biscuits, largely because of the influence of Hector Laing, is evangelical about its giving. It likes to be seen as a pioneer and a standard-setter in corporate philanthropy and social responsibility. It also seems to take a more than usually holistic view of its corporate personality. Whereas other companies seem to treat giving as separate from day-to-day operational matters, at UB, it is seen as part and parcel of the overall corporate reputation, one that includes a reputation for being ethical.

It will be interesting to see which, if any, of these styles becomes dominant, as corporate evolution unfolds. It seems to me, each of them has its strong points. Openness and UB-style evangelism are important in the differentiation of the corporate reputation; a systematic approach, like Tate & Lyle's, is necessary if investments in reputational assets are to be 'efficient', in the sense of yielding good returns; NFC-style consultation with employees helps to widen the 'ownership' of a company's reputation for citizenship, and will therefore make the company more attractive to potential recruits; Pearson's low-key generosity fits well with the hands-off style of its management, and with the self-sufficiency of its high-quality operating companies.

6

The New Intermediaries

One of the signs of maturity in an industry, a profession or a society is an increase in the number of institutions that serve it. It is a sign that it has acquired substance, and is becoming less transparent; that it has developed its own ecology and dynamic; that it is becoming a more complex organism which needs its own internal management system.

By this token, the charity sector is maturing rapidly. There are already a host of dedicated institutions specializing in particular, charity-related areas, and more are being set up all the time.

There is the non-profit-making Working For A Charity which prepares people for work in the sector, the National Council for Voluntary Organizations (NCVO) which involves itself in all sorts of matters including the management of charities, the Institute of Fund Raising Managers which trains people in fund raising, the Charity Finance Directors' Group which discusses financial, tax and legal matters, the Association of Charitable Foundations representing grant-making trusts, Charity Recruitment, a specialist job agency, the Council for Charitable Support, the Directory of Social Change, the Charities Aid Foundation, Business in the Community, the Per Cent Club, and a host of other organizations, all of which see the charity sector itself, rather than its 'clients', as their marketplace.

Much of the recent 'institutionalization' of the UK charity sector, particularly in the area of corporate giving, has been a matter of adopting and adapting US initiatives, such as Per Cent Clubs, community trusts and community leadership programmes, but oddly enough, one of the most important and long-established American institutions, 'federated' giving, through the United Way, has yet to be taken up here.

A local United Way is a non-profit, non-government, private voluntary organization, raising local donations for member health and human welfare charities. About 10 per cent of receipts is spent on overheads. United Ways raise money from companies, pay-roll giving, special charity events and other fund-raising activities. They are widely regarded as an efficient fund-raising system that allows the charities to concentrate on serving their clients.

It began at Denver in 1887, borrowing from a model developed in Liverpool a decade earlier. In 1920, sixty-one local United Ways raised $23m mostly from wealthy individuals. The 1920s were a period of dramatic growth – by the early 1930s there were 450 United Ways and by the end of World War II there were 800. Growth levelled out in the 1950s and the total number of United Ways is now stable at around 2,200.

The initial dependence on rich individuals began to fall in the 1940s when pay-roll deductions were introduced. Since then the emphasis has shifted to employee giving. The sums raised annually through the United Ways passed $1bn in the mid-1970s.

Though there is no direct equivalent of the American United Ways in the UK, the principle of specialization – where one organization does the fund-raising on behalf of fund-giving charities – has one prominent UK exponent.

Charity Projects

Charity Projects, best known for its innovative Comic Relief fund-raising campaigns, was started in 1986 by Jane Tewson who had been working with people with disabilities. She is now the full-time director of Charity Projects and must rank as one of the charity sector's most conspicuously successful entrepreneurs of recent times.

According to *Charity Trends*, Charity Projects was the 167th largest fund-raising charity in its first full year in 1987. In its second year, after the first Red Nose Day, it was up to 14th and it rose to eighth in 1989.

Tewson noted in the Charity Projects' 1989/90 annual review

that 'to date, we have raised over £45m, every single penny of which has been allocated to a specific project. We have supported over 1,000 charities working here, in the UK, and over 120 UK registered charities in Africa. In doing all this, we have tried to break new ground, reach where others can't and find new partners with new solutions to the difficult and growing social problems that we face'.

After squatting for a time in the offices of *aficionados* the twenty-strong organization established itself in its own premises. Tewson announced that, apart from 'minimal building costs', everything in the move was donated, and she thanked Taylor Woodrow, King-fisher, Bishops Moves and the Jenkins Group for their help.

There are five features of the Charity Projects idea that mark it down as a major evolutionary step for the charity sector. The first is that it recognized, from the start, that one of the things givers worry most about is how much of the money they give gets to where it can do some good. They know that charities cost money to run, especially these days, when it is necessary that they be run by professionals, but they also know some charities are more efficient than others.

Tewson wanted to find a way to guarantee to givers that 100 per cent of their contributions to Charity Projects would emerge from it. So she made it a principle that the organization would run very lean, and that as large a proportion of its running costs as possible would be donated.

As chairman Sir Tim Bell pointed out in his annual statement for 1989/90, the extra costs involved in doubling the size of the UK and African grant-making teams were met from bank interest, but accounted for less than 4 per cent of interest earned, and that 'other costs continue to be sponsored separately'.

Tim Bell, ex-Saatchi & Saatchi, ex-Lowe Group and adviser to Margaret Thatcher, exemplifies the second unique feature of Charity Projects: the recognition that the talented and the famous, from all walks of life, have more to give than money – that if they can be induced to contribute their fame and their skills, much more money can be raised from others.

Tim Lindsay, then joint chief executive of the UK's most creative advertising agency, Bartle Bogle Hegarty, and now managing direc-tor of Young and Rubicam, put it as follows: 'Working with Charity

119

Projects allows you to use the skills that you have developed in business to assist a fine cause. It's both more satisfying and more effective than simply giving money. And what's more they make it a lot of fun, so people come back keen to do it again.' The skill of Charity Projects is to dream up ways in which this largely untapped professional energy can be exploited. 'The Great Investment Race' exemplified the principle. In a competition sponsored by the Prudential, and organized by Charity Projects, teams of fund managers competed to produce the highest return on an interest-free loan, over a period of a year. 'The City couldn't resist it,' says Tewson, 'because it was competitive.'

In July 1989 comedian Lenny Henry's first movie, *Lenny Live and Unleashed*, had its world charity première at the Odeon, Haymarket, on behalf of Comic Relief. All the costs were sponsored or given free, and over £18,000 was raised.

In March 1990 five short BBC programmes called *Follow Your Nose*, were screened showing where the money from the previous year's Red Nose Day was being sent. (Red Nose Days are now biennial events, so 1990 was a non-fund-raising 'review' year.) Lenny Henry went to Uganda, Victoria Wood went to Ethiopia and a third comedian, Griff Rhys Jones, covered the UK. The programmes were produced as a joint venture with the BBC Documentary Department, and each contained a sketch with Postman Pat singing *You've Lost That Lovin' Feelin'* with the Righteous Brothers. The programmes were accompanied by three million brochures in the Radio Times to raise awareness of the issues surrounding Charity Projects' work.

Fun is the third ingredient of the huge success of Charity Projects. Jane Tewson hates the word 'fund-raising'. She regards Charity Projects as a 'one-off' organization. 'We have a lot of fun. We enjoy charity. We're trouble! People get involved because they buy a red nose. We're off-the-wall and we're filling a gap.'

This gap is important to her. The fourth principle, when she started Charity Projects, was that it should only raise new money. It's hard to be sure, but there is anecdotal evidence to suggest that the success of Charity Projects has not been at the expense of other fund-raising charities. For example, of the 46,000 cheques Charity Projects has received, only 103 have been from charity bank accounts, run by Charities Aid Foundation (see below).

The canon of non-duplication is also embedded in the fifth principle – that Charity Projects should not try to do what others are already doing. 'There are quite enough charitable organizations already,' says Tewson. 'We shouldn't be adding to the bunch. We could be one of the largest charities in Africa, but we prefer to get the legwork done by others.' This is where Charity Projects' similarity with the United Ways lies.

Charity Projects is a philanthropy broker, with a flair for dreaming up new fund-raising ideas. Like the United Ways, it gives the money indirectly, through the specialist charities concerned with its twin aims: 'to help the disadvantaged in the UK and Africa realize their aspirations and potential'.

Care is taken to ensure money goes to charities that really need it. 'We ask, could it function without us,' says Tewson. 'The big question is, are we filling a hole. We often help projects that have just lost government funding, but it's terribly important to know how the funding system works. The worst thing is to give money to a charity that could have got government funding, because they'll never get it again.'

The splitting of the raising and spending functions, and the care Charity Projects takes to spread its patronage widely, are great advantages. 'It means we can take risks,' Tewson explains. 'No people are absolutely dependent on us and our own risks are underwritten by sponsors. Woolworths paid for the red noses. We might have had to pull Red Nose Day because of the Gulf War. It was scary for a while, but we weren't at risk.'

Like Socrates, the more Jane Tewson learns about charity the more aware she becomes of her ignorance, so Charity Projects has set up an Education and Information Department, with two main functions: to tell givers why their money is needed and where it goes and to transfer knowhow. But Tewson emphasises that it's important not to preach while educating.

'It's a matter of heightening awareness. We've got a major project underway for all schools in the UK, and we feed the lessons we learn back into the public domain. We are hunting in new ground. We don't use the Charities Aid Foundation or the Directory of Social Change [see below] for fund-raising advice – they often use us. We believe in sharing our mistakes with others. We have a surgery time, when groups from charities come in to find out what we know. We tell them pop concerts don't work, for example, because the sector's not good at sharing. We should be doing bulletins and quarterly newsletters too.'

Tewson is full of passions and enthusiasms. She wants people to *feel* what their giving is about. 'Charity is terrifying for the rich and famous,' she says. 'Charity Projects offers another way. We don't work with them, unless they come out with us and talk to clients. Previously, the chairman of the Prudential wouldn't have dreamed of visiting hostels for the homeless in the middle of the night. It's *not* philanthropy – that's not the motivation. It's a very adult understanding. People visiting projects with us get angry. It's about how they feel about themselves and their clients. We cannot just represent the client group. We have to represent the clients as well.

'Advertising agencies used to be terrified of charity – now they're excited. They're asking me to use them more. I never ask them for money. We're trying to make giving OK; accessible, rewarding and fun.'

But she knows there is a mountain to climb. 'Once one or two people do it, it's very infectious, but it's not infectious enough. An MP was on the other day about 'the handicapped' – they're people, for heaven's sake! You've got to allow them their dignity. We haven't even begun. We have to change people's attitudes. I'm becoming aware of just how big the problem is. Charity is cropping up all over the place. It's having to take over. There's a big, big gap. I find the lack of support appalling.'

Tewson is very conscious of the ways in which the sector is changing. 'There are fewer Lady Bountifuls in the charity industry these days. It's more professional and better paid, because there's not so much spare time. Young people ring us up to ask what 'A' levels they should take for a career in development. We got oodles of calls after Comic Relief, but agencies don't want volunteers – they want professionals.'

There are aspects of the new professionalism that Tewson dislikes intensely. She is very worried, for example, about the impact on public opinion of rapacious fund-raisers. 'If I was on fifteen per cent, like some fund-raisers, I'd have £6.5m by now. It's very sad – it could go to clients. If there is a great scandal, the only sufferers are the clients.' She is hopeful the new fund-raising law will help.

Charity Projects has a grant from the Home Office to draw up a guide for good practice in producing high-profile media events such as Comic Relief.

Although Charity Projects leaves the tactics of giving to others, it has clear strategic objectives. Its priorities in the UK are young people in the 16–25 age group, disability, homelessness, drug and alcohol abuse and, more recently, older people. 'We try to address causes rather than symptoms,' Tewson says. The policy, in the UK and Africa, is to favour 'self-help groups and small voluntary organizations working directly at the grassroots', so the assessment process is hard work. The grant teams take up references, visit projects, consult advisers and assess the chances that the organization will survive after the grant runs out. They take into account the local background, the causes and scale of the problems, the capacity of the organization to achieve its targets, budgets and whether users and beneficiaries are involved in managing and organizing the supported projects.

In the case of UK work, staff write detailed reports each quarter for committees of experts. This restricts the ability to react quickly, but the main aim in the UK is to identify long-term solutions, so that charity will not be needed year after year. Progress is always monitored so that Charity Projects can learn from its experiences.

In Africa it can respond more quickly. In 1989/90 25 per cent of all funds earmarked for Africa were available for emergency grants. Grants in Africa are only made through UK registered charities like Save the Children and Action on Disability and Development. Of the money raised by Comic Relief, two-thirds goes to UK-based aid agencies working in Africa, and the rest goes to charities working in the UK.

Tewson says that although there are 'genuine philanthropists about, with whom we have very private relationships', there is also 'a new kind of person, who is giving more assistance in kind. They're making creative donations – they're putting their skills to work. Input comes in different ways'.

The comedian Lenny Henry, one of the organization's earliest and most loyal supporters, conveyed some of the flavour of the unique Charity Projects recipe in his tailpiece comment in the 1990 Annual Review:

I've been involved with Charity Projects for five years now – since a quick bit of acting with Frank Bruno in a dress blossomed into the tasty hugeness of Comic Relief. Three things make me feel particularly good about it. First, I've got complete trust that the cash is being spent by the grants people with care and passion. I've visited Ethiopia, Burkino Faso and Uganda in Africa and always come back with a total confidence (and a totally wobbly tum). Second, I do feel there's nowhere you can work where your time is more splendidly turned into cash: the back-up and imagination means even the smallest effort yields huge profit. And, finally, once in a while, when they're not getting at me and saying, 'Len, where's that 100 words you're meant to write for the Annual Report, you lazy git' – yes, once in a while, we do have some laughs.

Former Chief Charity Commissioner, Robin Guthrie, is also a fan. 'I have been particularly impressed', he said in his Wynford Vaughan Thomas Memorial lecture, 'by the work of Comic Relief in combining entertainment and successful fund-raising with mass communication in the difficult and sensitive human circumstances with which charity is necessarily concerned.'

Other commendations from the great and the good include the following:

'I believe that, from the point of view of both the charity recipient and the hard pressed charity worker/performer with the full diary, Charity Projects is the most efficient money-raising organization I know.' (Rowan Atkinson, comedian).

'Charity Projects are a great organization to work with because I think they really do understand the issues facing small charities. None of the money they raise gets swallowed up in the administration costs; it all gets through to where it's needed at the sharp end.' (Nick Hardwick, director of Centrepoint, the Soho charity).

'I now do almost all my charity work with Charity Projects. This is because I was taken to visit a project and talked to at length about the logistics and ethics of their spending. They place enormous emphasis on how they allocate funds, on educating people about why they are asked to donate and on changing attitudes as well as circumstances.' (Emma Freud, presenter).

Looking ahead, Tewson thinks it is conceivable that Charity Projects could set up something like Sock Shop. It already owns two companies, Charity Projects Trading Ltd and Comic Relief Ltd, which covenant their profits to Charity Projects, and there could be more. 'Companies are an interesting possibility,' she says. 'They may be the way forward. It's good to have product income (like American actor Paul Newman's salad dressing company, which covenants all its profits to charity). We could produce something healthy, like a vitamin, and create jobs. People should not have to pay for naff things from charity. We're very fussy about the quality of our products.'

But she is not sure what Charity Projects will do, or even if it will survive. 'We're not new now,' she says philosophically. 'We may have a limited life.' But for the moment Tewson seems content: 'We are making a difference, and we're enjoying our work.'

Business in the Community

Business in the Community was set up in 1981, with the aims, according to its mission statement, 'to make community involvement a natural part of successful business practice, and to increase the quality and extent of business activity in the community'.

'It is not about philanthropy,' according to Stephen O'Brien BitC's chief executive from 1981 to 1992 and now its Executive Vice-Chairman: 'Our objective is to persuade companies to get involved on the basis of enlightened, long-term profit maximization, and that is a very easy sell. In this respect, we are way ahead of the way it is talked about in the US, or anywhere else.

'It started with a recognition that the welfare state is not solving the country's problems. You began to see a public relations kind of corporate giving – in the form of arts and sports sponsorship – in the '60s and '70s, but the breakthrough came with the riots at the beginning of the '80s. They were incredibly traumatic for companies, and have had a lasting effect. Lloyds Bank's windows were broken in Bristol in 1981 – it became impossible to separate that kind of thing from the ability to generate profit. For the first time in living memory, trading was disrupted. It was really unpleasant for three or four days. That was when Heseltine went to Toxteth.

'Companies recognized that these riots were not caused by a group of militant left-wingers, but by the realization of ordinary people that they had no stake in what was going on. The companies caught on faster than the politicians and they realized that government couldn't do anything about it.'

O'Brien sees Business in the Community as a catalyst for the creation of new structures for developing relationships between companies and the communities they operate in. Local Enterprise Agencies, for example, provided a structure in which established companies can hold the hands of small businesses in their area, until they can stand on their own feet. The employer-led Training and Enterprise Councils are another conspicuous manifestation of the principle that if companies want to continue to be profitable, they must be concerned about the communities from which their profits come, and must take a more active role in community affairs.

'The private sector supported the Local Enterprise Agencies,' O'Brien explained, 'and it saw that they worked. It was the mechanism that was the important thing.

'We didn't have a "not-for-profit sector" here, like the US. Our corporate charity always had patronizing overtones; companies didn't listen to what was going on. There was no sense of partnership. The 300 Local Enterprise Agencies are all different, but they're all partnerships – it's a revolution.

'And the same principle of partnership is now being applied to education, with compacts and education partnerships. Companies are getting more involved in schools because they know that the raw material for their future employees comes out of the classroom. They realized our inner cities could become as bad as America's.'

Another principle that is fundamental to the BitC philosophy is its local approach. It is concerned with the regeneration of places and towns by partnerships between companies, local authorities and the voluntary sector.

O'Brien says that, partly because America is much larger and more decentralized than Britain, and partly because there was never such a comprehensive welfare state in America, US firms have always had more identification with place. 'Until recently, all the decision making has been in the bottom right-hand corner of this country,' O'Brien explains. 'Now we're getting a more regional sense, through the big privatized water and electricity businesses. It's true of British Gas and British Telecom, too. They're also beginning to think in a regional way and becoming more aware of their local consumers.'

But although O'Brien acknowledges that the idea of corporate involvement in local communities began in the US, and that American firms are still way ahead of British firms in the amount of money they give to charity, he is insistent that, because of BitC's evangelism, the principle of corporate involvement and particularly of the involvement of company leaders has been developed further in Britain. 'The level of personal involvement is probably higher here than in the US,' he says. 'Senior executives in the UK have got a pretty good grasp of the personal issues; of what roles they should play. It's on the agenda.'

BitC's former Chief Executive believes this is a considerable achievement because it means the talents of business people have become available to solve problems. 'Teams of business leaders worked out how to get small amounts of money to small businesses,' O'Brien pointed out. 'Venture capital didn't touch very small businesses. We asked bright business people to address that problem. That is what made the TECs (Training and Enterprise Councils) possible. Business people had ceased to see their role as just to give money away.'

An example of how BitC has been a catalyst in this process of conversion was the series of visits it arranged, for groups of upwardly-mobile top managers, to depressed areas where partnership schemes were making a difference. The managers were asked to consider what more businesses could do in the six areas identified in BitC's Agenda for Action: investment; marketing and communications; purchasing and sub-contracting; recruitment, education and training; employee volunteering; and management development. They were then asked to write a report and discuss it. 'They like it', O'Brien explains, 'because it involves networking with other managers and it allows them to set goals for us. One guy had no idea there was no retraining in prisons and he was horrified. They are driving it now. When I first got involved nearly ten years ago I used to be shown the door. Now the ideas are coming from them. Five years ago we were making the speeches. Now they are all being made by business people. The only limits are the imagination.'

In his view, the enthusiasm with which companies and company leaders have embraced the BitC philosophy is because of their awareness of the public's growing interest in the corporate names behind the brand names. He quotes the case of one of the BitC's early sponsors, the highly diversified hotels and restaurants group, Grand Metropolitan. 'It was hard to see what Grand Met was, a few years ago. It had no recognizable profile. That's changed. Even Hanson is talking about it now – its latest report acknowledges the community for the first time.'

O'Brien detects a hint of élitism among the large companies, which were in at the start of BitC. 'There's a group of fifty or so who think they do it all, but the extent of involvement is actually growing very fast although it's hard to measure. When a new Local Enterprise Agency was launched in Lancashire recently, it had sixty sponsors of which fifty were local companies I'd never heard of. It was the same thing in the Mansfield 2010 project. A group of seventy-five small companies can collect a lot of money. Some of the leaders of the big companies can't see that.'

A relatively new area for BitC is employee volunteering, widely regarded as another US import, although some British firms, particularly those with Quaker origins, might dispute that.

There is no doubt that the tradition is more advanced in the US. 'It has got to the stage there,' O'Brien points out, 'where it's seen as natural that employees, all the way down the organization, should be involved. At some American firms it's part of the appraisal process. Employees are asked what they have been doing in the community over the past year.'

BitC, in its UK Award For Employee Volunteering (sponsored by the Whitbread brewing group and the Home Office Voluntary Service Unit and organized by BitC), advises companies to bear in mind the following five requirements when promoting volunteering:

1. Support at board level.
2. A commitment of adequate resources to support activities.
3. An identified individual to co-ordinate activities.

4. Generating enthusiasm for activities to allay any reservations of potential volunteers.
5. Recognition for volunteering effort.

O'Brien sees BitC's job as unending. 'I proposed our demise a few years ago,' he recalled, 'but the trustees thought we were just beginning. The potential for the further involvement of the business world, and its skills, in local communities, is almost without limit.'

He says BitC is getting more involved in consultancy – in advising firms how to develop community programmes. 'We're going to companies and saying to them, do you know what you're doing? If not, let's help you formulate and plan and if you do, let's help you focus your efforts more. We act as catalysts and consultants.' He also predicts that BitC's horizons will extend beyond the UK's borders. 'If the arguments are valid here,' he says, 'they must be valid wherever a company operates.'

The Per Cent Club

The Per Cent Club was set up by Business in the Community, mainly as a marketing device, to promote the principle of corporate community involvement. The idea was that the Per Cent Club would get the corporate punters in, and BitC would show them how to do it.

Founded by Lord Laing, the UK Per Cent Club was launched, as part of Business in the Community, by the Prince of Wales on 15 December 1986, at a reception hosted by Margaret Thatcher at 10 Downing Street. Membership consists of a group of some 300 firms, mostly large, which are committed to making significant donations of money or kind to the communities in which they operate.

It has no written constitution, and does not try to influence its members' contributions. The annual meeting, at which the Archbishop of Canterbury, Dr George Carey, gave the keynote address in 1991, is the Club's only formal activity. In 1991 it also ran an award scheme for 'corporate volunteering' the awards for which were given out by Prince Charles.

The qualification for membership is the contribution of not less than half a per cent of UK pre-tax profits, or one per cent of dividends, to the community. Qualifying contributions include donations to charity, job creation schemes, local economic development, inner-city regeneration projects, education, the environment, the arts or music. Commercial sponsorship does not qualify. Contributions can be in cash, staff secondments or donations in kind (of equipment, premises, time or knowhow). Members are encouraged to publish details of their contributions in their annual reports.

Common Purpose

Common Purpose, a recent US import to Britain, is designed to identify community leaders and show them how to maximize their contributions to public life. It has been set up in Britain by Ms Julia Middleton and is half funded by the government's Action for Cities scheme, and half by Body Shop International, BP, BT, Coopers & Lybrand, Wellcome, National Westminster Bank and Grand Metropolitan. The first two projects were set up in Coventry and Newcastle in April 1990.

As in America, participants pay a fee, financed by employers, to be taught how their cities work. Subjects covered include health, social services, education, the local economy, crime and the city's image. 'People at senior levels can't operate well within a city', says Middleton, 'if they've no knowledge of sectors beyond their own.'

Public/Private Sector Partnerships

In the US the Allegheny conference on community development, based in Pittsburgh, has pioneered public/private sector partnerships and the Boston Redevelopment Authority has been a leader in their application to urban development. Boston developers pay a levy, determined by the size and location of their projects, to help finance social projects like low-income housing. Massachusetts banks help too, by providing a special loan facility aimed at inner cities.

A conspicuous example of this partnership principle at work in America was a decision by General Motors to improve a run-down area in Detroit, instead of deserting it. In a $60m public/private sector redevelopment, the company bought up houses and helped to fund the relocation of tenants and the construction of new housing in the New Centre Commons area.

British oil giant BP is making a name for itself in the US as a socially responsible company by expanding community projects in Cleveland, Ohio, begun by its Sohio subsidiary. It spent more than $11m on community projects in 1989 and $13m in 1990. The programme is run by a special division and senior managers are directly involved. BP has also involved itself in housing in the US, taking advantage of federal tax credits on social investments.

In the UK company-backed City Technology Colleges (CTCs) and the Training and Enterprise Councils are good examples of the public/private sector partnership principle at work in education. CTCs and City Colleges for the Technology of the Arts are a new breed of technology-orientated secondary schools, being promoted and supported by a registered educational charity, the CTC Trust (funded jointly by the government and private sector sponsorship).

The first CTC was opened in September 1988 at Kingshurst, a suburb of Birmingham. By the end of 1993 there will be fifteen CTCs and CCTAs. Typically, individual CTCs are sponsored by charitable foundations and companies but the mix varies. The chief sponsor of the Harris CTC, for example, at Norwood in East London, is the Philip and Pauline Harris Charitable Trust but the fifteen supporting sponsors include nine companies, four charities and two individuals. Chief sponsor of the original Kingshurst CTC was Hanson plc, one of the UK's largest companies, and all the forty-five supporting sponsors are also companies.

Other firms that have played prominent roles in establishing CTCs and CCTAs include ADT Group, Dixons Group, Forte, BAT, British Steel, British Aerospace, Cable & Wireless and Tarmac.

British Gas, a supporting sponsor of the ADT College (a CTC in Wandsworth, London) has chosen to make its greatest social effort through schools and universities. Tony Wyatt, the group's head of social policy, explained the rationale to *Management Today* (June 1990): 'These are not only tomorrow's consumers but potential recruits as well. Regular contact with teachers has a lasting effect too; they are likely to be around for several years after the students have gone.' According to the 14th edition of *Charity Trends*, British Gas gave £10m to UK-based organizations in 1990/1.

National Council for Voluntary Organizations

The NCVO was established in 1919 as the representative body for the UK voluntary sector. Its declared aims are to:

1. Promote the common interests of voluntary organizations, particularly among policy makers at government level.
2. Provide, and encourage others to provide, a range of resources that will increase the effectiveness of voluntary organizations.
3. Extend the scope of the voluntary sector and to identify new areas for action.

It operates through a network of 208 councils for voluntary service, working at local level, and through a powerful head office in London. As well as acting as an authoritative and persuasive lobbyist on behalf of the voluntary sector, with a constant stream of publications on topical issues such as contracting, Europe, the environment, training, management and fund-raising, it has proved remarkably fertile. Over the years it has been instrumental in the formation of a number of other organizations, including Age Concern, the Citizens Advice Bureau network, and the Charities Aid Foundation (see below) which spun-out from the NCVO in 1974 but still works closely with its parent and, like a dutiful child, helps to finance the NCVO's running costs. (CAF's contribution of not far short of £750,000 in the 1990/1 financial year amounted to 20 per cent of the NCVO's revenue.)

The NCVO's quasi-official status has also caused it to play a prominent role in the deployment of public sector funds, including the local development agencies' Development Fund, and the Employment Action Fund.

Sir Geoffrey Chandler CBE, 'chair' of the NCVO's Executive Committee, explained the NCVO's position in his foreword to the 1991 Annual Review:

> NCVO looks two ways: to the voluntary sector's external environment, of which the Government is the most important element, and to the voluntary sector itself. The impact of Government policy on voluntary organizations is of crucial importance: it can be creative or crippling depending on the

degree of consultation in the making of policy and of pre-
dictability in its implementation.

Looking towards the external environment, the NCVO was busy,
in the year to March 1991, providing a continuing response to Sir
Philip Woodfield's 1987 report, *An Efficiency Scrutiny of the Supervision
of Charities*, and spent much of the following year lobbying, with
some considerable success, for amendments to the Charity Bill.

It has also been concerned with the impact on the voluntary
sector of European integration – it commissioned the only major
piece of research on the impact of the single market on the sector
(published as *Changing Europe* in 1991) – and with the need to
uphold what it insists is the 'legitimate campaigning role of charities'. This latter concern was stimulated by the Charity Commission
enquiry into Oxfam (see chapter 8). The NCVO's view is that the
Oxfam affair has revealed a need for guidelines in the delicate area
of political campaigning to be clarified.

Looking towards the internal environment, the NCVO has been
particularly concerned with 'quality assurance'. As Chandler
explained, the voluntary sector

> is as vulnerable as any other activity to the rare case of mal-
> practice being used to tarnish the whole. The training of tru-
> stees and of paid staff therefore remains a key target, the
> ultimate aim being to stimulate a local capability throughout
> the country to provide such training from a variety of sources.

Perhaps one of the NCVO's most enduring contributions to the
voluntary sector will turn out to be its decision, in 1977, to ask
management guru Charles Handy to lead a working party to look at
voluntary sector management. This produced the Handy Working
Party Report and the establishment of the NCVO Management
Development Unit.

Handy published his *Understanding Voluntary Organizations* in
1988 and the NCVO has maintained its emphasis in this area with
its National Management Forum and the launch, in 1990, of the
'Advancing Good Management' pilot scheme, with Government
and private sector support. The idea is to form a network of 'hub'
agencies to provide management support on a local basis.

The emphasis on management was affirmed by the Nathan Report in 1990 which set out an agenda for action for the NCVO in particular and for the voluntary sector at large. Following another Nathan Report recommendation the NCVO has set up a joint working party, with the Charity Commission, to provide training and support for charity trustees.

The NCVO appointed a new director, Judy Weleminsky, from the National Schizophrenia Fellowship in September 1991, but has since lost one of its three Assistant Directors, Richard Gutch (see chapter 8).

Charities Aid Foundation

When Margaret Thatcher requested that her foundation should be a charity, the Charity Commissioners turned her down, on the grounds that its goals were political. But in the nick of time the Charities Aid Foundation (CAF) put forward a solution to what seemed like an insurmountable difficulty. CAF proposed that the cash raised by the foundation could be sent to a separate charity fund – the Mrs Thatcher Fund – and distributed in her name. By mid-1992, Baroness Thatcher's private office was estimating that the foundation would have accumulated between £5.5m and £8m by the end of the year from businesses and individuals in Britain, the US and the Middle East.

This anecdote exemplifies the way in which CAF has involved itself in charity matters, of all kinds, since it spun out from the NCVO in 1974 and particularly since its present executive director, Michael Brophy, was appointed in 1982. Brophy had spent the previous six years as Appeals Director for the Spastics Society and is now widely regarded as one of the sector's most energetic and innovative entrepreneurs.

His style – a blend of charity professional, advertising man and fighter pilot (he worked for J. Walter Thompson after leaving the Fleet Air Arm) – does not always sit comfortably with the sector's more passive and circumspect ethos, but what Brophy has done at CAF, and what he plans to do, are striking proof of the falsity of the belief that only the profit motive has the power to invoke the energy, ambition and imagination that are the engines of capitalism.

CAF, under Michael Brophy's leadership, has been transformed from a small, specialist charity, with about £500,000 to give away each year, into a mini financial conglomerate that looks more like a full service stockbroking firm than a run-of-the-mill, traditional charity.

What makes CAF so interesting, and such an intriguing signpost to one of the many possible futures for charities, is that its 'diversifications' into areas like tax planning and fund management all seemed, at the time they were started, to be perfectly logical developments of existing activities. Since it had its own Grants Council, for example, to decide how best to deploy its own charitable funds, it seemed logical to offer other givers the opportunity to have their funds deployed under the same umbrella of expertise.

After all, it makes no difference to CAF's respected Grants Council, an autonomous advisory body of thirteen members chaired by Sir Harold Haywood, if its decisions are applied to money in the gift of individuals and companies other than CAF. In this way CAF began to resemble a wholesaler of charity in a way not dissimilar to Charity Projects, although on a much smaller scale.

And since effective and responsible giving requires a great deal of information and research, was it not logical to 'package' the information, so it could be made more widely available? This was how CAF's Research and Statistics Unit (RSU) got going. 'We needed to have data to make giving effective,' Brophy explains. 'It was part of the professionalism. We're a sort of merchant bank offering an investigating service to advise donors on the range of charitable interests and needs.'

CAF quickly became the authoritative source of statistical material on the UK voluntary sector. Its annual *Charity Trends* is much quoted (in this book, and elsewhere), its annual *Directory of Grant-Making Trusts* is widely used by fund-raisers and the RSU's Individual Giving Survey (formerly the Charity Household Survey) is an invaluable monitor of changes in individual giving.

And since such customer givers are often unfamiliar with the fiscally privileged charity environment, is it not logical to offer to relieve them of the burden of having to reclaim income or corporation tax on the money they give? This was how CAF's 'Charity Cheque Book Scheme' began. By the end of April 1990, 37,000 donors to charity, including over 50 per cent of Britain's most generous firms, had CAF charity accounts that give them tax-free cheque book services for their donations.

The client donor makes out a cheque to a charity, and then CAF honours the cheque by payment from the client donor's account which can be 'fed' through the Gift Aid scheme, for example, Give as You Earn or other forms of untaxed income. Thus CAF became a retail banker, specializing in non-taxable income. It can make disbursements from client accounts with cheques or standing orders, and can treat accounts as either current or capital (with its Trust Account service).

Since an important result of these banking-type services is that quite large sums of money flow into CAF, and stay there for a while, before donors give instructions for it to be paid out, is it not logical to offer to manage the money, so that it earns a reasonable rate of return? CAF's career as a fund manager began in 1986. By the end of 1990, CAF had almost £75m under management in three funds. CafCash, which is supervised by the Bank of England, takes money on deposit from 600 charities. An elegant consequence of CAF having both donor and charity customers is that a simple clearing entry at CAF can, with the appropriate instruction, transfer money from a CAF donor account to a CafCash charity account.

More recently CAF has launched an Income Fund and a Balanced Growth Fund, both of which are managed, on CAF's behalf, by the City's most blue-blooded broking firm, Cazenove & Co. At present CafCash accounts for over two-thirds of funds under management, but Brophy thinks there is a lot more to go for with the two managed funds. 'The total assets of our donors are £20bn, at least. We reckon we could get to £75m in three years (the two managed funds contained £26m in 1991). We have some advantages – we know the charity sector and we are not in it for the money. We should be able to offer schemes every bit as competitive as anyone else.'

Brophy has plans for the further development of CAF's newly forged City links. 'We're going into Europe,' he says. 'The idea is to combine our links with Cazenove with our knowledge of the voluntary sector, to sell CAF services to France and Germany. We also want to form a European Association of some kind, to represent voluntary sector concerns, in areas like the Social Charter.'

Brophy acknowledges that, as the scale and variety of CAF's

operations grow, conflicts of interest could arise. For example, if CAF has a large number of charities as clients of its fund-management operations, or large numbers of firms as clients of its grant deployment and cheque book services, the objectivity of its statistical publications might be called into question. But he is sanguine about CAF's ability to resolve such difficulties and has established an Advisory Board for the research and statistical unit, to ensure its objectivity.

Brophy sees CAF as a bridge between donors and charities: 'the bigger the bridge, the more the traffic'. He believes that an organization like CAF, which makes giving easier, also increases the amount given. But Brophy is not content with CAF's role of lubricator. He also plays a full part in the sector's advocacy campaigns. He is involved with the Council for Charitable Support with Lord Whitelaw, is a tireless campaigner for more and simpler tax incentives, has given his full support to the Windsor Campaign, to increase levels of giving, and is a passionate advocate of the use of television advertising in fund raising.

And he also sees CAF, with its rich statistical knowledge, as having a whistle-blowing responsibility. In his foreword to the 1990 edition of *Charity Trends*, Brophy warned that a fall in median giving in 1989, from £1.97 to £1.28 a month, was serious, and suggested individual giving was getting stuck on a plateau. In his foreword to the following year's edition of *Charity Trends* he said those warnings had been vindicated and that a new, equally worrying development was that charities had begun to liquidate their assets in their efforts to maintain their spending levels.

He regrets the evidence that suggests the proportion of people engaged in volunteer work has fallen from 80 per cent, three years ago, to 74 per cent now and chastises the government for not making the right political moves. 'The civil service has the same attitude as social workers,' he says. 'They see the role of the statutory sector as sacrosanct.'

However Brophy believes there are signs of a welcome change in the voluntary sector. 'There's much more professionalism,' he says. 'The HQs are unrecognizable, from what they were ten years ago. There are professional appeals systems now, using computers. National Trust membership has risen from 250,000 to 1.3m in ten years and the large charities are beginning to pay people properly.'

In addition to these intermediary organizations, there are dozens of others, each of which plays a role in the internal workings of the charity sector. Together they are adding coherence and substance, and a feeling of solidarity and common cause, to an area that was previously fragmented and which lacked much in the way of an infra-structure. Their emergence and rapid growth in recent years is yet more evidence that the charity sector is undergoing a period of fundamental evolutionary change.

7

The Charity Industry

They call it 'caritas', and they say it means love and care. They say they know how important management is, and some of them even say they have read Charles Handy's *Understanding Voluntary Organizations*, but they say you should not be paid £70,000 a year to run a charity. They say that when most of your helpers work for nothing but love, salaries like that are not appropriate; they say the new hardheaded, professional philosophy in charity is going too far, and has begun to undermine the ethos of the sector.

They are bewildered when the National Council for Voluntary Organizations (NCVO) runs seminars on competitive tendering, and they find the language spoken by the new breed of people who seem to be taking over the sector unintelligible and deeply disturbing.

In the old days, charity people were charity people – a bit flaky, perhaps, but their hearts were in the right place. You knew where you were with them. They were dedicated and passionate, full of that quality of 'caritas' which was the fuel that drove everything.

Nowadays, it is a bit vulgar, a bit too 'professional'. There is all this talk of competition, product differentiation, market segmentation, niche strategies, brands and 'clients'. It is as if the magic is leaking out of fairyland, and being replaced by the prosaic and the banal. The charity sector is becoming less special and, for the old charity people, it is becoming a less attractive place to live and work.

The new people see it differently. They see themselves as the vanguard of an army of charity professionals, dedicated to applying their knowledge, skills and flair to a sector brim-full of great brand names that, for far too long, have remained under exploited and woefully mismanaged.

They see the old 'charity person' stereotype as a worthy relic of an amateur past, standing in the way of progress. And they resent the implication that lies behind the teeth-sucking of the 'social workery' old guard, namely that the new breed are sacrilegious invaders of a temple they do not understand and are unworthy to enter.

They say they care just as much and that, anyway, caring is an over-rated quality in a competitive market. They say it is better for the recipients of charity when charities are run by professionals, rather than well-intentioned amateurs who regard such things as direct mail and expensive full-colour brochures as at best extravagances, and at worst, inventions of the devil.

The way the new guard sees it, it was never what a charity *was* that mattered, so much as what it did. And they say that what it does will be done better, and to the greater benefit of charity clients, if it is done professionally.

The culture clash is not as violent as I depict. It was the old guard, after all, who invited the money changers and the brand managers into the temple in the first place. They may not find all the consequences entirely to their liking, but they knew things had to change.

They had pleaded guilty to Charles Handy's twin accusations of 'strategic delinquency' – putting ethos before strategy – and the 'servant syndrome' – making virtues of shabbiness and parsimony. They knew the old style, where virtue was its own reward, was off the pace in the modern world and, being doubtful of their own ability to adapt, they recruited their change agents from the nether world of commerce and Mammon.

Chris Chestnutt, head of marketing at the Imperial Cancer Research Fund, exemplifies the new breed. She came from the commercial world three years ago, from the leisure and service sector, where she worked for Trust House Forte (now Forte) in its corporate hospitality division. 'It was about the marketing of intangibles,' she recalls, 'and there are parallels here, because cancer isn't a single issue. There are more than 200 different types.'

She describes herself as a humanitarian who loves marketing.

'I wanted to do it in a way that didn't make me ashamed. I didn't want to be a "charity person" though – I wanted to be a professional. There are stereotypes, the old and new sorts of people, but for me, although professionalism comes first, I want to be involved in an ethical area.

'I'm very ambitious, a professional woman, and it is important to me to be professionally respected. But enough of a light has dawned about what area I want to work in.'

Chestnutt has realized there are different types of people in different charities. 'In the Third World charities, you get more of the "social workery" types but in the UK-based medical organizations, there are more professionals now. I'm part of the new look.'

But though, by and large, the old and the new types seem to mix reasonably well, there is real tension between them and real issues divide them. It is true that the old guard failed to respond quickly enough to the challenges of commercialism and that their clients suffered from this tardiness. But it is also true that there is something special about the charity sector – an ethos of compassion that the commercial world would do well to learn from – that is both precious and in jeopardy.

It remains to be seen how this tension – between the demand for professionalism on the one hand, and the need to preserve charity's traditional ethos on the other – will be resolved. It is clear, though, that just as it is hazardous to pour new wine into old bottles, so the tension contains a potential for destruction as well as creation.

The charity industry has reached a stage of transition, and it is against this background that its current structures, management styles and strategies must be considered.

Structure

Though all charities, by definition and law if not in fact, spend all their income on giving, by no means all charities receive all their income through gifts. The first thing to note about British charities is that 'charity' defines how their income is spent, much more than it defines how it is raised.

In an analysis of the *Charity Trends* data, I identified different types of organized charity, distinguished by their sources of

revenue. The types, or themes, are usually mixed in various proportions in particular charities and it is the balance between the
themes that determines the natures of the organizations.

There are four basic sources of charity income: voluntary contributions (donations, covenants, legacies), fees and grants from
central and local government, investment income and trading
income. Each revenue source reflects a different theme or business
idea.

The 'Pure' Charity

A charity that receives all or the bulk of its income from voluntary
contributions can be described more or less as a 'pure' charity, in
that both the source and destination of its income are in tune with
the conventional idea of what a charity is. Most of the effort of
such organizations goes into fund-raising, whether done internally
or with the help of external fund-raisers.

Some of these pure charities are also active in education, and
in the provision of information about charity matters and a few are
politically active, too, in ways that, as we shall see in the next
chapter, often inspire controversy.

A striking feature of Britain's top fund-raising charities is how
relatively few derive the bulk of their income from voluntary
sources. Of Britain's largest 100 fund-raising charities, less than a
third derive more than 80 per cent of total revenue from voluntary
sources. Of these, the purest is the Jewish Philanthropic Association, which derived all of its £9.3m of income from voluntary
sources in 1988 (see Appendix, table 7.1).

The 'Agency' Charity

Though most of Britain's 165,000 charities receive nothing from
central or local government, apart from the tax relief they enjoy
by virtue of their registration as charities, a significant proportion
of the larger charities (185 of the 400 top fund-raising charities,
according to the 13th edition of *Charity Trends*), receive money from
government in the form of fees and/or grants.

In 1989 contributions to charities by central and local government amounted to not far short of £400m (nearly 20 per cent of

the total income of the top 400 fund-raising charities). In addition, these same 400 charities probably benefit to the tune of at least another £400m a year in the form of tax relief. It is clear from these figures that the charity sector acts as the agent of government for the provision of various kinds of welfare to a very significant extent.

The degree of dependence on government support ranged from the modest £3,000 of the Licensed Victuallers' National Homes, representing 0.1 per cent of their total income, to the £4.9m received by the National Autistic Society, which represented nearly 87 per cent of its total income. The largest recipient of government support was the Leonard Cheshire Foundation which received nearly £26m in state assistance in 1989, representing over 72 per cent of its total income. Other large 'agency' charities include the Spastics Society (see chapter 2 and ponder the implications), Barnardos, the Salvation Army, the National Children's Home and the Royal Opera House, Covent Garden. Smaller grants went to charities such as Voluntary Service Overseas, the British Trust for Conservation Volunteers, Welsh National Opera, the National Trust and Help the Aged.

It is possible to detect some inkling of government policy priorities in the ranks of the 'agency' charities, but it would be wrong to set too much store by this. Some charities are much richer than others and so need less support, and some have much more scope for voluntary fund-raising. Policy should be reflected in the patterns of support, but other considerations inevitably obscure its significance.

It should not be surprising, therefore, that apart from the evidence of an oddly open-handed enthusiasm for the minority 'art' of opera, the pattern of government support is mixed, as the selected list of UK charities, more or less dependent on state sponsorship, indicates (see Appendix, table 7.2).

The 'Trading' Charity

I define 'trading' charities as those deriving a relatively large proportion of their total income from the same kind of activities that normal commercial companies engage in.

These can be divided into three main categories:

1. Trading and sales: profit from trading companies; net income from activities like mail order, cards and calendars; sales of new items in charity shops; gross income from publishing, other goods made by the charity, entrance fees, box office receipts, royalties, fees and income from contract research.
2. Rent and investment: income from capital assets in the form of rents, dividends and interest.
3. Charity shops: net income from the sale of donated goods in charity shops.

Table 7.3 in the Appendix gives a table derived from *Charity Trends*, ranking the top twenty fund-raising charities by the percentage of total income they received in 1990 from each of these categories.

Although Oxfam just pips the National Trust, the largest UK fund-raising charity by quite a margin in 1990, most of its trading income came from its huge network of charity shops selling donated goods and earning about £18m in 1990. Though clearly lucrative, these shops are not strictly comparable with private sector retail operations. The National Trust has no charity shops but it earned nearly £14m in 1990 from trading and sales, over £5m of which came from its offshoot National Trust Enterprises which runs its much admired gift shops, restaurants and tea-rooms.

The National Trust's 1991 accounts show that NT Enterprises actually increased its contribution in 1991 from £5.1m to £5.3m, during a year in which most private sector retailing groups recorded lower earnings. This achievement reveals the existence of retailing skills of a very high order in NTE.

The large trading charities like Oxfam, the National Trust, the British Red Cross and the Imperial Cancer Research Fund (ICRF) are 'company-like' organizations. Those with a speculative turn of mind might see them as hybrid organizations – part charity, part company – that are in the vanguard of a long-term evolutionary trend that will lead, ultimately, to the effective convergence of the two species.

We shall return to this idea in chapter 9. For the moment, I want to make two points. First, there is an obvious next step in this direction for charities with large charity shop operations. They can decide – as the ICRF (see below) seems poised to do – to begin selling new goods, in addition to (or instead of) donated goods.

Second, some contributions classified as 'voluntary' in *Charity Trends* are, in reality, more like trading revenues. We shall see in the St John Ambulance case study that services ostensibly supplied free of charge are sometimes provided on the understanding that recipients will make a donation to the charity, and that it is not uncommon for charities to make it clear to the recipient what size of contribution would be acceptable.

To my mind there is precious little difference between this ostensibly 'charitable' transaction and a simple commercial transaction between two companies.

Charitable Trusts and Foundations

As is the case elsewhere in the UK charity sector, accurate figures about the number and significance of grant-giving trusts are hard to come by, but they are thought to account for around 3 per cent of total giving, or roughly £400m in the 1989/90 financial year. (See Appendix, table 7.4 for a list of the top ten UK grant-making trusts.)

Partly because of the way in which their giving and, to a lesser extent, their income has held up in the recession, while that of other voluntary organizations has fallen, the relative financial importance of the grant-giving trusts has been rising in recent years.

Trusts have a significance, in the charity sector, that extends beyond their financial contribution because they, more than any other kind of charitable organization, have the discretion to select and focus. John Stuart Mill saw this as the main distinguishing, redistributive quality of charity.

Unlike pure fund-raising charities, trusts are not dependent on the caprice and whim of public opinion and unlike the agency charities, they are not dependent on contracts and, hence, on the political priorities determined by the government of the day. Their wealth makes them independent of fashion and policy. They are free to experiment and to deploy their largesse as they see fit, unconstrained by the exigencies of contract-hunting and the changing patterns and levels of giving.

This freedom has been preserved, over the years, despite the fact that trusts enjoy the same fiscal privileges as other voluntary organizations, but it has recently become a matter of growing controversy. Diana Leat points out, in her report *Trusts in Transition*, that the dependence of some trusts like the Family Fund, the Independent Living Fund, Motability and AIDS trusts on the government shilling (rather than on endowments) has made them more like 'agency' charities than endowed trusts (like the Wellcome Trust). This has sometimes caused their grant-giving freedom to be characterized as a lack of public accountability.

As Leat explains, trusts can be convenient conduits for the deployment of government money for this very reason. She quotes Sir Patrick Nairne, ex-Permanent Secretary at the (then) DHSS: 'The advantage for government is that people can't ask questions in the house ... [The government] can simply say, if necessary, "Well, that's done by the Family Fund".' (*Trust Monitor*, February 1990).

Moreover, because such non-endowed trusts are surprisingly not required, under present charity law, to present regular accounts to the Charity Commission, it is possible for largely state-funded organizations to be controlled by trusts that are subject to no statutory supervision. And even the permanently endowed charities, which are required to submit annual accounts, are far from assiduous in doing so. The House of Commons Public Accounts Committee expressed astonishment and dismay recently, when it found that of a sample of 122 charities, only nineteen had submitted annual accounts in the past year.

Estimates by the Directory of Social Change indicate that in grant-giving the trusts favour:

1. national health and welfare organizations (accounting for some 40 per cent of grants from the 400 largest trusts)
2. medical and scientific research – Wellcome Trust is the dominant giver here, see below – (accounting for 30 per cent)
3. religion (accounting for 9 per cent)
4. education (accounting for 7 per cent)

There is evidence to suggest that trusts prefer to fund on a project-by-project basis, rather than to act as providers of 'core' funding. Diana Leat's survey also indicates that recipients of trust funding are mostly in southern England, although, no doubt, this is partly a reflection of the heavy concentration of charity head offices in London.

An interesting development, in recent years, is the tendency of some trusts to engage in syndicated funding, known as 'partial' or 'multiple' funding. The development appears to have been driven, not by the trusts themselves, but by the desire of their recipients to reduce their dependence on a single source of finance.

A similar appetite for syndicated financing – by the banks and venture capital funds – is evident in the corporate world although, in these cases, it is more often a reflection of the desire of fund suppliers to spread risk.

Syndicated funding is an important development because it improves the efficiency of the funding market. It allows applicants to offer 'packages' to grant givers, tailored to the latter's size and inclinations, and makes it easier for the voluntary sector to co-operate with the statutory sector in the funding of recipient organizations.

Some say the main disadvantage of multiple funding is that it makes it more difficult to evaluate the effectiveness of grant giving, at a time when evaluation is an increasingly important issue. In the parallel world of corporate finance, where syndication is driven by the suppliers rather than the recipients of funding, this difficulty has been addressed by the practice of assigning a leadership role to one funder.

The 'lead investor' in a venture capital financing package, for example, gets the business in the first place, does all the ground-work – the 'due diligence', as it is known – puts the syndicate together, and subsequently becomes the conduit for information between the portfolio company and the other syndicate members. The portfolio company sees a lot of the lead investor, and relatively little of the other syndicate members.

The system can work with charity funding too. Instead of putting a 'package' together itself, a recipient would ask a loyal supporter to become a 'lead funder', and to assemble a group of fellow funders for a particularly large project. In agreeing to play this role, the loyal supporter would assume the lead funder's responsibility to evaluate performance and to report back to other grant givers.

Management

When the Third World charity, War on Want, was discovered to be potentially insolvent in March 1990, the Charity Commission announced an Inquiry under section 6 of the 1960 Charities Act to

> ascertain the circumstances which have led to the current potential insolvency of the charity and the extent to which members or past members of the Council, employees or past employees and the charity's professional advisers may have contributed to this state of affairs, with particular reference to the treatment of special trust funds and special project funds in the hands of the charity.

At the end of March 1991 David Forrest, Secretary of the Charity Commission, wrote to Ms Susanne MacGregor, chair of War on Want. He acknowledged that 'the Council and staff of the charity have devoted considerable time and effort to meeting the needs of the poor and deprived in many parts of the world' but said the Inquirers' report had identified 'many grave deficiencies in the administration of the charity', namely:

> the production of misleading accounts for five successive years
>
> failure to account separately for separate funds from different sources for a given purpose and their wrongful disbursement
>
> failure to recover £36,745.98 owed to the charity by WOW Campaigns Ltd. (a War on Want subsidiary)
>
> failure to recover £66,385 owed to the charity by War on Want Trading Ltd.
>
> failure to control the charity's programme of work in accordance with the resources available
>
> failure to define the relationship between the charity and the consortia of charities to which it belonged
>
> the absence of proper membership records
>
> unresolved internal disputes

other serious failings of management and financial control

The Commissioners assigned responsibility for these failures to the members of the Council of Management, but said that since the report had also identified failures on the part of War on Want's auditor, a copy had been sent to the Institute of Chartered Accountants in England and Wales.

'The Commissioners have concluded', the letter went on, 'that all those assets which have been misapplied must be restored to the charity in the shortest possible time and acceptable standards of accountability must be established immediately.'

They gave the Council a month to say how they would identify funds received on trust, for special purposes, since April 1985 which were not so spent; two months to come up with an acceptable plan for their early restitution (plus quarterly progress reports, thereafter); and a month to prepare a plan 'showing how the solvency of the charity may be restored and maintained'.

The Commissioners also demanded 'steps forthwith' to recover money owed to the charity by its two companies, and gave the Council a month to say how and when this would be achieved.

They demanded, within a month, a statement of sums for which the European Commission awaited a full report, and plans for improved accounting and budgeting systems (and a report, six months later, that the changes had been implemented).

Money, other than general funds, held on a trustee basis by the charity was required to be identified and then held in separate trust accounts and the charity secretary was given two months to prepare a statement, for the Commissioners, on the accuracy of the statutory books, and how they would be maintained in future.

War on Want failed to comply with all the demands and is no more, but its collapse still reverberates grimly around the voluntary sector. The can of worms uncovered by Charles Raikes and David Spence, the Inquirers, is reminiscent, insofar as it involved misapplication of funds, of the Robert Maxwell scandal, although there was no suggestion here of deliberate fraud. War on Want's collapse exposed incompetence, rather than dishonesty, although, as we saw in chapter 2, there is plenty of that around in the voluntary sector, too.

Perhaps the most disturbing feature of the affair, to which the new powers granted to the Charity Commission by the 1992 Act were partly attributable, was that, to all intents and purposes, War on Want's situation was irretrievable by the time the official charity watchdog was able to act.

It remains to be seen how effective the Charity Commission's new powers will be in policing incompetence in the future. It is clear, however, to many within the voluntary sector as well as to many outside it, that there is a great deal the charities themselves must do to smarten up their management act.

One problem is that the charity 'ethos', or rather the way the ethos is perceived by those in charge of charities, has meant the much-needed and vaunted 'managerial revolution' in the voluntary sector has been proceeding at rather less than breakneck speed.

Tim Gauvain, executive director of St John Ambulance (see below), put his finger on one of the central dilemmas when he pointed out that 'if you're in the voluntary sector, the determination of policy must be a volunteer matter'. At St John Ambulance, all members of the policy board, except Gauvain, are volunteers. 'They make the decisions,' he says. 'I am like a managing director, responsible to a mainly non-executive board.'

Developing the corporate analogy further, Gauvain suggested that St John Ambulance could be regarded as an important subsidiary of the Order of St John, whose shareholders were the Order's members and donors. This is reminiscent of what is known in the corporate world as a 'mutual' company, like a building society, or the Co-Operative Wholesale Society.

Mutual organizations owned by their customers or depositors look very good for customers, on paper, because they do not have to pay dividends to outside shareholders. But history suggests this technical advantage is more than offset by the practical difficulties such organizations have encountered in hiring and keeping high-quality managers.

The constitutional peculiarities of mutuals, which charities frequently exhibit to an even greater extent, often exclude senior executives from policy making and strategy formation, and ambitious managers find this very frustrating. They have no wish to be mere caretakers. They want to be leaders, to have the power to change things.

One of the new breed of 'professional' managers illustrated this classic frustration by saying: 'People recruit people like themselves. Lots of charities are run by wing-commander so and so, who wouldn't know a new management idea if it bit him. We're trying to be market-led but change comes from the top. There has to be a new generation there, too.'

Another, older hand was even less circumspect. 'The trustees are the problem – so many of them are yo-yos. Technically, many charities are bankrupt, because of trustee incompetence. We have to professionalize the trustees. Too many come for the gong [being a charity trustee is reckoned to increase one's chances of a knighthood]. They should be more like directors – they should have a contribution to make.'

But, in some ways, this profound managerial conservatism is inescapable because givers demand it. Research shows that givers are particularly concerned with two things: 'What happened to my money – what proportion went where it was supposed to?' and 'I want real evidence of benefit'.

The first indicates a widespread belief, on the part of most givers, that the best-managed charity is the one that gives the highest proportion of the funds it raises to 'clients'. It is an integral part of the Charity Projects strategy, for example, (see chapter 6) that, insofar as it's possible, running and marketing costs should be donated and that those that must be supplied 'in-house' should be more than covered by bank interest.

The trouble with this cost minimization strategy is that it is a manifestation of Charles Handy's 'servant syndrome' (making a virtue of shabbiness and parsimony) and militates against investment in marketing campaigns, for example, that could generate improved net donations. If the quality of a charity's management is measured by how little it spends the charity will often end up with very little to give.

The decision by the Imperial Cancer Research Fund (ICRF), for example, to switch from black and white to colour printing of its marketing materials and advertising literature, added to costs but, according to Chris Chestnutt, was well worthwhile. She is convinced that the reasons why the third edition of the ICRF's *Conquest* newsletter raised £350,000 compared to the £100,000 raised by the first edition were that it was more positive and was printed in full colour. 'The colour approach is in contrast with the approach where everyone sees cancer as the "big C" – a bottomless pit where there's no progress. We have to emphasise hope and progress, and be seen to be positive. We don't want to sell doom and gloom. People have to see that progress is being made – that it *has* worked. We need more optimism – the positive, not the negative thinking.'

Of course, the second demand of givers, for more 'real' information about the good the charity has done on their behalf, conflicts with the demand for minimal costs because it is expensive to provide regular, detailed information.

The best that can probably be done is to impose an arbitrary limit on administration and fund-raising costs of, say, 10p in the £. But it should not be hard and fast. As in business there are times when the expensive marketing campaign is the one that achieves the lowest cost per £ raised.

The arrival of these new management ideas is influencing the way charities are organized, as well as how they're managed. There is a tendency for more specialist departments to be set up, to accommodate the new, specialist skills being hired in areas such as market research, direct mail, corporate fund-raising, merchandizing, promotion and event organization.

Since all this extra 'functionality' is steadily increasing the complexity of many large charities, and so adding to the leadership task, it is hard to see how the volunteer trustees can continue, for much longer, to deny the senior, salaried professionals a lead role in policy formation, and strategic decision making.

And it is equally hard to see how the voluntary sector, if it really wants its managerial revolution, can continue to pay its senior executives low salaries and no bonuses. There is no denying the power of the charity ethos to inspire good people to work hard for relatively low pay, but it cannot be too low and it needs to be performance-linked.

Pay

It will not be surprising to learn that charity people are generally paid significantly less than people of comparable rank in the corporate sector. Moreover, although over half the larger charities (£3m plus revenue) have introduced some form of performance-related pay (the proportion is expected to grow), the sums involved are small, by company standards, and there is precious little in the way of bonuses or perks. However, the gap in rewards between companies and charities has been narrowing, and there are some important differences in relative pay, depending on seniority, and on the size of the charity.

It is useful to think of the charity/company differences as reflecting the influence of the charitable 'ethos'. One can talk in terms of the 'ethos discount' in charity pay, and try to understand how it works and how it interacts with other, commercial pressures on human resource management.

Figures derived from Charity Recruitment's 1991 survey (see Appendix, table 7.5) show the pattern of these 'ethos discounts'. They indicate how much less, in percentage terms, the average charity executive is paid, compared to executives in equivalent positions in companies and they also suggest that charity's 'ethos discounts' are larger in senior jobs and smaller in the larger charities.

The tendency for more junior people to be paid at rates that are closer to company rates increases all the way down, to the point where clerical and secretarial rates of pay in the voluntary sector are practically the same as in companies. The main reason for this is probably that those in lower-paid jobs are at the periphery of the labour market. The alternative, for such employees, is not to work at all, so they need something pretty close to market rates to induce them into employment.

As their pay rises to accommodate higher levels in Maslow's 'hierarchy of needs', charity people feel they can afford to sacrifice more for partaking in the charity ethos. They buy, with their 'ethos discount', either the appearance of virtue or the reality of increased job satisfaction.

The generally lower 'ethos discount' in the larger charities is a reflection of their greater 'professionalism'. Because they are dealing with larger organizations, and larger sums of money, the need of charities for competent people offsets the desire of such people to partake of the 'charity ethos'. They still need to make sacrifices, but not such large ones.

There are signs, in the figures, of the emergence of a cadre of charity executives whose pay expectations are influenced as much by their need for professional self-esteem as their wish to partake of the 'charity ethos'. There is also evidence that the 'charity ethos' keeps a lid on top pay in the sector. The discount for chief executives is lowest in the mid-sized charities (£10–25m revenue) but rises again in the large charities which suggests there is an 'exposure' effect at work here. Though, unlike companies, charities are not obliged to disclose in their accounts the emoluments of their highest-paid directors, it is common for top jobs to be advertised, and the industry seems to balk at salaries much above £70,000.

Even at that level, top salaries are controversial. Some say that charities should be legally obliged to disclose top salaries. 'The punter should know,' said one charity old-stager. I agree. It is inconsistent with the sector's ethos for charities to be unduly coy about what they pay their top people.

There are also significant pay differences between charity types. Generally speaking, senior people are paid rather more in the medical and disability charities than they are in the so-called 'developing countries' charities. Here too one can detect the influence of the ethos. It seems to be less acceptable for the leaders of charities dedicated to the relief of destitution or famine to be paid conspicuously 'high' salaries.

Sex

I have argued elsewhere that there are distinctively masculine and feminine 'styles' of management, and that one way of characterizing the modern trend in management thinking is to say the balance of emphasis is shifting from the 'masculine' style to the 'feminine' style.

This has nothing to do with the abrasively ambitious female manager who acts as if she believes the only way to breach the ramparts of sexual discrimination that surround senior management jobs is to be more macho than the male. In this case, management responsibility changes women more than it changes management, with the consequence that we end up, not with more feminine managers, but more masculine women.

The management writer and thinker Mary Parker Follett (1868–1933) exemplified, in her life and work, how the feminine approach to management is different from, but complementary to, the masculine approach. Pauline Graham in her fine book *Integrative Man-*

agement presents Follett to the modern world in the context of her own experience as a manager and a consultant. She tells of her time at the John Lewis Partnership, and of a special position in each of its stores called the 'registrar'. The function of the registrar, who, though lacking executive responsibilities, is equal in status and authority to the general manager in charge of the branch, is to embody the conscience of the branch.

The extraordinary thing about the 'registrar' is that it is laid down, in tablets of stone sculpted by John Spedan Lewis himself, the founder of the partnership, not only that every store should have one but also that the registrar should *always* be a woman.

Quite how one squares that stipulation with the contemporary legal principle of equality of opportunity between the sexes is hard to see, but there is no mystery about the basic idea behind it. John Spedan Lewis saw companies as families, writ large. As Graham puts it: 'Just as in the family, the husband was the go-getter and aggressive breadwinner and the wife the peacemaker and the upholder of the family's conscience, so, Spedan Lewis deduced, it had to be in business.' The branch head's job was to make profits; the registrar's job was to ensure those profits were come by with justice and fairness.

Graham was a branch manager and she recalls that she used to joke with her registrar that since she, herself, was a woman the 'hard and soft attributes' were already combined, rendering the registrar's role superfluous. 'It was not of course so,' Graham says. 'She was actually a tremendous support and comfort, always providing sensitive and wise advice and guidance. She was also more than a "conscience". Being in a way outside the hurly-burly of the business side, she was an impartial and disinterested observer and thus a confidante whose business judgement I valued highly.'

The gender of the registrar in the John Lewis Partnership is controversial, but Pauline Graham approved, and Mary Parker Follett would probably have concurred. Graham believes that the fact that Follett, who was never herself a practising manager, should have made such an enduring contribution to management thinking had 'something to do' with the fact that she was a woman. The parallels between Follett's ideas and the contemporary themes of management theory half a century after her death are almost uncanny.

Follett wrote passionately about the importance of groups and group dynamics; of what she called the 'law of the situation' according to which conflicts and disagreements should be resolved; of the reconciliation of the idea of competition with the principle of co-operation and of what she called 'power-with, not power-over'.

All these ideas are echoed in modern management theories and, arguably, all are examples of the growing influence of the feminine in company management. But there is nothing 'soft' or 'weak' about them. They are entirely compatible with the goal of profit maximization.

History may judge that Mary Parker Follett saw further than her male contemporaries because she looked through the heart of a woman. It may also judge that the greatest strength of the charity sector, as it emerged from its amateur period and entered its professional period in the late 20th century, was its regiments of women. 'We're divided into nine regions,' Seymour Fortescue, of the Imperial Cancer Research Fund told me, 'and all the regional directors are women. There's been no discrimination, it just so happens. The job is reasonably well paid, so it should be attractive to men.'

*   *   *

CASE STUDIES

With 160,000 or so charities to choose from, it is simply not possible to find a representative sample. In this chapter I shall look in some detail at three large charities: the Imperial Cancer Research Fund, one of Britain's largest medical research charities; the Order of St John (including the St John Ambulance Brigade), one of our oldest charities; and the Wellcome Trust, Britain's and the world's wealthiest charitable foundation.

My purpose is to shed some light on what kind of creatures they are, how they work, how the people who run them think, what concerns they have about their own charities, and about charities in general, and to try to glean from all this a hint or two about where they, other organizations like them, and the voluntary sector as a whole, might be going.

Imperial Cancer Research Fund

When the Imperial Cancer Research Fund advertised in 1991 the job of director of finance and fund-raising at a salary of £70,000 a year, more than 300 people applied. After sifting through the applications, the Council appointed Seymour Fortescue as its front-line marketing chief.

Fortescue exemplifies the new breed of professional managers who are moving into senior positions at some of the major UK charities, and who are injecting the charity sector with the experience and the attitudes of modern corporate man.

The Imperial Cancer Research Fund (ICRF) was established in 1902 by the Royal Colleges of Physicians and Surgeons whose Presidents have, traditionally, been vice-presidents of the Fund. In addition its voluntary policy-making Council includes eminent representatives of these and other colleges and of other research bodies, such as the Royal Society and the Medical Research Council. A royal charter was granted in 1939 defining the objectives of the Fund as the promotion of 'investigations into all matters connected with or bearing on the causes, prevention, treatment and cure of cancer'. The Queen is the ICRF's patron.

After borrowing and leasing research laboratories for over sixty years, the Fund's researchers moved into the first phase of the

ICRF's own laboratories in Lincoln's Inn Fields in London in 1963. An extension was opened in 1973 and No. 44 Lincoln's Inn Fields now houses sixty-five research groups. New laboratories at Clare Hall in Hertfordshire were opened in 1986 to house another nine research groups and support services for all 1,200 or so ICRF scientific personnel.

In the 1970s the Fund began setting up new clinical units in hospitals where its scientific and medical staff work with colleagues in the main ICRF laboratories to expedite the transfer of research benefits to patients. There are units at Guy's Hospital, St Bartholomew's and St Marks' in London, at Western General Hospital in Edinburgh and at the Churchill Hospital in Oxford. There is also a new clinical research group at the Frenchay Hospital in Bristol and a Proton Therapy Group operates at Moorfields Hospital in London and at Clatterbridge Hospital in the Wirral.

Chairs in oncology (the study of tumours) have been endowed at Guy's, Bart's, Western General and Churchill. A tumour immunology unit was set up at University College in 1978 and an epidemiology and clinical trials centre was acquired in Oxford, to collect and examine cancer statistics.

Oxford is also the home of the Fund's Developmental Biology Unit, a new Cell Cycle Group studying the controls for cell division, a 'research hotel' at the Institute of Molecular Medicine for scientists studying the biomolecular aspects of diseases, and the General Practice Research Group working with GPs to encourage prevention and improve the efficiency of screening programmes. The latter works closely with the ICRF Health Behaviour Unit at the Institute of Psychiatry in London, studying the psychology of tobacco addiction.

The distinguishing feature of the ICRF is that, in contrast to its main 'competitor', the Cancer Research Campaign, it funds long-term research at its own facilities, rather than financing individual projects through universities. It says this approach 'permits continuity in particular fields of study and the closest collaboration between the scientists of many disciplines and the clinicians working for the Fund, whose results are made available for patients everywhere.' The Fund also supports research co-operation in the UK and Europe, as well as the International Union Against Cancer.

In the year to September 1990 voluntary income amounted to

£42m, making the ICRF Britain's fourth largest fund-raising charity thanks largely to legacy income of just under £29m. The ICRF is also a trading charity, earning £7m from its 460 charity shops in 1989/90. Charitable spending was just over £50m and, at the end of September 1990, ICRF's net assets amounted to almost £103m. 'It's quite a large business,' says Fortescue. 'Total income last year was £53m, we employ 1,800 people, including 1,200 scientists, and we've got more shops than Marks & Spencer, a lot of them in good sites. It has to be run like a business. It's important you should be managing this money sensibly.'

Before joining ICRF in 1991 Fortescue had worked at Barclays Bank for twenty-six years, latterly as chief executive of Barclaycard and director of UK personal banking. He felt twenty-six years was long enough in a sector he admits he was never passionate about.

His aim on the administration side of ICRF is to achieve the same standards of professional excellence that exist on the scientific side. He has hired a professional retailer, to attack what he sees as the wasted opportunity of the charity shops. 'Their combined turnover is only £20m a year because they're only dealing in second-hand clothes,' he said. 'I see no reason why they shouldn't sell bought-in merchandise too.'

When I spoke to him, Fortescue was also trying to recruit a corporate fund-raiser. 'It's not that we're doing it badly,' he said, 'it's that we're just not doing it at all. At the World-Wide Fund for Nature and the NSPCC, for example, firms are a major source of income.' He thinks that the charity sector has much to learn from the company sector and evidently believes that the old idea of charity – retired colonels and elderly spinsters working in drafty church halls – has outlived its usefulness. 'We are poor on the personnel side. There is no performance appraisal, no job evaluation and people are paid on Civil Service scales according to length of service. We have to change the pay structure but it's difficult and expensive because you can't make anyone worse off. There's a general recognition that management performance needs to be improved – my appointment is indicative of that. There is the monkeys and peanuts syndrome: if you pay peanuts, you get monkeys.'

Fortescue believes that now City salaries have fallen, basic charity salaries 'are reasonably competitive'. It is in fringe benefits where the difference lies. Car policies, in particular, are necessarily less favourable. Fortescue had a Jaguar at Barclays. Now he has no car at all. ICRF cars are all small and are allocated on the basis of need, rather than status. It seems to fit with the charity ethos. 'We don't eat out and there are no stock options,' Fortescue says. 'I'm very conscious that the money is voluntarily donated. I don't take a taxi as readily because I know some old lady might be paying for it. I don't wear a hair shirt, either, but there's more of a consciousness about money.'

He likes the idea of performance-linked rewards but says it would be a mistake to put fund-raisers on a commission only basis. 'Donors wouldn't like it,' he explained. 'There is a danger that some people would get six-figure salaries and it would encourage short-termism. We had profit-related pay at Barclays linked to the employment contract. You got a bit more if you performed better than contract and a bit less if you performed worse. I'm very keen on that – on say 10–20 per cent of pay being performance-related.'

One of the features that has struck Fortescue most forcibly about the charity sector is its lack of external sanctions. 'It is pretty unregulated,' he said 'and not very answerable to donors or the commissioners. It was different at Barclays – analysts were looking at us constantly and the press would always comment on results. There is nothing like that here.

'I'm honorary treasurer of Lepra [the Leprosy charity]. We had a very difficult year and lost £1m which was half of our reserves. But management was not called to task and required to give a full explanation. It was seen largely as an internal matter.'

Another area where Fortescue believes the charity sector may be able to learn from the corporate sector is in mergers and acquisitions. 'Why are there so many cancer charities?' he asks. 'There are very few charity mergers because it is not seen as an appropriate mechanism. But War on Want went bust. If it had been in our area and had had some good assets like research, donor files or good people, we might have wanted it. Mergers would help the reputation of charities generally – there are 170,000 charities, and that is far too many. But there is no obvious way to do it, without being accused of megalomania.'

But he suspects a winnowing could be in the wind, following the passage of the Charities Act. 'Maybe greater regulation will encourage some of them to throw in the sponge. For the smaller charities, the compliance burden may be too large. A similar thing happened at FIMBRA; a lot of small independent intermediaries have just given up.'

Right now, though, things appear to be getting less, not more, concentrated. 'There has been a lot of market segmentation already,' Fortescue observed. 'There are specialist charities for children's cancer and leukaemia, and there's a new one – Breakthrough – for breast cancer. Market research shows that a lot of people prefer to give to local causes, so there are now local cancer charities for Yorkshire and Wessex. There is excellent co-operation amongst the scientific community, both nationally and internationally. However, one must be concerned that research activities are becoming fragmented, with too many smaller players.'

From the fund-raising point of view, however, it is harder to segment. There are a few regional ICRFs in Scotland for example and clinical units outside London get local support (such as in Oxford). 'But it is like banking,' Fortescue explains. 'You cannot say that this deposit funds this loan. We do try to enable a donor to associate with a particular activity or piece of equipment, but there's more to do here. The Cancer Research Campaign [the ICRF's main "competitor"] is very different. It is a slightly smaller fund-raiser but a much smaller employer. It should be easier for us to identify particular work with particular donors, because it's all in-house.'

ICRF's head of marketing Chris Chestnutt points out that the reason the ICRF runs no special appeals for lung cancer is that its purpose is to cure cancer. 'That's why we have the newsletter, to show people we're attacking the whole range. We do believe people are interested in particular forms of cancer, though, so we'll probably try it – we'll do a test.'

As we shall see, for reasons to do with the charity 'ethos', the issue of competition is a vexed one for the voluntary sector (see chapter 9). Fortescue believes the ICRF's brand image is not at all well differentiated. 'We are the fourth largest fund-raising charity, but many people don't even get our name right. We're not like the RNLI or the RSPCA.'

But orthodox brand differentiation stratagems are not always possible. In the past, Fortescue's brand sharpening efforts have been frustrated by internal resistance to the use in promotional material of arrogant, self-serving words such as 'leading' and 'largest'. He sees an irony here. 'In the corporate sector, monopolies are generally abhorred; competition is seen as a good thing. With charities, competition is bad because it is duplication of effort. But there is really a very good case for not being a monopoly.'

Chris Chestnutt affirms the point: 'We believe competition increases the total.' She suggests heart disease evokes the same kind of public concern as cancer but points out that the British Heart Foundation, which has a monopoly, brings in £26m whereas between them the two major cancer charities – ICRF and the Cancer Research Campaign – bring in £85m.

Ten years ago, ideas like these would have seemed heretical to the charity ethos, but these days, the idea that charities are competing with each other for market share is, as a metaphor at any rate, almost a statement of the obvious. There is still a lot of thinking to be done in the voluntary sector about competition (we will do some in chapter 9) but the idea is now definitely on the agenda.

'The charity cake is a certain size,' says Fortescue 'and we are fighting for a slice. The key is to increase the size of the cake. That's what the Windsor Group, with Lord Whitelaw and Sir Adam Ridley is about. They recently raised commitments of £500,000 from the thirty largest charities for a TV advertising campaign. With government support and sponsorship it would amount to £9m worth of airtime, at rate card prices.'

Chestnutt is very conscious of the need for such initiatives. She agrees with Fortescue that 'the size of the cake is not increasing, and more and more people are going for a slice. It's very hard. It has made us look at ways of giving something back to the giver. *Conquest* [the ICRF newsletter] is one of the most successful mailing campaigns we've ever done because we give our supporters information. We have over 120,000 donors on a database – it's our own list and we don't rent it out. The affinity card scheme with the Leeds and Visa is another way of using it.'

She is also anxious to diversify the ICRF's types of income. 'We are particularly keen to increase our covenant income. The ones that do well in covenant income usually deal with tangible projects. It's harder for us. Our covenant income is low – £500,000 out of £48m. We want to increase it. There is a huge amount of tax people are paying that they needn't be paying. People don't know how to give.'

Research by the Charities Aid Foundation (see chapter 6) showed that 50 per cent of people do not understand how covenants work, and that the top ten UK charities still only receive about 10 per cent of their income in tax-free covenanted form. The Windsor Group is trying to raise people's understanding of giving.

I have sometimes wondered how people working in a single-cause charity, like the ICRF, feel about the prospect of realizing the charity's dream and finding a complete cure (for cancer, in this case). Fortescue smiled at the question. 'The intractability of the disease should see me through. There are 200 different kinds of cancer – only a few have been conquered. Hodgkins disease is 95 per cent cured now, but there's lots of work still to be done. The biggest killers are the most intractable. Leprosy is totally curable now with multi-drug therapy but fifteen million people still have it.'

The Order of St John

As Robin Hood was establishing the legend of the charitable outlaw in Sherwood Forest, members of the First Crusade were capturing the Holy City of Jerusalem and endowing, with land and money, the hospital of St John of Jerusalem named after St John the Almsgiver.

The hospital had been established (or re-established) in the 11th century by a group of Amalfi merchants, and was being run, when the Crusaders arrived, by monastic brothers led by the Blessed Gerard. In 1113 the Pope recognized the hospital and its Hospitaller brothers as an independent religious order of monks and nuns who took vows of poverty, chastity and obedience, and whose special task was to care for the sick.

In response to the need to defend the states established by the Crusades, Raymond du Puy, the hospital's second master, instituted a military role for the brothers. With the other military religious orders, the Teutonic Knights and the Knights Templar, the Knights of St John became the principal defenders of the Holy Land employing mercenary soldiers and building castles and establishing garrisons. When the Holy City fell to the Saracens, the order moved its headquarters and its hospital to Acre on the Mediterranean.

After the fall of Acre the Knights withdrew to their estates in Cyprus and then expanded again into the pirate-infested waters of the south-eastern Aegean, capturing islands from the Byzantine Greek Empire and finally re-establishing their headquarters, or 'Convent', in the City of Rhodes in 1309.

They developed Rhodes, and other islands in the Dodecanese, into a heavily fortified base for crusading warfare, mostly against Egypt and Turkey. Trade flourished and settlers from Western Europe came to live and work alongside the local Greek population, under the rule of the Order. A convent was built within the city of Rhodes with a palace for the Master (then the Grand Master); inns and *auberges*, as the communal houses for the Brothers of different nationalities; a church and a great infirmary. Within the strongly fortified city walls there were other hospices, also for the care of pilgrims calling at Rhodes on their long voyage between Europe and the Holy Places of Palestine.

In 1312 the Pope endowed the Order with the lands of the Knights Templar (who had similar military responsibilities but no duty to care for the sick). This greatly increased the Order's already burgeoning wealth.

For more than two hundred years the Knights defended Rhodes against the rising power of Imperial Turkey but in 1522 they were forced to surrender the city and its islands, together with their castle at Bodrum on the Turkish coast, to the overwhelming might of Sultan Suleiman the Magnificent. The Sultan was magnanimous and allowed the Grand Master and his Knights to return to Europe.

After the loss of Rhodes, the Knights were given the Maltese islands by the Christian Emperor Charles V in 1530 in the frontline of the struggle for mastery of the Mediterranean between the Turks and Christendom. In 1565, under the Grand Master Jean de la Valette, the Knights and the Maltese people repulsed a great siege by the Turkish armada under their old enemy, Suleiman. This victory and the building and fortification of the city of Valetta brought the Order great renown.

In addition to acting as the frontline in Christendom's war against the Turks, the Knights helped to keep the seas clear of the Barbary corsairs, operating from the North African ports and their advanced hospital and quarantine services in Malta were of international value at the centre of the sea routes of the Mediterranean.

With the decline of the Turkish empire in the 18th century, the military role of the Knights faded. Napoleon expelled the Knights from Malta in 1798 and although the British drove out the French two years later, the Order of St John never returned to rule in Malta.

Since its inception many in Europe had found the work of the Order inspiring, and it attracted not only recruits of both sexes but also considerable amounts of land and money. Despite its members' vows of poverty, the Order itself became very wealthy. It organized its lands into 'commanderies', each of which included an estate with peasant tenants, a church, a hospice and a manor house where the Knight Commander lived. There were hundreds of commanderies in Europe, grouped into twenty-five Priories, each under a Prior. It was the Prior's duty to send to the Order's headquarters in the Holy Land, and later in Rhodes and Malta, new Knights, armour, horses, clothing, food and drink and large sums of money. The Order was entirely dependent on these gifts from Europe for its crusading warfare and its medical work.

For 700 years the Hospitallers who wore the eight-pointed cross took a prominent part in church life. They cared for pilgrims and the sick and served their respective states as lawyers, diplomats, admirals, generals, artists, scholars and scientists.

Lands in England were first given to the Order in the early 12th century and a century later churches, hospices and legacies of money had been donated to the Hospitallers in most English and Welsh counties. The Prior of the English and Welsh Knights established his headquarters in the great Priory of Clerkenwell, on the northern fringes of the City of London. A Scottish Priory, headquartered at Torpichen, Midlothian, was in being by 1153 and an Irish Priory, at Kilmainham, near Dublin, was founded in 1174.

Following Henry VIII's dissolution of the monasteries, the Order was suppressed in England and Ireland. Queen Mary restored the Order, but it fell into abeyance again under Queen Elizabeth I and was not revived until the early 19th century following encouragement by a group of French Knights of the Order.

In search of a new role for the order in England, members of the revived English branch sent observers to the conferences in Switzerland that drew up the Geneva Conventions on the humane care of battlefield casualties and inspired the formation of the International Red Cross. Feeling that a similar system for the treatment of accident victims in civilian life was needed, the English branch of the Order of St John formed the St John Ambulance Association (SJAA).

The Association was founded in 1877 to provide instruction on first aid and ambulance transport to the public, at home and at work. Within six months over 1,000 people had been granted a first aid certificate. In the first year, classes were run for women, railwaymen, the police and the fire brigade, and the first industrial centre was formed at Tibshelf Colliery in Derbyshire. In October 1878, the first ambulance textbook was published and soon afterwards ambulance equipment, such as first aid hampers and wheeled litters, was available from the Stores Depot at St John's Gate in London.

The St John Ambulance Brigade (SJAB) was formed in 1887 to supply ambulance transport and volunteers trained in first aid at public events. Soon, groups of first aiders with SJAA certificates began to group together as Ambulance Corps. An early example was the Invalid Transport Corps at St John's Gate. These corps formed the basis of the Brigade. Within ten years, five Brigade districts had been established, and a uniform and drill had been adopted.

The Brigade's first major public duty was to provide first aid cover for Queen Victoria's Golden Jubilee celebrations in 1887. It has been providing the same service ever since 'wherever crowds gather'. Another Brigade role is to provide trained personnel to act as a reserve to the Armed Forces Medical Services in time of war. It first saw service in this role in 1899 during the Boer War. During the two World Wars the St John Ambulance joined with the British Red Cross Society under a Joint Committee to provide Voluntary Aid Detachment personnel to casualty hospitals and to supply numerous auxiliary medical services to the public. It also supplied what it called humanitarian services for prisoners of war.

To maintain standards, members received regular instruction and examinations in first aid and nursing subjects, and, to stimulate interest and nurture an *esprit de corps*, regular members' meetings were arranged, competitions were held and camps were introduced.

The Association and the Brigade were merged in 1971, to co-ordinate the roles of training and voluntary service more effectively. The modern St John Ambulance comprises the SJAA and the SJAB and includes:

St John Ambulance Cadets, formed in 1922, in which children between the ages of ten and sixteen receive first aid and nursing training.

St John Badgers, formed in 1987 (to celebrate the Centenary of the Brigade), to provide basic first aid and nursing training, plus fun activities, for six to ten year olds.

St John Aeromedical, a joint venture with the AA to provide skilled medical attendant service for those injured or taken ill abroad, and to ensure a safe return home.

St John Air Wing, which flies human organs to where they are needed for transplants accompanied by specialist surgeons.

St John Ambulance Schools Project, for first aid training in schools.

St John Overseas, providing primary health care programmes in the Third World.

The Association, as the country's leading supplier of first aid training, works closely with government departments and local authorities. Between 1983 and 1985 nearly 200,000 men and women were trained by St John, and achieved the new 'First Aid at Work' qualifications, now required by Health and Safety Regulations.

The other half of the Order, which is both the Association's dependant and the symbol of its long charitable history, is the St John Ophthalmic Hospital in Jerusalem. The Order returned to the birthplace of the Hospitallers in 1882 when the Sultan, head of the Ottoman Empire which held Jerusalem at the time, granted the request of the Order's Grand Prior, HRH the Prince of Wales (later King Edward VII) for permission to build a hospital and opthalmic dispensary in the Holy City. The Order had decided to specialize in eye disease because it was particularly prevalent in the Middle East at that time.

Its original home was a house on the road to Bethlehem. It was used by the Turks as an ammunition dump during the 1914–18 war and blown up. Though the damage was severe the Order began rebuilding immediately, and by 1918 the hospital was treating patients again. It was extended and developed during the 1920s and 1930s and remained open throughout World War II.

In 1960 the Order opened a new hospital in the Sheikh Jarrah district of Jerusalem. It now has training schools for post-graduate doctors and Arab nurses and its own opthalmic Research Institute. In an average year, the hospital carries out 5,000 eye operations and treats 45,000 out-patients. It also operates an 'Out-stretch' programme of visiting villages to train villagers in primary health care. The hospital is almost entirely supported by donations. Only 19 per cent of its 1990 income of £2m came from charges.

Tim Gauvain, St John Ambulance's first 'executive director', regards the Order of St John as a 'service charity' like the Royal National Lifeboat Institution and the Red Cross, and is proud of the fact that it is one of only three with a royal charter.

He was in the RAF for eighteen years before leaving to start his own business, Eskimo Ice, in London. Gauvain then joined the accountancy firm BDO Binder Hamlyn where he spent five years helping to develop a national management team.

He says his main interest is in people; how to get the best out of them and, now, how to marry the voluntary ethic with the business ethic. 'All charities that mean business,' he says, 'have to be professionally managed. Of course, they have to be relevant, but they've got to be well managed too. It is a fallacy that management and volunteering do not mix. The volunteering is simply more cost effective if the volunteers are properly managed.'

Being the charity's first executive director Gauvain is charting his own course. He sees his main job as ensuring that the Order's headquarters are managed efficiently, so the operating units can have confidence that they will get a good service.

Like those of the other 'service' charities the organization structure of St John is very decentralized. 'The HQ has no purpose except to support the counties,' Gauvain explained. 'Most counties have a small nucleus of salaried staff, but all the top jobs are held by volunteers.

'It is very hard to establish national fund-raising figures, because the counties are virtually autonomous. We make no levy on them and we don't have a percentage contribution target at HQ. However, the provisions of the Charities Act will require consolidation of accounts and changes in the financial relationship between HQ and the counties.'

Being very interested in management, Gauvain has doubts about the wisdom of this convention. 'Management has to be cost effective,' he says. 'It must be possible to set targets, to introduce job evaluation and even an equivalent of profit-related pay, so that we can be sure that we're producing the right range and quality of training.' He had no business plan when I spoke to him, but was working on one.

One of the purposes of the plan he was at work on was to try to anticipate how the pattern of headquarters revenues was likely to change in the future. At present there are four main sources.

The Order applies to trusts for funds, is left some money – according to the 14th edition of *Charity Trends* it received £2.5m in legacies in 1990 – and also raises voluntary income from direct mail campaigns and sponsorship.

It earns money from the supply of uniforms and a small mail-order operation and also sells first aid courses. 'We're the market leader in first aid courses,' Gauvain pointed out. 'We earn a registration fee from the counties for them. We issue 200,000 certificates a year.' First Aid at Work courses are nice little earners too. 'It's a captive market,' Gauvain smiled, 'because any business with more than fifty employees is required, by the Health and Safety Executive, to have at least one qualified first aider.'

A third source of revenue is publications – first aid books and pamphlets – where St John's strong brand image ensures a high market share.

Perhaps the most interesting source of revenue, though still quite small, is from the endorsement of commercial products based on what Gauvain says is 'the very best medical advice, by eminent people'. It is usually an endorsement of a first aid product but St John was prepared to stretch a point when endorsing Dettol, Reckitt & Colman's home hygiene fluid. 'It has no place in first aid, so we had to find a form of words,' Gauvain recalled.

It is risky using one's brand to endorse other people's products, but it can also be very lucrative. 'If something is head and shoulders above the competition,' Gauvain says, 'that's OK. And if it's safe and good, that's OK, too. But we expect to earn fees and prestige. St John is the voice of authority in first aid and in health care generally, and that brand value has to be professionally managed.'

The current fund raising climate is very tough, according to Gauvain. 'Small donations are not much affected. It's always those with least, who give the most. It's quite inspiring. Big companies are much less eager now – more tightfisted – though we've recently got major sponsorship from BP for our schools programme.'

Gauvain feels bound to look at other ways to raise money. But he sees the challenge as a bit of a catch 22, where you are damned if you don't and damned if you do. 'We have to be very careful that what we do is consistent with our overall charitable mission and we're forbidden by law to indulge in political activity. We are also constrained by EEC law; new regulations on the liabilities of suppliers of services will effectively reverse the burden of proof.'

The Order regards the threats to its freedom, and to that of UK charities in general, posed by EC laws on advertising, or the endorsement of medical products, as well as EC definitions of 'non-commercial organizations', as so serious that it has established a lobbying operation in Brussels.

But a charity is more damned if it does not seek new ways to raise money, and Gauvain believes there are some interesting possibilities in corporate giving. 'Big companies would like long-term relationships with charities – giving annual lumps for specific projects, but also contributing to their long-term security. We have a relationship like that with Safeway. It's been supporting us for three years. It gives an annual donation, to help with our ongoing projects, and has also underwritten our major "Over to you John" appeal.' He would like more such relationships. 'You can't have more than one in a particular industry, of course, but it would be nice to have a major pharmaceutical company or a major producer of first aid equipment.'

Another possibility for earning additional revenue is to develop the publishing business, and Gauvain also thinks HQ could earn good revenue by becoming a central supplier of ambulances for the counties.

And with the advent of the so-called 'contract culture', (see chapter 8) government, which in the past has restricted its contributions to the Order to a few small grants, is now becoming a much more interesting prospective customer. 'We may develop a long-term relationship with the Department of Health by becoming an official ambulance reserve,' Gauvain speculated. 'It would be very useful in training and for the acquisition of ambulances. We shall bid for local authority ambulance services contracts, too, although we'll never be a frontline emergency service. There are a number of things we could do on behalf of the NHS but we don't want to pinch anyone else's job.' The St John Ambulance is already a *de facto* reserve. As Gauvain pointed out, the ambulance dispute, the Gulf War and the Hillsborough disaster, were all good for the Order. 'We are paid the costs of running the ambulances, members get their expenses and the organization gets donations.'

Although, so far, there has been no attempt to encourage the adoption by the counties of common policies, there are signs that the counties themselves, though they still differ greatly, are becoming more 'commercial'. Gauvain cited the case of a three-day Tina Turner concert in the grounds of Woburn Abbey. The local SJA division was asked to supply the ambulance cover required, by law, at such events. The division chief agreed, and then asked the organizers for a donation. They offered £50. The County Commissioner, when told of the proposal, was indignant. 'Tell them that if we don't get £5,000 we'll pull out,' he insisted. The organizers said no, so St John pulled out. The organizers, conscious of their legal obligations, came back and eventually it was agreed that the service would be provided if a 'donation' of £4,000 was forthcoming. As Gauvain put it, 'donations have to be realistic, and some people don't play cricket but there's no policy imposed from here.'

Each division has twenty to thirty active members, and one or more vehicles of their own. They cost money to maintain, which has got to be raised, and in Gauvain's view, it's unrealistic to expect to get all of it by tin rattling. 'Most members hate tin rattling,' he says. 'They would much rather invite donations for a service.'

Which raises what is a crucial philosophical question that all charities seeking to reduce their dependence on voluntary income (and so become more like companies) would do well to address: 'Do we have a moral obligation to be a receptacle for those who want to give?' If the answer to that question is yes, another question – less philosophical maybe but more pregnant with practical implication – arises: 'If we have such an obligation, and must therefore accept if not actively solicit, voluntary donations, and then use them to further the charitable purposes for which they are given, how can we set targets and plan?'

There are no unequivocal answers to these questions and each charity finds its own accommodations. For Gauvain, a number of principles provide some guidance in this moral minefield: 'You must be innovative in fund-raising, you've got to apply funds properly and you have to respond to needs, such as the need for a human-organ transport service, for an aeromedical service and for the eye hospital.'

In Gauvain's view, if charities build up their resources they're not doing their jobs properly. They should not hoard money, they should spend it, so that it can do some good. However, he thinks it is reasonable for the Order to seek modest real growth in its reserves because it needs more security and he also thinks headquarters should invest in the future, on computers, for example. 'We're under-ITd here,' he says. 'HQ is well behind the counties in that respect.'

But otherwise he thinks that the money that comes in should go out. 'It doesn't look good to have a healthy surplus. We are conscious that it's not ethical. You can have a debate about what's a reasonable level of reserves, but all the money belongs to the Order, and there is another foundation, St John's Ophthalmic Hospital in Jerusalem. Our surpluses can fund the hospital's losses. St John Ambulance should be the flagship of the Order, and should raise money for the hospital.'

The question of surpluses raises another issue. How should a charity that is good at raising money behave if it finds it hard to spend it all in ways consistent with its charitable purposes? Gauvain thinks such charities should be allowed to acquire more 'needs', to match their revenue, by taking over other charities in related fields.

There are other ways for a charity to unburden itself of an embarrassment of riches. The British Heart Foundation, for example, which raises huge amounts of money each year, spends some of it on helping other charities. By arrangement with the Jockey Club the BHF supplies expensive defibrillation equipment, for use in St John ambulances, at racecourses. It also helps the Red Cross with its equipment needs. 'We might do the same,' says Gauvain.

The point seems to be that a charity's fund-raising power must be exploited to the full, whether or not the charity can readily spend all it raises. It is difficult to measure the brand value of a charity, and hence establish whether it is being fully exploited, but it is not impossible. What firms are prepared to pay for endorsements is not a bad guide. 'We're trying to establish what our name is worth by negotiation,' Gauvain says.

The Wellcome Trust

Henry Solomon Wellcome was born in 1853 in the American Mid-West, the son of a farmer-preacher. He studied pharmacy in Chicago and Philadelphia and, after graduating, worked as a salesman for a large drugs firm. He travelled widely and in South America he conducted a study of the cinchona forests, the source of quinine.

In 1880, he accepted an invitation from Silas Burroughs, an old college friend, to help set up a company in England to sell medicines in tablet form. The partners were able and diligent, and Burroughs Wellcome prospered. It pioneered direct mailing to doctors, registered the 'tabloid' brand name and its 'ruggedised' portable medical chests travelled with Stanley to Africa, Peary and Amundsen to the North and South Poles and with Princess Mary on her honeymoon.

After the premature death of Burroughs in 1895, Wellcome was left in sole ownership of the business. He became a British subject in 1910 and was knighted in 1932. He died in 1936. A gifted and visionary businessman, Sir Henry was the first in the drugs industry to recognize the importance of fundamental research. He was also a deeply compassionate man – he financed missionary and medical work in Uganda, and was active in the support of the North American Indians.

When he died, Sir Henry bequeathed the entire share capital of Burroughs Wellcome to the Wellcome Trust for the purposes of scientific and medical research, medical history and for the improvement of the condition of mankind. In the immediate post-war years, the Trust endowed chairs, built laboratories and bought equipment for universities in the UK and North America. When public money began pouring into higher education in the 1960s, the Trust switched its focus to individuals, granting senior clinical fellowships and establishing links with Europe. By 1976, the Trust was spending £2.5m a year on supporting individual work in various research fields.

More recently, in the wake of the public spending cuts, the emphasis has switched back again to the maintenance of the research base through the provision of research posts and other support for young scientists who might otherwise have emigrated or taken up more lucrative careers.

The 1980s was a period of dramatic expansion for the company and for the Trust. The former was floated on the stockmarket in 1986, with the Trust retaining 75 per cent of the equity, and the Trust's annual research expenditure soared from £12m in 1980 to a budgeted £100m for the 1991/2 financial year. After the sale of a further £2.2bn of Wellcome plc shares in July 1992, the Trust was expected to be able to double its annual spending.

Wellcome Trust is the largest foundation in the world, with an asset base worth around £6bn, depending on Wellcome plc's share price. It dwarfs all other UK foundations. It is a key pillar of UK medical research, spending around half the sum spent each year by the state-financed Medical Research Council. Notwithstanding the enormous success in recent years of Wellcome plc, dividends from which have multiplied fifty-fold since 1976, Dr Bridget Ogilvie, the formidable new Director and Chairman of the trust's board of management, feels under pressure to spend more.

She points out that despite a trebling of grants since 1987, the funding rate – the proportion of applications approved – has fallen from 60 per cent to 22 per cent in the same period as a result of the changes in the way government does business. 'Pressure from the universities has soared,' she says, 'and, because of the "sophistication factor" [the need for more high-tech and more costly equipment] the cost of research far outstrips the Retail Price Index. The universities are under such ferocious and unrelenting pressure from the government that they are in danger of collapsing as research organizations. By progressively reducing the unit of resource [the funds provided per student], the government has forced staff-student ratios down which has forced academics to do more teaching so the quality of research has to drop.'

Dr Ogilvie insists that, in saying this, she is not making a judgement about government policy – it would be impolitic of her to do so – but she stresses that 'the government needs to understand what it's doing and there is no evidence that it does understand.' She also points out that Wellcome Trust is very dependent on Wellcome plc and that, notwithstanding the company's massive growth in recent years, pharmaceuticals are a very high-risk business.

She regards the effect of the impoverishment of the universities on Britain's ability to keep able people as very serious indeed and points out that a recent Royal Society study suggested the main problem wasn't so much the number of people leaving, as their quality. Although stemming the medical science 'brain drain' does not rank as a specific objective of the Trust, Dr Ogilvie is gratified when it succeeds in particular cases. 'We've just induced a medical professor to come here from the US,' she said proudly. 'The clinical side here has real attractions because, in a way, the National Health Service still exists. It means that research involving patients can be done more easily than in many other countries.'

She sees the task of the Trust as looking after its research customers and clients, some 2,500 people in all. 'We back good people with good projects through the universities and medical schools.' This is unlike the Imperial Cancer Research Fund (see above) which has its own institutes.

The existence of the big cancer charities (the ICRF and the Cancer Research Campaign between them spent £91 million in 1990, against Wellcome Trust's £81 million) has encouraged the Trust to steer clear of cancer, but it has recently done a joint venture in Cambridge with the CRC, which Dr Ogilvie regards as a 'natural partner'.

The neurosciences, particularly in the psychiatric area, are a growing interest for the Trust. 'We're very impressed with the work that's being done here,' says Dr Ogilvie. 'It's the most rapidly growing subject in biomedical research at present.'

All the scientific trustees are university people and there are two business trustees. They are always re-examining policy and new ideas come along with new trustees. Both Henry Wellcome's will, which refers to the improvement of the physical condition of people, and his actions during his lifetime, direct Trust policy. When considering a new proposal, the trustees will often ask themselves whether it was something of which Henry would have approved.

Dr Ogilvie thinks it is very unlikely the general direction will change – like building hospices for AIDS victims. She says the Trust's interests will remain in 'basic, biomedical science and the history of medicine, as directed by Sir Henry Wellcome's will.'

The Wellcome Trust has been funding visiting fellows from Europe for years, from countries like Czechoslovakia, Italy and Scandinavia but, by and large, salaries on the Continent are too high for UK fellowships to be attractive. In 1989, a new scheme, the Hitchings-Elion Travelling Fellowships, was launched to enable senior and post-doctoral US scientists to spend up to two years engaged in research in the UK, and one year back in the US. The scheme is operated by the Burroughs Wellcome Fund and the Fogarty Foundation in America and is named after 1988 Nobel laureates, Drs George Hitchings and Gertrude Elion.

8

Philanthropy and Politics

The charity sector inhabits a world saturated with economic, political and philosophical ideas and pulsating with debates about everything from the hole in the ozone layer, to the ethics of foxhunting. It is a morally rich sector, because its business is altruism, and because those working within it are perceived to speak with authority about the needy and the disadvantaged, but there is, as yet, no consensus about charity's proper place and role in the world. It is clear, however, that the area of the sector's competence to act, and to engage in the important contemporary debates, must be defined, in some way, by its privileged position.

Society has seen fit to grant to the sector freedom from tax (though not yet from VAT), but the freedom is a qualified one. The sector's fiscal privilege has been granted on the condition that charities 'stick to their knitting' as modern management parlance has it. The freedom from tax is granted, not because of what charities are, but because of what they do. If they decide to do things that are not charitable, they should not be surprised if some people question whether they deserve to retain their tax privilege and charitable status. Also, if they comply with requests from government to involve themselves in areas of activity that were previously seen as the responsibility of the state, they should not be surprised if they become subject to the kind of scrutiny and criticism under which the administrators of modern welfare societies have to operate.

If, armed with their considerable moral authority, they start to engage in debates, or exert their influence in the furtherance of

177

causes that are beyond their competence, then they should not be surprised if they are chided or censured, with more or less vehemence, for speaking out of turn or for wrongfully wasting the money given to them by donors, and by society, on purposes for which it was not intended.

In accepting the privileges of charitable status, therefore, a charity incurs an obligation to maintain the purity of its purpose. This stricture has become increasingly significant in recent years. As the charity industry has grown it has become more sophisticated and professional, and has acquired a momentum and aspirations of its own which transcend its role as mere conduit for the generosity of others.

This transformation of the voluntary sector into an industry consisting of a wide range of goal-seeking organizations is begging a whole series of questions about the definition of a charitable act and the right of charities to impute causes to the symptoms it is their purpose to address. They also have to face the question of what their precise relationships should be with the state, the company sector, the political system, and with each other. In this chapter I shall look at these questions and try, if not to provide answers to them, at least to show what kind of questions they are and in what sort of places the answers to them might lie.

The Charity Sector and the State

The first serious attempt, in modern times, to differentiate between the proper roles of the state and the charity sector in the provision of alms and, of what later came to be known as social welfare, was made by John Stuart Mill.

In his *Principles of Political Economy* Mill laid the foundations of the modern welfare state in the following credo:

> I conceive it to be highly desirable that the certainty of subsistence should be held out by law to the destitute able-bodied, rather than that their relief should depend on voluntary charity. In the first place, charity almost always does too much or too little: it lavishes its bounty in one place, and leaves people to starve in another.
>
> Secondly, since the state must necessarily provide sub-

sistence for the criminal poor while undergoing punishment, not to do the same for the poor who have not offended is to give a premium on crime.

And lastly, if the poor are left to individual charity, a vast amount of mendacity is inevitable.

What the state may and should abandon to private charity is the task of distinguishing between one case of real necessity and another. Private charity can give more to the more deserving. The state must act by general rules. It cannot undertake to discriminate between the deserving and the undeserving indigent. It owes no more than subsistence to the first, and can give no less to the last. What is said about the injustice of a law which has no better treatment for the merely unfortunate poor than for the ill-conducted, is founded on a misconception of the province of law and public authority.

The dispensers of public relief have no business to be inquisitors. Guardians and overseers are not fit to be entrusted to give or withhold other people's money according to their verdict on the morality of the person soliciting it; and it would show much ignorance of the ways of mankind to suppose that such persons, even in the almost impossible case of their being qualified, will take the trouble of ascertaining and sifting the past conduct of a person in distress, so as to form a rational judgement on it.

Private charity can make these distinctions; and in bestowing its own money, is entitled to do so according to its own judgement. It should understand that this is its peculiar and appropriate province, and that it is commendable or the contrary, as it exercises the function with more or less discernment. But the administrators of a public fund ought not to be required to do more for anybody, than that minimum which is due even to the worst. If they are, the indulgence very speedily becomes the rule, and refusal the more or less capricious or tyrannical exception.

Since Mill's time, the role of the state, in Britain and in most other modern societies, has burgeoned enormously and colonized vast tracts of redistributive territory that were previously the preserve of the charity sector. Throughout this time, all British governments have studiously declined to tackle the issue of a definition of charity and, therefore, of its proper relationship with the institutions of the welfare state.

The government's 1989 White Paper *Charities: A Framework for the Future* outlined proposed new legislation based on a number of recommendations in the Woodfield Report, published two years earlier. There were five areas of particular interest: the propriety or otherwise of political activities by charities, the updating and computerization of the Charities Register, the keeping of charity accounts, powers to deal with abuse, and charitable appeals (with special reference to the new fund-raising techniques that had emerged in recent years).

The White Paper expressed grave concerns about the degree and quality of regulation and monitoring in the voluntary sector and acknowledged the need for a clearer division of responsibilities between the Home Office and the Charity Commission, but it broadly concurred with the historical principle of basing charity law on common law rather than statute law. In much modified form, it emerged as the Charities Bill, and this, in turn, after the inclusion at the request of the charity sector of many amendments, became the Charities Act of 1992.

The voluntary sector was seen in the White Paper as a thing in itself that should be allowed to develop according to its own internal dynamics. 'It is part of the make up of Man to want to give,' the White Paper declared, and it is important that the legal framework within which this fundamentally human activity takes place should be 'sensitive to changing needs whilst maintaining the fundamental principles on which the concept of charity rests.'

Despite the untidiness that had accumulated in common law in the four centuries since the Elizabethan Charitable Uses Act of 1601, the government continued to baulk at establishing a definition of charity. It said any attempt to define charity would be 'fraught with difficulty' and would jeopardize the valuable flexibility of the present law.

It was content to leave charity undefined and living loosely within the 'classification' proffered by Lord Macnaghten, in his seminal judgement in the Pemsel case, in 1891:

Charity in its legal sense comprises four principal divisions –

trusts for the relief of poverty, trusts for the advancement of education, trusts for the advancement of religion, and trusts for other purposes beneficial to the community, not falling under any of the previous heads.

According to the White Paper, the authority of Macnaghten's judgement would be threatened if it were to be used as the basis for new law. 'As a classification, the formulation has proved of enduring use,' the White Paper said. 'As a definition, its advantages are much less compelling.'

There is a similar feeling within the charity industry, among its *aficionados* and some of those who are involved in regulating it (there is a well-documented tendency for regulators to 'go native' and adopt the world view of those it regulates). This vagueness – this lack of precision about what charity is – is nonetheless a strength because it endows the sector and the legal environment within which it exists with flexibility.

But vagueness can also be a vice in times, like the present, of dramatic change because it is too easy for flexibility to become a licence for unwarranted adventurism. Law, even common law, depends on precision and clarity for its power, and there is a new breed of entrepreneur in the sector now who see an opportunity to push parameters and construct for themselves a wider stage.

The increasing availability of funds for charitable purposes from the European Community is further muddying the waters for those seeking a clear definition of charity. The Social Chapter, for example, though specifically excluded from the 1992 Maastricht Treaty, remains dear to the hearts of many leading Europeans. In its attempts to harmonize the welfare arrangements of EC members, the European Commission will continue to threaten to overlay the British charity system, based on common law, with a pan-continental, codified patina of statute law. At the same time, as the trend towards harmonization brings the welfare systems of community members into closer contact with each other, comparisons are being made.

'Look at the Dutch and the Swedes,' runs the argument. 'The state looks after everyone there. How can we be sure, if the state passes some of its responsibilities to the charities, that they'll provide a better service than the statutories?'

181

But the Charities Aid Foundation's annual Charity Household Surveys suggest that, during the 1980s, the government had some success in persuading the population at large of the merits of its proposed shift from public welfare to caring citizenship. The proportion of respondents who agreed with the statement: 'it is the responsibility of people to give what they can to charity' rose from 46 per cent in 1987 to 49 per cent in 1988/9 and to 52 per cent in 1989/90. It should be noted, however, that 48 per cent of people still disagree with the statement and there is no evidence at all that this increased acceptance of an individual duty to give to charity has been accompanied by a belief that the government's responsibilities have correspondingly declined.

The proportion of respondents who agreed with the statement: 'the government has a basic responsibility to take care of people who can't take care of themselves' increased from 80 per cent in 1987 to 88 per cent in 1988/9 and to 91 per cent in 1989/90. Similarly, the proportion of respondents who agreed with the statement: 'the government ought to help more, not rely on charities to raise needed money' rose from 80 per cent in 1987 to 88 per cent in 1989/90.

Part of this sharp increase in the belief in the government's primary role in the provision of welfare can, no doubt, be attributed to reduced optimism about the economy, associated with the onset of recession. For it is natural that when the material well-being of individuals and their assessments of the security of their employment begin to weaken, the 'safety net' role of government should come to be seen as relatively more important.

Even so, it is hard to escape the conclusion that there is a very long way to go before the public is fully persuaded of the need for, or the desirability of, a fundamental re-balancing of the welfare responsibilities of the state and the voluntary sector. But there is a strong argument that says there *must* be a re-balancing of welfare responsibility from the state to the voluntary sector because, notwithstanding public opinion, it is simply not possible for the state to continue in the role assigned to it by Beveridge.

Even Mill's more limited formulation of the state's role as welfare provider, which he proposed long before questions about the 'efficiency' of state provision began to be asked or the ideas of 'contracting' and the 'agency' charity had been conceived, appears to assign too much to the state, by modern standards.

Moreover there are positive reasons to welcome an increase in the scale and influence of the voluntary sector's role. As Professor Ken Young said in his Gresham College essay on *Meeting the Needs of Strangers*:

> Voluntary action in today's changed circumstances has a wider role – and is of greater social and political significance – than that of an adjunct provider of special services alongside mainstream state provision. It contributes to the representative process, to the development of public policy and to the processes of social integration and cohesion.

The campaigning style of the voluntary sector, particularly when it is concerned with the predicament of minorities, is seen by some as a valuable protector of small, disadvantaged groups against the tyranny of the majority. But the lack of a clear definition of charity has prevented the emergence of a clear and durable consensus about where charitable purpose ends and political agitation begins.

Political Charity and Charitable Politics

In May 1991 Oxfam was formally censured by the Charity Commissioners for political campaigning. The reprimand involved two particulars: Oxfam's Free Front Line Africa campaign in 1990, advocating the continuance of sanctions against South Africa, and a similar campaign in 1989 urging the British government to change its policy towards Cambodia's Khmer Rouge regime.

It was the fifth time in ten years that investigations into allegations of improper political activity by Oxfam had led to formal censure, and the Commissioners were running out of patience. They acknowledged Oxfam had been acting in good faith but warned that if it happened again they would not hesitate to ask the Attorney General to mount a civil action to reclaim charitable contributions spent on political campaigns.

There were those who felt the Commissioners had been far too lenient with Oxfam's apparently incorrigible politicking and that the Commissioners' insistence that it was not their intention to bar Oxfam and other charities from contributing to public life and debate gave altogether too much 'wriggle room' for politically-motivated charities.

Conservative MP Sir George Gardiner reflected this widely held view. 'Oxfam has been in flagrant breach of the law on charities for years,' he said. 'Well-meaning people have been running jumble sales and raising funds for what they thought was the relief of famine, little knowing that they are also financing a rag-bag of left-wing causes across the world.' Another Conservative MP, Gerald Howarth, went so far as to call for the resignation of the then Chief Commissioner Robin Guthrie. 'It is simply not acceptable', said Howarth, 'that Oxfam, which is not alone among left-wing charities, should get away with a rap over the knuckles.'

The International Freedom Association, the Washington-based free-market think-tank which had lodged the allegations that had led to the latest reprimand, called for the appointment of an independent ombudsman to investigate Oxfam and prevent a repetition of the abuse of charity law.

Simple party politics explains some of the heat generated by the row – Oxfam's then director, Frank Judd (now Lord Judd), was a former Labour MP and an Overseas Development Minister – but there is more to it than that. Oxfam received £8m worth of grants from central and local government in 1988/9 and a further £4m worth of tax relief on its income from legacies, covenants and trading. Taken together, grants and tax privileges accounted for not far short of a fifth of Oxfam's total income of £67m that year. Whatever one's political allegiance, it is reasonable to question the extent to which a fiscally-privileged charity should be free to engage in activities not directly related to its charitable purpose.

It was, after all, quite within the power of Oxfam's leaders to set up, and solicit separate contributions to, a separate advocacy foundation dedicated to political campaigning. It would not, of course, get tax relief on that income but the example of Amnesty International suggests that tax relief is not a necessary condition for success in the advocacy area.

But there is also a good case, which the Commission's alleged leniency with Oxfam recognized, for resisting the temptation to gag charities. It is, after all, their passion that makes some of them so outspoken, and to deny them the freedom to speak their minds, when they understand the causes of the suffering it is their purpose to alleviate, runs the risk of diminishing that passion, and obscuring matters that are best revealed.

Charities as Social Innovators

The second reason why Professor Young expects the assignment to the voluntary sector of a more prominent role in welfare provision to prove beneficial is that he believes that its passionate and enthusiastic pluralism makes it an inherently more innovative and dynamic public benefactor than the state can ever be.

There is no 'party line' in the advocacy of voluntary groups – no sameness of view. While the state tends to react, often to causes and issues identified by charities, the voluntary sector initiates. Unconstrained by the Treasury's parsimony, it is constantly identifying new causes, raising new money for them, attracting public attention to them, and doing all it can, with its limited resources, to pursue its charitable purposes. It is exploratory and experimental and has no concept of political or economic risk. Because it lives on need it is always seeking it and often finds it in places where the state would not even think of looking.

Perhaps more important than this, the voluntary sector acts, by virtue of its dependence on the donations of millions of individuals, as a high-fidelity sensing system for the concerns of society. As Ken Young says:

> The history of social policy in Britain is largely one in which the agenda for action has been set by the voluntary bodies turning hitherto tolerated conditions into problems and claims for action. Their representations and arguments are part of that larger conversation from which policy change flows.

Finally Professor Young argues that because the effectiveness of the voluntary sector as a social antenna depends on its informal nature (part of the charity ethos), it can act as a force for 'social and political integration' by bridging the gap between mainstream community life and 'the dispossessed and alienated'.

Young asserts that these three crucial contributions: to the representative process, to the development of public policy, and to social integration and cohesion, together constitute a strong case for taking voluntary action seriously 'as an integral part of the polity'.

The Government's Duty of Care

The National Council for Voluntary Organizations argued, in its 1990 paper *Investing in the Voluntary Sector*, that government has a two-fold role in funding voluntary action: 'to further its own policy objectives (and) to foster the health, vitality and development of the voluntary sector'. There are some in the sector who believe the government has yet to acknowledge the second role and that its interest in the sector, such as it is, has been more concerned with the details of regulation and other bureaucratic matters than with a positive desire to foster the 'health, vitality and development' of voluntary organizations.

On the face of it, this neglect is consistent with the free-market ideology of the Thatcher era; organizations should not be helped to help themselves but should be given the freedom to take their fates into their own hands. But government action promoting freedom in one area can take it away in another.

In 1991, ninety years after Florence Nightingale made the following plea: 'I ask and pray my friends who still remember me not to let this truly sacred work languish and die for want of a little more money', two London hospitals, Guy's and St Thomas's and their United Medical and Dental Schools, set up the Florence Nightingale Fund and hired Derek Robertson, former head of fundraising at the NSPCC, to run it. He was the first professional appeals director the hospitals had appointed and he symbolized the arrival of a large bunch of hungry new kids on the voluntary sector's block.

Hospital appeals for new wings or expensive items of medical equipment have been commonplace for years, but the partial emergence of some hospitals from the public sector to become self-governing trusts is causing their managers to adopt an altogether more vigorous and professional approach to fund-raising.

'It has been made quite clear to the Charity Commissioners', Robertson told the *Financial Times*, 'that the objective is to raise funds which will be supplementary to income from the National Health Service and the Universities Funding Council. We will not be replacing public funds by collecting money to polish the ward floors.' But Robertson's assurances notwithstanding, there is plenty of evidence that hospitals, and thus the NHS, are claiming an increasing share of voluntary income.

A report by the Directory of Social Change (DSC), in March 1992, alleged that the role of charity in the NHS 'has altered fundamentally, with charity now being called on to fund both major capital projects and also basic medical services. In the past, charitable income has only had a peripheral part to play in the NHS, concentrating on providing small comforts for patients and staff and supporting research and the development of new treatments. However, the former consensus, that charity should not pay for the costs of core services that were the proper responsibility of the state, has now all but collapsed.'

The DSC said the number of hospital appeals registered each year rose five-fold in the 1980s and there were now 2,300 such appeals. 'Charity is called upon', the report continued 'to build new NHS hospitals or to develop existing ones; to equip special care baby units; to keep operating theatres open; to sponsor intensive care cots in a children's hospital; to buy new operating tables, life support machines and cardiac monitors; to train ambulance crews and to equip ambulances with resuscitation equipment; and to shorten waiting lists.'

According to DSC's estimates, total charitable income to the NHS had risen above £370m a year, and charitable assets held by authorities and NHS Trusts were worth nearly £700m. In a carefully aimed jab at the philosophical inspirations of the NHS reforms the DSC observed:

> Charity represents a significant artificial subsidy that distorts the operation of the market. A hospital could achieve success in the internal market not because its services were particularly efficient, or of good quality, but because it had a large charitable income.

Similar considerations apply to the education reforms. It is true the universities have long depended on appeals and that Oxford University's massive £340m appeal, for example, is attracting considerable support from overseas, but there is every reason to expect that 'opted-out' schools will become yet another group of hungry mouths for charity to feed. Whatever the theoretical merits of the health and education reforms, in terms of fostering good management and improving allocative efficiency, their incidental effects on voluntary organizations could be very serious.

It has to be said that a government that suddenly decides to go fishing for serious money in a charity pool that shows, for the moment, little signs of real growth, does not seem to be a government conscious of its duty 'to foster the health, vitality and development of the voluntary sector' (*Investing in the Voluntary Sector*, NCVO, 1990). This must also apply to the government's continual refusal to relieve the sector of its VAT burden.

Contracting

The aspect of the relationship between the state and the voluntary sector that has inspired the most heated debate is not the state's emergence as a big competitor for charitable funds but its growing role as a big buyer of human services from the voluntary sector.

The coming of the 'contract culture' – the sub-contracting, by central and local government agencies, of welfare and 'human services' provision to voluntary organizations – is widely seen as one of the greatest challenges facing the UK voluntary sector in the 1990s.

Until the 1980s the role of the voluntary sector was seen as supplementing statutory welfare provision, innovating and monitoring mainstream provision by local authorities, health authorities and other government agencies. Voluntary organizations received grant aid from government, sometimes as core funding from local authorities, sometimes through partnership funding arrangements, such as the urban programme, and sometimes through government agencies such as the Manpower Services Commission. By 1987/8 local authority funding of the voluntary sector exceeded £500m a year.

The new 'Thatcherite' philosophy which became influential in the 1980s envisaged a greater role in the provision of human services for the 'independent sector' and regarded local government as an 'enabler and purchaser of services', rather than a direct provider.

At the same time there was a growing disenchantment with the open-ended grants made to voluntary organizations. They were unreliable sources of finance for the agency charities which received them, and the system suffered from an inherent lack of accountability. So 'contracting' became the new buzz-word.

Sometimes it simply meant replacing open-ended grants with more tightly specified agreements and sometimes it meant contracting-out services previously supplied by the state. Usually it involved negotiation, but occasionally it meant competitive tendering.

Contracting is not totally new to Britain. Social housing has been provided by housing associations, under contract to the Housing Corporation, for many years and special training has also been subcontracted, at first by the Manpower Services Commission and the Training Agency and now by the Training and Enterprise Councils (TECs), in England and Wales, and by the Local Enterprise Companies (LECs) in Scotland.

But the implementation of the 1990 National Health Service and Community Care Act in 1992, and the introduction of new financial arrangements in 1993 mean that many more voluntary organizations are becoming involved in contracting. The Act requires local authorities to develop a mixed economy for the provision of community care and makes special mention of the role voluntary organizations must play as contractors.

The housing associations are becoming involved in managing local authority housing stocks as well as providing social housing. Other voluntary organizations are entering into contracts to provide adult education, youth services, advice work, probation work, environmental improvement, leisure and conservation services.

Some see the advent of contracting as a major threat to the traditional and valued independence of the voluntary sector, which has enabled it, in the past, to act as a monitor of statutory provision of welfare as well as a provider in its own right. When it was beholden to no one but givers, it was free to engage in the major debates of the day without fear of jeopardizing large proportions of its income. Within the 'contract culture', it is argued, charities will be forced to adopt a far more deferential attitude to their government principals. Their campaigning vigour will be muted and, over time, they will have to adopt the world view of the agencies for which they act as sub-contractors.

Others fear that these new 'big buyers' of welfare services will favour 'big suppliers', and that this will lead to the extinction of the smaller, more innovative, community-based organizations.

Some of the big charities welcome the 'contract culture'. They see it as a major opportunity to expand their operations and to exchange some of their dependence on volatile voluntary donations and grants, for more reliable sources of revenue.

The new training arrangements, launched in 1989, illustrate how the contracting model works. The TECs are effectively run by local businesses through their representation on the TEC Boards of Directors. Each regional TEC is charged with delivering local training programmes, designed and funded by central government, and with carrying out all other functions previously discharged by the Training Agency's area offices. The TECs have considerable flexibility in matching training provision in their areas with the expected needs of their local labour markets.

They do not supply training directly, however. This task is sub-contracted to training providers, which are sometimes commercial companies and sometimes charities. There has been considerable unease about the contracts between the TECs and the training providers. John Plummer, managing director of Community Industry, declared in an August 1991 Bridge Group memorandum 'Contracts for Success – Or Failure', that 'the TECs and LECs are presently not empowered to negotiate or enter into commercially sound contractual arrangements with suppliers'.

If such problems are being experienced in the training area, where contracting has been operating for many years, how much steeper must the learning curve be in other human services areas such as health and welfare, where registered charities play a more important role?

The prospective scale and extent of the sub-contracting of human services in the UK dwarfs the contracting pioneers in training and social housing. It is true government agencies currently contribute around 18 per cent of the voluntary sector's income, mostly through grants, but it is hard to exaggerate the psychological and operational gulf that divides the old grant culture from the new contract culture.

Previously, governments (local and central) played the roles of more or less reliable patrons. Under the new deal they are obliged to act as cost-conscious principals giving clear briefs to their agencies and taking account of the financial and planning requirements of the ultimate service providers. Where will contracting lead and what effects will it have on all the parties involved?

A partial answer to this question is that the relationship between the state and the voluntary sector in Britain will come to resemble, more and more, the kind of relationships that have prevailed for many years in America.

In 1991, Richard Gutch, the former Assistant Director of the National Council for Voluntary Organizations (NCVO) and now chief executive of the charity, Arthritis Care, was asked by the Calouste Gulbenkian Foundation to study what lessons the UK voluntary sector could learn in this area from the US. In his report, *Contracting lessons from the US*, Gutch concludes that American-style contracting, towards which the UK is moving, works, but not very well. He says that in the last twenty years the US voluntary sector has been overwhelmed by the emergence of an incoherent morass of contracting bureaucracies, and that the relationship between the voluntary sector and government has been severely strained by policy mistakes.

According to Gutch, the Reagan administration's policy of cutting public sector spending on welfare services and encouraging voluntary and private sector organizations to fill the gap

> failed to recognize the significance of public sector funding for the voluntary sector. What happened, therefore, was that the voluntary sector was forced to become more commercial. Most of the income needed to replace lost government funding came from additional service charges and fees, with some coming from private charitable support. In order to secure this income, voluntary organisations had to focus more and more on clients who could afford to pay. Generally speaking, those agencies with the best access to paying clients – such as health agencies – did best in response to budget cuts, while those with least access – such as employment agencies – did worst.

Moreover, the American experience shows the alleged advantages of contracting over grant giving – greater security, longer-term funding agreements, more emphasis on output than input and more equality between funder and funded – are chimeras.

Most contracts are for only one year, over-spending is not reimbursed (but under-spending is clawed back) and, as local government funders struggle to manage their own cash-flow problems, the squeeze on funding levels is being aggravated by chronic late payment, which transfers cash-flow problems to the voluntary organizations. 'If anything,' Gutch concludes, 'financial security has been reduced by contracting rather than improved.'

US estimates suggest most contracts are 'subsidized' by the voluntary organizations that undertake them, to the tune of 15–20 per cent. The subsidy is in the form of lower wages (charity wages are 10–30 per cent lower than public sector wages); longer hours; the substitution of paid staff by volunteers; and the use of charitable funds, in addition to contractor fees, in the performance of contracts. One commentator told Gutch the constant downward pressure on costs coupled with late payments and increasing demands was 'bleeding the voluntary sector dry'.

But there were encouraging signs too. The problems seem to be widely recognized and, in a number of areas, the trauma of Reaganomics appears to have concentrated the minds of those on both sides of the contracting divide on improvement and reform. Gutch's description of recent developments in New York City provides a case in point.

The City of New York spends $7bn a year – about a quarter of its total budget of $30bn – on contracts for goods, services and construction. Some $3bn of the 'contracted out' spending is devoted to 'human services', like foster care, day care, home care and services for the mentally ill. Most of these are supplied by voluntary organizations.

Over the years, a huge bureaucracy has grown up around New York City's contracting. There have been allegations of corruption and malpractice and concern has been expressed about the lack of competition, diversity and equality of opportunity in the contracting procedures. To cap it all, the US Supreme Court ruled that the voting system on New York City's Board of Estimate, the body responsible for contracting, violated the US constitutional requirement for equal representation.

Accordingly, in 1990 the old Board of Estimate was replaced by a Procurement Policy Board (PPB) to establish and then to monitor new contracting procedures, and responsibility for contracting decisions was delegated to City agencies. The new PPB consists of five members, three appointed by the Mayor and two by the Comptroller. There is now a City Chief Procurement Officer, based in the Mayor's Office, and Chief Contracting Officers in each agency involved in contracting.

The PPB's rules govern the whole contracting process, from the initial decision to contract out, through selection of suppliers, contract negotiation, administration, evaluation, invoicing and payment. All approved contractors are sent details of contract opportunities and the latter are also published in a daily edition of the City Record. Contracting forms have been simplified, and there is a Contract Dispute Resolution Board.

It was recognized that human services, where sub-contractors are voluntary organizations, posed particular difficulties because the relationship between the sub-contractor and the principal (NYC) was more like a partnership and because it was harder to define and achieve quality. It was also felt more flexible forms of funding were appropriate to encourage innovation and start-ups, so a joint voluntary sector/NYC Task Force on Human Service Contracts was set up to examine six issues of concern:

1. Length of contract. At the time, 90 per cent of NYC's 2,000 human services contracts were on a one-year basis so a lot of City and contractor time had to be spent on contract prep-aration, approval and registration, all in a two-month period at the end of the City's financial year. It created uncertainty in the voluntary organizations, causing higher staff turnover than would otherwise have been the case. So the Task Force rec-ommended the phased introduction of multi-term (usually three-year) contracts, staggered so that they did not all expire at the same time.
2. Paperwork. The Task Force recommended a central register be established to collect, review and certify all contract docu-mentation on behalf of all agencies.
3. Auditing. The Task Force wanted to see if the procedures here could also be streamlined, so it conducted a pilot scheme where a single audit covered a number of contracts with a single voluntary organization. It seemed to work.

4. Cash-flow. The Task Force estimated that in 1990 payments on 80 per cent of contracts were over thirty days late. The PPB's new 'prompt payment principle', requiring bills to be paid within forty-five days of performance or invoicing and interest to be paid on late payment, helped. The Task Force also proposed direct deposits into the voluntary organization's bank accounts, front-end funding for those with cash-flow problems at the beginning of a funding cycle, and a study of the feasibility of forming an interim financing system, to address cash-flow problems, using City and voluntary sector funds.

5. Standardization. A serious administrative problem for the voluntary organizations was that each agency had different policies on whether contract funds could be used to pay for the voluntary organization's pensions; on how 'direct costs' were defined; on whether or not interest on contract funds could be retained by the voluntary organization; on whether separate bank accounts were needed; and on audit, legal and bonding arrangements. One voluntary organization said it had to close and open 100 separate bank accounts every year. The Task Force recommended standardization and simplification of these arrangements.

6. Monitoring. At the time, monitoring procedures focused on paperwork rather than actual performance. The Task Force recommended more work here and proposed experiments in ways to make monitoring more of a partnership and less a policing of paperwork process.

From the Task Force exercise emerged the Procurement Policy Board's draft rules for human services, applicable to all contracts (not grants), including those for the provision of services that are 'social, health or medical, housing or employment assistance, training, educational or recreational in character'. The declared aims of the rules are to:

1. Ensure City funds are most effectively applied to the provision of needed services of a high quality.
2. Maintain continuity of service relationship between the client and the provider, while encouraging competition and innovation.

3. Minimize paperwork, give administrative and technical assist-
    ance, allow providers to look after their staff and evaluate them
    on quality of services.
4. Publicize contracting opportunities widely and provide oppor-
    tunities for new, small, minority and women-controlled service
    providers to qualify for contract awards.
5. Recognize that service programmes may help preserve or
    strengthen the social and economic fabric of the communities
    where they operate.

There are two lists: one of potential proposers, organizations
that ask to be on the list, plus providers with current contracts; and
a more select list of prequalified providers, including organizations
that are licensed or meet established criteria to provide the particular service, including those providers performing satisfactorily
on current contracts. Each agency must publish notices of the
availability of list membership each quarter.

Each contracting agency is also obliged to develop an annual
plan for all its human services contracts, detailing when existing
contracts expire, if and when the agency intends to exercise options
to renew and describing planned contracting in the coming year.
These plans must also be made available for public inspection for
use of new contractors or dissatisfied clients.

The PPB has identified four contractor selection procedures:

1. competitive sealed proposals
2. competitive sealed proposals from prequalifiers
3. sole source
4. emergency
5. small contracts (less than $25,000)

The PPB recommends the first as the most appropriate. Under
this procedure the agency's contracting officer develops a brief
including a statement of selection criteria and a request for information on staff and the proposed manner of delivery. Bidders must
be given at least twenty-five days to respond.

Contract terms are capped at three, six or nine years, with three
years as the standard term. Six year contracts are deemed more
appropriate when provision is centre-based and involves obtaining

complex permits and approvals or where there is a need to establish links with other providers. Nine year contracts can be appropriate when long-term care giving or residential care is involved.

The PPB urges agencies to co-ordinate and review monitoring procedures and insists on new, competitive solicitations on contract expiry. Public hearings must be held on contract renewals at least once every three years to solicit input about the provider's performance, and evaluation procedures must include unannounced site visits and client satisfaction surveys.

New York's contracting reforms identify some of the problems Britain's embryonic 'contract culture' is likely to encounter in the coming years, and also suggests some possible solutions. Gutch regards the formation of a joint task force for human services contracting as a good sign, and thinks the new system has the flexibility to improve itself, in the light of its experience. He sees the most positive features of the reforms as the distinction between contracts and grants; the special arrangements for smaller contracts; a recognition of the need for technical support; the emphasis on planning and publicizing; the introduction of longer-term contracts; and public hearings involving users and advocacy groups.

But he wonders how reasonable it is to apply common rules to conventional and human services when, in the case of human services, there is a strong case for involving the providers and, arguably, the clients in planning and specification. He also finds it hard to reconcile the emphasis on competitive, sealed bids, select lists and multi-term contracts, with the desire to provide opportunities for new, small, minority and women-controlled service providers.

Looking ahead, Gutch speculates that the city of New York might, at some stage, grasp the decentralization nettle and delegate the planning and delivery of human services to the neighbourhood level, leaving the centre with only a regulatory role.

Pushing the provision of human services, whether financed by charity or government, down to a level at which clients have more say over the manner of their provision, is a theme that runs through most of the debates about the future of giving.

9

The Future of Philanthropy

In the previous chapters I have tried to describe what seem to me to be the salient points about the present condition of charity in Britain and I have pondered the significance of the substantial broadening of its base into the popular culture.

I have discussed the charity 'ethos', the spirit which seems to guide and inspire those who work in the voluntary sector, and how it is being modified. I have compared the charitable ethos with the corporate ethos, and have tried to show that, although differences remain there is also, as the traditions approach each other, a growing similarity.

I have explored the history of charity's relationship with the state and have tried to indicate what seems to me to be the important consequences of the profound changes in this uneasy welfare partnership, some of which have occurred already, but most of which are threatened, or still pending.

It is clear that there is a great deal going on, in and around the voluntary sector; so many trends that are converging, so many debates of great import that remain unresolved, so many threats and so many opportunities that it's tempting to talk of revolution. But I believe in evolution, not revolution. The seeds out of which charity's future will grow and blossom have already been sown. If we only knew where to look we could watch them germinate.

In this chapter I shall speculate about the nature of these seeds and about the pattern of their development. I do so from the point of view of a business economist who has a deep interest in management and has become convinced that goal-seeking organizations, such as charities and companies, are best seen as life-forms that are evolving in response to changes in their environment.

Looking back it may seem quite obvious and quite abrupt, but for the moment, the future of the voluntary sector, and of the welfare society within which it lives, is obscure. My speculations are certain to turn out wrong in many important respects, though I hope to score the odd hit here and there.

The important thing for charities and companies as they face an uncertain future is to have some kind of framework within which to think and make long-term plans. The framework may turn out to be misconceived, and wrong in certain details, but it can be modified along the way, and at least it gives you a guide for action in the meantime.

My speculations will be divided into three sections. I shall start by looking at the relationship of the voluntary sector with governments, I shall go on to consider the changes that are happening within the voluntary sector itself, and where they may be leading, and I shall conclude with a discussion of what, for me, is the most fascinating possibility of all: that companies and voluntary organizations will enter into a 'symbiotic' partnership and progressively displace the state as the primary provider of welfare.

Charities and Government

Despite all the Thatcherite talk over the past decade or so – of shifting the responsibility for welfare provision from the public to the private sector; of 'rolling back the frontiers of the state'; of the *quid pro quo* of the Tory's tax cuts being an obligation, on individuals and companies, to give more – there has been precious little sign of any major re-balancing of public service financing.

Giving, in real terms, rose steeply during the economic boom in the second half of the 1980s, but has been on a plateau during the past three years, and charities have been obliged to dig into their reserves to maintain a modest increase in their spending.

But this should not be seen, as it is by many of the charity sector's cynics, as conclusive evidence that the whole idea of a re-balancing is fatally flawed, that in expecting the private sector to take up some of the state's welfare burden the government has been pushing on a string.

Changes of this magnitude do not happen over night. It takes time for people and organizations to adapt to new realities and to feel comfortable with them. It may be that the notion of a 'welfare society' replacing the 'welfare state' will, in the end, prove an illusion but the jury is still out. There is still plenty of time for the hoped for increase in giving to materialize.

For my part, I am sanguine. I believe that over the next ten years or so, if government keeps its nerve (and, for reasons we have discussed, it will be hard for it to do otherwise), a significant real increase in giving and in volunteering will occur. There are two reasons for this.

The first is that, notwithstanding frequent claims by left-wing politicians to the contrary, it is society, not the government, which ultimately makes these decisions. In the past it has been quite easy for people to delegate this decision-making role to the state by voting in a government committed to a particular pattern of wealth redistribution.

Nowadays it is far less easy to believe that any government, whatever its promises or commitments, will be able even to maintain welfare services let alone to increase them. The public finances of most developed nations are in a mess, and most governments are under severe pressure to reduce public spending. The relative health of Britain's public finances, brought about during the Thatcher years, is not an exception – it is becoming a model.

The so-called 'convergence' of national economic policies in the European Community, and the tight constraints that were imposed on domestic policy by membership of the ERM (European Exchange Mechanism) are discussed constantly. There is less room now for pluralism in economic policy. This does not mean we are creating less wealth; it is simply that world financial markets have decided, on the basis of pretty clear evidence, that there is an inverse relationship between economic health and proportionate size of the public sector.

How would a compassionate society respond to the realization that it can no longer delegate the task of providing what it deems an appropriate level of welfare to the state? It might take a while to understand the full implications of the state's loss of power and there might be under-provision for a while, but sooner or later society will recognize that it must assume greater responsibility for

199

welfare, and it is hard to see how it could discharge this duty without a sharp increase in giving and volunteering.

The second reason why I am sanguine about the prospects for a substantial increase in the level of giving, is that the voluntary sector has stopped moaning about its problems and is starting to act. The Windsor Campaign, for example, which aims substantially to increase the level of UK giving reminds me a little, in the grandness of its goals and the co-operative way in which it is setting out to achieve them, of Japan's Ministry for International Trade and Industry – and look how well MITI did. (The willingness of charities to co-operate with each other exemplified by the Windsor Campaign is, in my view, one of the voluntary sector's greatest strengths, and I shall have more to say about it later.)

One of the arguments of the Windsor group is that, from the point of view of individual givers (whether companies or people), a very small change in their giving habits would have an enormous effect on voluntary income. Because giving is so meagre in Britain, relative to America for example, there is considerable built-in leverage just waiting to be exploited by mass-marketing campaigns, of the kind advocated by the Windsor group, to persuade non-givers to give and to persuade givers to give more. And it is relatively easy marketing, by the standards of the company sector, because there is still so much ignorance in Britain about how to give.

Michael Brophy, the executive director of the Charities Aid Foundation (CAF), gave an indication of the enormous scope for increasing levels of giving in his foreword to the 14th edition of *Charity Trends*:

> In a situation in which only 3 per cent of wills contain a gift to charity it makes sense to promote more legacy giving. In a situation in which the very existence of gift aid is still known by just a few it makes sense to tell more people about it. (The minimum for gift aid should be lowered from £600 to £100.) After four years payroll giving is still considered to be complicated. It makes sense, surely, to demonstrate to people how simple it is? Giving in fact remains a marginal activity for most of us. It really is time to make the case for more giving: this means giving more, more often.

There is a feeling, now, in the voluntary sector that after the disappointments of the past few years, it is no longer sufficient to wait for a spontaneous welling up of public generosity, and that a concerted effort is now needed to get the bandwagon rolling. It seems to me that the time is ripe for such an initiative.

The government has a contribution to make too. As we saw in the last chapter, it is doing the voluntary sector no favours in its efforts to attract more charitable funds into the health and education sectors. If it is really as keen as it protests to help nurture a vigorous and financially sound voluntary sector, it should think through, more thoroughly, the consequences for the sector of its other policies.

For it is obvious that those welfare functions traditionally discharged by the state are precisely those functions that will have the most charity pulling power if the state ceases to discharge them. And as the Directory of Social Change has pointed out, it is benefiting no one if badly managed hospitals and schools respond to state finance 'cuts', not by improving efficiency but by hiring full-time appeals managers.

But the government is on a learning curve too. These are uncharted waters, the hazards need to be mapped and new habits of mind and policy design need to be acquired before the two traditional partners, in what former Chief Charity Commissioner Robin Guthrie calls the 'public benefit sector', can work in harmony together.

Perhaps, as a gesture of good faith to the voluntary sector, the government might accede to its persistent requests to be relieved of VAT, and might also give serious consideration to Michael Brophy's demand that the minimum limit for gift aid be reduced to £100.

The Charities Themselves

It is a feature of evolution that environmental changes that appear to threaten a species often end up by strengthening it. My friend Hugh Thompson put the point more vividly when he said, 'if you have to hang on by your fingernails for any length of time, you tend to get very strong fingers'.

The voluntary sector in general and individual charities in particular, are confronted today by numerous threats. They are finding fund-raising more and more of a struggle. Their relationships with government – particularly in the area of contracting – are becoming more problematical. The burden of compliance with a much tougher regulator has increased greatly since the passage of the 1992 Act. And all the while the needs of their clients, their *raison d'être*, are becoming ever more pressing.

There can be little doubt that the combined effect of these numerous pressures will be to increase greatly the mortality rate of voluntary organizations in the years ahead. Though here, as elsewhere, the figures are not reliable, there is reason to believe that the attrition rate in the sector had already risen considerably during the 1980s, and there is no reason to suppose the rate of the upward trend will slacken. In retrospect, the collapse of War on Want may well be seen as the harbinger of a 'great dying' in the voluntary sector during the 1990s.

Faced with this coming shake-out in the sector, which will in all probability be brought about as much by mergers and takeovers as by failures and closures, some observers fear the enormous diversity of the voluntary sector, in terms of size, wealth, sources of income and styles of management, is likely to prove a serious weakness.

I see it as a strength. It represents, in an evolutionary sense, a rich 'gene pool' from which new styles, new strategies, new concepts and new cultures will be constantly emerging, to be tested by the environment and there to be selected for advancement and success, or to be consigned to the dustbin of failed experiments.

An important consequence of this struggle to survive will be a heightening of self-awareness amongst charities. When you are hanging on by your fingernails, you may spend the odd moment pondering the meaning of life, but most of the time your attention will be devoted to the strength of your fingers, the possibility of grabbing that tree stump, whether you can afford to spend energy on another scream for help, and how desperately you want to live. In the past, one of the features of voluntary organizations that has distinguished them from companies has been a much clearer sense of purpose.

Charities have never, for a moment, been in any doubt about their *raisons d'être*. They are defined by their purposes. In a sense, they are, or at any rate have been, nothing but their purposes.

Hence former Chief Charity Commissioner, Robin Guthrie, stressed the importance of winding up clauses in a charity's articles of association. It is necessary, in his view, for a charity to acknowledge the inevitability of its death, in the event that its purposes are achieved or are rendered superfluous, and to make appropriate dispositions beforehand.

Companies on the other hand, have managed for centuries to muddle through quite well without having a very clear idea about what they are and what their ultimate purpose is or should be and the great evolutionary advantage of this, of not having a single, unequivocal purpose to which all else is merely a means, is that you do not have to die if you lose your purpose. You are not at the mercy of your success. Companies, like biological organisms, have a powerful instinct to survive, and that, I believe, is something that charities have begun to acquire as they take up arms against their sea of troubles.

I am not suggesting that charities are losing their sense of purpose, but I am suggesting that many of them are becoming something more than their purposes – that they themselves, not just the things they do, are becoming important to them and are influencing the way they behave. In general they are becoming less transparent, less like mere conduits for the generosity of their donors, and more like corporeal creatures with a concern for their own well-being. In a word, they are becoming more like companies.

It is ironic that charities that were once nothing but their purposes should be finding 'corporate identity' now, at the time when companies, in their efforts to hire and keep the good people they need to remain competitive, should be busily trying to create a sense of purpose, by drafting 'mission' statements and articulating bold and inspiring 'visions'.

It is as if companies and charities were made for each other or were the two halves of a sixpence (perhaps it should be a widow's mite) that, having been severed long ago, are now coming together again.

Company/Charity Convergence

The process of convergence has two components: charities are becoming more like companies and companies are becoming more like charities.

In my book, *The 'nice' company*, I borrowed ideas from the theory of games to show how companies were under considerable evolutionary pressure to become more generous, more ethical and generally 'nicer'. I used a game called 'The Prisoner's Dilemma' – a conundrum that has played an important role in Game Theory in recent years – and explored the business implications of the 'iterated' version of the game featured in Robert Axelrod's *The Evolution of Cooperation*.

The analysis demonstrated how 'nice' strategies are very strong in the long-term. Marks & Spencer, ICI, Pearson, NFC, Virgin and Body Shop, are examples of British companies pursuing nice strategies, in this sense. Their general outlook often seems to be at odds with the traditional tough, hard-headed attitude (exemplified by the assertion that in business 'nice guys finish last') but it has proved of enduring worth for their shareholders, as well as employees.

Since there is a tendency for strategies that deliver long-term value to shareholders to spread through the corporate population (because strategies that do not, die and because managers are motivated to emulate successful strategies), it is reasonable to regard companies as being under a strong, evolutionary pressure to become 'nicer', in the sense outlined in chapter 5. And since charities are nice by definition, notwithstanding the nastiness that occurs from time to time (see chapter 2), it seems reasonable to characterize the adaptive processes set in train by this evolutionary pressure on companies, by saying that companies are becoming more like charities.

In their efforts to accumulate the reputational assets they need to maintain their competitiveness, companies are likely to become more assiduous, and more systematic in their giving. Some large companies may even take the distribution of their largesse 'in-house'. In such cases, the company's reputation managers will begin to resemble fund-raising charities, with one donor. Because corporate reputations are multifaceted these 'in-house' charities are unlikely, except in special cases, to be dedicated to a single cause. They will act more like wholesalers of charity, like the United Way in the US, or Charity Projects in the UK.

Their work will consist of:

1. Identifying weaknesses in the company's reputational assets
2. Preparing plans to make good these weaknesses, and putting these plans to the company
3. Selecting appropriate causes
4. Preparing briefs for specialist charity sub-contractors
5. Inviting tenders and holding 'beauty contests'
6. Monitoring the performance of sub-contractor charities
7. Reporting back to the company

Smaller companies may use a new kind of intermediary to plan their giving, in the same way as investors use mutual funds (unit trusts) and investment trusts to spread their risk and to reflect their prejudices.

Looking further ahead it is possible to imagine a time when a wholly new kind of organization emerges, that contains elements of both the charity and the company. (I have suggested the word 'comparity' to describe this hybrid although I am not sure if it is elegant enough to catch on.) Such an organization could take many forms but let us try to imagine one, possible, variant.

The company would be owned by institutional shareholders but by then, the segmentation of the fund management industry would have progressed apace. Building on the small but growing group of tiny, specialist funds that have emerged in recent years – the so-called 'conscience' funds (including 'ethical' funds and 'green' funds) – it will have produced a group of large cause-related funds.

Let us suppose that in this case the company's policies and strategies have attracted the attention of specialist funds that offer their subscribers, in addition to the prospect of a reasonable return, the guarantee that by subscribing, investors will be helping to support children's hospitals.

The company could attract such investment support in various ways. One possibility is that it could covenant 50 per cent of its profits, over and above what is needed to finance all viable investment projects, to a selected group of hospitals. Or it could establish its own, in-house, charity or it could agree to covenant profits to an external charity that specialized in children's hospitals.

One could imagine, if such 'comparities' become commonplace, that the prices pages of the *Financial Times* might, one day, classify listed companies according to the causes that they support, rather than the type of businesses they are in. Probably this is too fanciful but it is clear that charities and companies have a lot to learn from each other and this potential for mutual enlightenment will draw them closer together.

The company will contribute its survival instinct, its undoubtedly superior management skills (including its cost-consciousness) and its understanding of the dynamics of competition. Lord Laing (see chapter 1) argues that management skills are the most important of all the contributions companies can make to social progress. 'We all want a better society,' he said. 'It is better to get the help of business, leading local partnerships of local government, central government and the voluntary sector [rather than merely assisting such partnerships], because leadership is our strong suit. It's about more than just giving money for worthwhile projects – secondment of managers is invaluable. We're helping people to help themselves but they usually need experienced leadership – someone to ask the difficult questions.'

The charity, for its part, will bring its sensitivity about what ordinary people care about, its sense of purpose and vision and its much better understanding of the dynamics of partnership and collaboration. Charities have always known that their's must be a positive sum game. The frequent references by fund-raisers to the 'newness' of the money they receive demonstrates this. An appeal that raises new money is invariably regarded, in the voluntary sector, as more successful than an appeal that has clearly diverted money away from other causes. The Windsor Campaign is a good illustration of the sector's inherently collaborative nature.

Companies can learn from this insight. It can help them to understand that it is in their long-term interests that their customers, suppliers and, in some respects, even their competitors, should remain healthy. Charities can learn something from the debates about how companies should be organized and structured that are currently exercising the minds of the leaders of some of the world's largest firms.

The idea of the integrated organization that controls all of its outposts from the centre is becoming unfashionable. Modern management thinking favours a more federal structure, in which business units are given a great deal of autonomy. Some large charities are already organized in this way, for historical reasons, but others appear still to be wedded to the centralist model. They might do well to consider, as the pressure on them grows to make their services more relevant to their clients, and more local, reorganizing themselves along federal lines.

Charities can also learn from the analytical rigour of the corporate approach: the emphasis on monitoring and feedback; the importance of standard systems of measurement; and the healthy discipline that comes from a constant attention to the detail of their operations.

Richard Fries, who was appointed Chief Charity Commissioner in mid-1992 on Robert Guthrie's departure for the Council of Europe, brought with him to the job a strong conviction that the voluntary sector needs more accountability and openness. As a senior civil servant Fries had been involved in the management of the Woodfield scrutiny report, the White Paper and the new Charities Act which emerged from it (see chapter 10).

In an interview with *Trust Monitor* (June 1992) he said the Commission was halfway through the programme of reform that had begun under Robin Guthrie and that the task now was 'to digest these changes and make use of the new instruments that we have at our disposal. It's all very well having a new database. The thing is to make it into a resource for the whole charity sector.'

The charity meta-brand is extremely valuable, but the value of individual charity brands will be assessed, increasingly, by how charities perform on cost/revenue ratios, the returns they achieve on their investments in people and computers, as well as money, and the extent to which they succeed, each year, in meeting the targets they set themselves and in furthering their charitable purposes.

Organizations like the Charities Aid Foundation (see chapter 6), the Directory of Social Change and business publisher Hemmington Scott, which publishes a Directory of Britain's top 1,000 charities, all have important roles to play in the development of reliable measurement and monitoring systems. These are also going to be needed to track the charitable performance of companies, as they begin to exploit the opportunities to accumulate reputational assets, offered by corporate giving. How should corporate generosity be judged? Should it be measured in terms of the percentage of pre-tax profits, as the Per Cent Club criterion assumes, or is giving reflected more accurately in relation to sales, the number of employees or the value companies add to their inputs of resources?

It is likely that British companies will increase the value of their giving, from considerably less than 1 per cent of pre-tax profits to the 2 per cent or more, common in the US, but Lord Laing thinks it unlikely that quoted American or British companies (those owned by institutions, rather than individuals) will ever give much more than that. He insists however, that companies can do far more to promote the generosity of their competitors and their employees. 'When you involve your employees with matching funds [under this arrangement, the company undertakes to match their employees' fund-raising on a pound for pound basis], you get corporate Britain involved in the community. The young people I see these days are less materialistic and more interested in things like the environment.'

He believes organizations such as Business in the Community (BitC), with which he has been closely associated, have a role to play here. 'BitC will be asking companies if they are aware of what they and their people are already doing – because many are not. And if they are not, BitC can help them formulate and plan their programmes. Because it is only when you know where you are starting from that you can direct your efforts effectively. Even if a company does know exactly what they are doing, BitC can help them focus, by acting as a catalyst or consultant.'

Focusing effort is the interesting point when one asks oneself what sort of intermediate steps are likely to be necessary in the journey from here to the comparity. St John Ambulance's relationship with the Safeway retailing group is particularly interesting in this respect. Could it be that, in a few years, this pioneering relationship will lead to a situation in which it is quite common for a large company to 'adopt' a particular charity under an arrangement that provided substantial support for the charity's core funding needs, in return for the reputational assets that the company would derive from such an association?

Such a partnership could involve regular, mutual secondments of staff, which would modify the cultures of both organizations, and also transfer knowledge and insight between them.

10

Philanthropy Around the World

The habits and practices of giving are intimately linked to national cultures; they are the products of a country's history and of the economic, political and religious forces that have driven its cultural evolution. Giving is different from time to time, and from place to place. The liberal economic traditions of America, for example, have produced very different patterns of giving from those that have evolved within the social democratic traditions of Europe.

The traditions of philanthropy in other regions of the world – in Asia, the Far East and in Communist countries – also reflect cultural, historical and religious differences. It is probably fair to say, however, that the reassessment of the problem of welfare is not confined to Britain, but is a matter that is of concern to all societies. There are no certainties anywhere, and almost everywhere, government is in retreat as a welfare provider.

Moreover, as society increasingly concerns itself with the needs of 'strangers' elsewhere in the world – whether living in the parched farmlands of Africa or in Romanian orphanages – charity finds itself poised, just as business was, decades ago, on the threshold of an international future. There are, already, calls for common definitions of charity, and common international tax treatments for giving.

In this final chapter, I shall endeavour to place giving in Britain in an intelligible international context by briefly reviewing philanthropy around the world and then considering the constitutional status of giving in the UK and how it has evolved over the centuries.

The USA

Perhaps because of the strong philanthropic traditions that were bequeathed to the American culture by the Pilgrim Fathers, information on giving in the US is more widely available than in most other countries. It is convenient to look at the published data in two ways – from the point of view of the donors and from the point of view of recipients.

Donors

The independent, or non-profit sector in the United States, is defined as those organizations which are tax exempt, and eligible to receive tax-deductible gifts. This sector includes a wide range of organizations, from schools, hospitals and social service organizations, to religious institutions and a plethora of smaller charities of all different kinds. There is no doubt that the US non-profit sector is the largest of its kind in the world.

According to *Giving USA*, the most authoritative source of US independent sector statistics, there were 907,000 such organizations in 1987, representing 4.2 per cent of all organizations (including companies and other profit-making concerns) and commanding resources equivalent to 5.8 per cent of US national income, which includes an estimated $86.5 billion's worth of so-called 'volunteering'.

The figures show that overall contributions rose by 120 per cent in a ten-year period, indicating only a modest real increase, after adjusting for inflation. Within the total, proportions given by donor-type (individuals, corporations, foundations or bequests) remained pretty stable. Individuals gave a fractionally smaller percentage of the total in 1990 than in 1981, and companies a somewhat higher percentage but there is little evidence of a trend. (See Appendix, table 10.1.)

Corporate giving as a percentage of the total reached a peak of 5.8 per cent in 1984, but after a 4 per cent nominal reduction in company giving in 1987, its share dropped, and had returned to its 1982 level by the end of the decade, indicating that in the US, as elsewhere, company giving is peculiarly sensitive to the economic climate.

Though the general US picture looks flat, it should be noted that total giving as a percentage of gross national product, rose from 2.23 per cent in 1989 to 2.24 per cent in 1990, the highest for twenty years.

Recipients

Religious organizations received well over half the $122.6bn given in the US in 1990, but, as table 10.2 in the Appendix shows, the grip of religion on American generosity, though still strong, appears to be weakening a little, in favour of social, environmental and international causes.

The sharp increase in 'public and social' giving, including so-called 'advocacy' organizations, is an important feature of the US 'non-profits' sector. It may have implications for how the UK debate, on the extent to which charities should be free to engage in political activity, develops.

Canada

According to the Canadian Centre for Philanthropy, giving in Canada in 1986 (the latest year for which figures were available at the time of writing) totalled C$3.9bn, an increase of 11 per cent on 1985. Individuals, including bequests, accounted for 86.6 per cent, foundations for 4.9 per cent and corporations for 8.5 per cent.

Declared corporate donations fell marginally, from C$375m to C$370m in 1989, but profits fell further, and the percentage given rose from 0.6 per cent to 0.62 per cent. Over a longer period, though, the trend of corporate generosity in Canada is downwards; in the early 1980s, Canadian companies were giving about 1 per cent of pre-tax profits.

The family expenditure survey shows that in 1987, some 75 per cent of Canadian households made donations and that some 70 per cent of these went to religious organizations, many of which act as retailers of more general charitable donations, to community and social causes.

According to a survey by Canada's Institute of Donations and Public Affairs Research, 45 per cent of corporate donations went to health and welfare organizations, 25 per cent to education, 14 per

cent to the arts, 7 per cent to civic causes and 1 per cent to sport.
The companies surveyed also gave C\$8.3m worth of gifts in kind.

Australia

The first serious attempt to analyse Australian patterns of philanthropy was a report entitled *Giving Australia*, published by the
Australian Association of Philanthropy in 1991 (see Appendix,
tables 10.3 and 10.4). The surveys on which the report was based
only covered cash donations, but they revealed some striking con-
trasts with patterns of philanthropy elsewhere in the world, notably
the important role of companies and the modest role of religion.

Some 77 per cent of Australian households made one or more
donations in 1988/9 amounting to an average of A\$123.77 or 0.38
per cent of average household income. Within these averages, there
were wide variations – 3.2 per cent of large donors accounted for
37 per cent of total giving by individuals. The authors of the report
were unimpressed by the generosity of their compatriots: 'For
Australian individuals,' they concluded, 'philanthropic giving is
not a mainstream activity governed by economic variables. It is a
marginal activity loosely associated with social customs which do
not give it high priority.'

They found that smaller Australian companies were relatively
generous and suggested this could be construed as individual generosity by their wealthy owners. They noted a selectivity favouring
special human services and health.

Japan

The further one travels from the English-speaking world, the less
confident one can be that one is comparing like with like. In Japan,
there are difficulties with the translation of the word 'foundation'
and it is clear that some donations regarded as 'charitable' in Japan,
would not be so regarded in Britain or America. However, if one
takes the view, as I do, that company giving is fast becoming a crucial
part of the strategic management of a company's reputational assets
(see chapter 4), there is evidence to suggest that Japan is leading
the rest of the world in the development of corporate philanthropy.

Individual giving seems relatively underdeveloped in Japan, as it is in a number of European countries, like Sweden and the Netherlands, where the state has traditionally been the main provider of welfare. And Japan's patriarchal, corporate tradition also renders unnecessary some areas of giving that are the preserve of individual giving in the West. In addition to these cultural differences in the pattern of welfare provision, corporate giving in Japan has received an additional stimulus.

In response to growing public criticism of Japanese business since the early 1970s, the Japanese corporate sector has spawned scores of huge corporate foundations. According to the Japan Association of Charitable Corporations, there are 341 corporate foundations, of which 183 (54 per cent) have been set up since 1970. A 1990 survey also identified 253 major grant making trusts of which 157 (62 per cent) were corporate foundations. (See Appendix, table 10.5.)

A survey by the National Tax Administration Agency indicated that Japan's corporate sector donated ¥398.7bn in 1987, or about 1 per cent of their net income, though by no means all of this was charitable in our meaning of the word. Favoured recipients are research and development (19 per cent), the promotion of science and education (18 per cent), international scientific and cultural exchange (16 per cent), and social welfare (15 per cent).

Important though the corporate foundations are in Japan, their significance is exaggerated by a lack of information about the many thousands of small, non-profit private sector organizations, mostly of a religious nature. It is thought that the non-profit sector as a whole could be worth as much as ¥7.4 trillion (£23bn) a year – some 2 per cent of Gross Domestic Product.

France

According to Bernard Latarjet, director of the Fondation de France, the French do not donate generously to the non-profit sector, compared to Americans, preferring – in line with the French social democratic tradition – to fund them indirectly through the tax system and government spending.

Partly because there is no legal obligation to register the death of a French association (non-profit organization), it is hard to know how large the sector is. Professor Edith Archambault, of the Paris-based Laboratory for the Social Economy, estimates there were 680,000 French associations in 1989, most of which were rather small.

Figures published by the Fondation de France (see Appendix, table 10.6) show that sports, hunting and fishing associations account for about a quarter of the total, and that charities, in the English meaning of the word (associations operating in areas such as health and social welfare, civic and humanitarian causes, housing and the environment and education and training), together account for about 43 per cent of the total.

But an analysis of salaried employees in French associations (see Appendix, table 10.7), shows charity-type associations are much larger than the rest. Together they account for about four-fifths of total, salaried employment in the French non-profit sector.

There are relatively few French foundations, perhaps because the law obliges them to have a government official on their boards and a minimum capital of five million francs. These stipulations have distorted the development of foundations in France, and encouraged foundation-type organizations to adopt different legal structures.

Giving in Britain

According to the 14th edition of *Charity Trends*, voluntary income of Britain's top 400 fund-raising charities rose by 12 per cent (1 per cent, adjusted for inflation) in 1989/90, to £1.3bn.

Donations also rose by 12 per cent, to £623.3m, and accounted for 47 per cent of all voluntary contributions. Legacies grew by an impressive 20 per cent, to account for 35 per cent of the total, the contribution of covenants (tax-free giving) increased by 10 per cent and there was a significant increase in income from the sale of goods and services. The Charities Aid Foundation estimates the shops run by the top 400 charities raised over £38m in 1989/90, some 3 per cent of voluntary income.

CAF's Charity Household Surveys show that individual giving, after rising sharply during the previous year, was hit hard by the recession in 1989/90 (see Appendix, table 10.8). Another CAF survey showed that company giving was also hit by the recession. Total giving by companies fell, in real terms, by 3 per cent in 1990/1, compared to a sharp real increase of 6 per cent in 1989/90.

Most of this can be explained by the contraction in the scale of the corporate sector. Because companies can and do make losses from time to time, particularly in recessions, their 'disposable incomes' are intrinsically more volatile than those of individuals. In my view the best measure of corporate philanthropy is the amount given per employee, because it takes redundancies into account and avoids some of the problems associated with the accountancy profession's often misleading definitions of 'profit'.

As table 10.9 in the Appendix shows, there is reason for optimism about the continued development of the British company as an important contributor to the charity sector. As we have seen, firms, for strategic, self-interested reasons, are likely to become increasingly important donors to charities, and charitable causes, in the years ahead.

Another important trend is a continuing increase in the government's contribution to the voluntary sector. In addition to the government's philosophical desire for a re-balancing of the welfare responsibilities of the state, on the one hand, and of individuals and companies on the other, there is also a policy of sub-contracting larger proportions of the state's provision to the voluntary sector. (See Appendix, table 10.10.)

The Housing Corporation, and the housing associations which it finances, constitute a model for the future relationship between government and the voluntary sector in Britain, as grants to charities, from central and local government, are progressively replaced by contracts. The coming of this so-called 'contract culture' – a key feature of the state/charity relationship in the US for more than twenty years – is one of the most crucial and controversial challenges facing the British voluntary sector (see chapter 8).

The British Voluntary Sector

Robin Guthrie, the Chief Charity Commissioner from 1988 to 1992, was regarded by many in the sector as a breath of fresh air. He sees charities as part of a Public Benefit Sector, the other main contributor to which is government. 'It's the public sector,' he says, 'but it is not controlled by government. It's fuelled by both [charity and the state]. Our job is to protect that sector – from any failure by trustees, from abuse and from government interference.'

As Guthrie sees it, the principle that there should be some kind of balance of public and private welfare provision is much more important than exactly where the balance should be struck. 'There's a very broad band within which the line can be drawn,' he says. He acknowledges that the law of charity has been caught up in the political argument about public welfare and government responsibility, but suggests that it matters less where the balance lies, than that it should be clear. 'It's all about "benefit to the community",' he explains. 'In the beginning Tudor businessmen got involved, for the public benefit, in building roads and bridges, and in the provision of education and training. Most of those things, like roads and education, were taken over by government, but lifeboats were not.

'There has never been a permanent consensus about what the balance should be. Each generation finds its own answer. They thought they'd found an answer after World War II but that required adaptation. It is not simply a matter of calling for less government; there must be a statement of what government is for.'

Is it, for example, for research in the public interest? I had occasion to ask this question of the then Secretary of State for Health and Social Security in 1979, soon after the general election of that year. His answer was positive, even at the moment when his civil servants were interpreting the Conservative manifesto call for less government to include a dismantling of the government's structure for research in the health and social services. (It was not dismantled.) The point is echoed by Dr Bridget Ogilvie, the new Director and Chairman of the board of management of the Wellcome Trust, the world's richest charitable foundation, and a major supplier of funding for British medical research (see chapter 7). She warns that because of what she calls the 'ferocious and unrelenting pressure from the government', the universities are 'in danger of collapsing as research organizations'.

Guthrie believes the move towards the contract culture is a positive one. 'Until now,' he explains, 'grants have been the language with which the government speaks to the voluntary sector. I'm unhappy with this because it creates a dependence without any clear criteria. It's been bad for the voluntary sector because there are no proper criteria and there's no proper discipline. Contracts are a much better relationship.'

The former Chief Commissioner sees the advent of contracting as part of a more general change in the nature of British charities. 'They're increasingly operating as businesses,' he says, 'but although they have to be business-like, they're not like businesses. They must make sure they have their own sources of funds, and they should be allowed to earn surpluses out of contracts, so they can continue to operate as independent organizations.'

Guthrie very much approves of the legal independence of the British voluntary sector, and is at pains to emphasise the extent to which it is embedded in the constitution. 'There is a fundamental right for anyone to engage in activity for the public benefit, as defined in law,' he insists with some firmness. 'It is not a right conferred by government.' To emphasise the point, Guthrie recalled the time when the government announced plans to divest the assets of a charitable research organization it had funded. 'The trustees had already agreed, but we [the Commissioners], stepped in to prevent it. No one can interfere with the assets of a charity.'

The way charities die is of constitutional significance too, according to Guthrie. 'A charity should be wound up if it completes its purpose or loses its driving force,' he says. 'We advise charities to put in winding-up clauses, which say something about where the assets should be distributed. When the Regional Arts Associations became Regional Arts Boards, for example, winding-up clauses were included.'

A corollary of the constitutional right of Britons to engage in activities for the public benefit is that the abuse or betrayal of this privilege is peculiarly abhorrent to us. 'It's like putting sugar in the wine in France,' says Guthrie. It is for this reason that charity fraud and mismanagement is such a hot issue for the voluntary sector (see chapter 2). The arrangement, whereby the independence of the voluntary sector is enshrined in common law, will only continue to command public support if the charities maintain the utmost vigilance in the defence of their reputations for honesty and good management.

A related concern is that the 'advancement of religion' is a charitable purpose under common law. This has sometimes been a matter of some controversy, as in the cases of the Moonies and the Scientologists. 'They could be taken out completely,' Guthrie observes, 'but the established church would not like it. It does worry me, though, that an extreme sect of any religion can exploit their charitable status for political ends.'

Notwithstanding Guthrie's belief that the English system for charities is superior to systems based on some kind of Napoleonic Civil Code – and that includes Japan and much of Africa and South America, as well as all the countries of continental Europe – it is far from certain that the 'common law' system will survive.

Voluntary sectors, in nations with common law jurisdictions, like Canada, Australia and New Zealand, have ceased to regard America as a legal model because of the large amount of administrative law that has grown up around charities in that country. And some believe their allegiance to English common law will fade, too, as Britain's membership of the EC reduces the development of common law precedents. The Canadian lawyer E. Blake Bromley was against a statutory definition of charity in Canada but he urged Britain to legislate such a definition, while it can, so that a foreign definition is not enforced by default. Bromley believes it is inconceivable that the EC's civil code members will abandon their system of codifying legal principles, and that it is, therefore, inevitable that the EC will, eventually, adopt a statutory definition of philanthropy.

He believes that, in view of the welcome increase in trans-national charitable activity, as networks of charities with common aims link across borders to act in concert, it is important that Britain and America should not sit on the sidelines, and on their common law laurels, but should involve themselves in the drafting of a statutory definition of charity. Now Director of Social and Economic Affairs at the Council of Europe, Robin Guthrie is more sanguine about the survival chances of the English common law system. He says that, following a period of mutual misunderstanding, 'the English system of charity law is now attracting appreciation and respect on the continent.'

There are some new definitions in the 1992 Charities Act, but they relate to the control of fund-raising activities and add little statutory flesh to the common law bones. In Part 2 of the Act a 'charitable institution' is defined as an organization 'established for charitable, benevolent or philanthropic purposes', which leaves the meanings of the words 'charitable', 'benevolent' and 'philanthropic' secure in their common law ineffability.

Bromley observes that English-speaking common law 'purists' can take comfort from the fact that the natural place to begin a search for a statutory definition of charity is the preamble to the Elizabethan 'Statute of Charitable Uses' of 1601. Its list of purposes that were considered charitable included the relief of the aged, impotent and poor, the maintenance of schools of learning, the repair of bridges, churches and highways and the relief and redemption of prisoners.

Three centuries later, Lord MacNaghten, in his judgement in the Pemsel case of 1891, offered a classification of charity under four headings: the relief of poverty, the advancement of education and religion, and trusts established for other purposes beneficial to the community.

Developments since then that have led to the cusp of change at which the UK voluntary sector now stands (symbolized by the 1992 Act), include the 1960 Charities Act, which laid down the modern system of charity regulation, and the 1985 Charities Act (now repealed and replaced by the 1992 Act) which made it easier for small, local charities to alter their objectives and modernize their activities. There have also been a number of influential reports.

The National Council for Voluntary Organizations published a report in 1986 on *Malpractice in Fund-raising for Charity*. It blew the whistle on various dubious forms of fund-raising and recommended new law, giving greater power to the Charity Commission to deal with the problems of bogus charities and dishonest fund-raisers. In 1987, the Home Office asked Sir Philip Woodfield to carry out an *Efficiency Scrutiny of the Supervision of Charities*. He also recommended new law and more power for the Charity Commission. In the same year, the Comptroller and Auditor General published a report on the *Monitoring and Control of Charities in England and Wales* and the House of Commons Public Accounts Committee, in an outspoken report, concluded that the risk of abuse was unacceptable (see chapter 2). In January 1988 the government announced its acceptance of the Woodfield Report and its intention to legislate; a Home Office White Paper appeared the following year and, delayed somewhat by political events, this was duly transformed, via a bill and numerous amendments, into the 1992 Charities Act.

At the same time, the charity sector was starting to get to grips with its own problems. In 1977, the NCVO recruited the distinguished management thinker and writer Charles Handy to lead a management development working party for charities. It published the *Handy Working Party Report*, and led to the establishment of the NCVO's Management Development Unit.

Handy's fine book, *Understanding Voluntary Organizations*, was published in 1988, and in 1990 the NCVO published *Effectiveness and the Voluntary Sector* (alias the *Nathan Report*), which included a list of initiatives needed to increase effectiveness in voluntary organizations.

In a very real sense, therefore, the UK voluntary sector is at a new beginning. It has a new legal framework in which to work and a powerful watchdog, in the form of a strengthened Charity Commission. It has been studied, analysed and at times fiercely criticized by numerous experts and committees and has developed considerable internal momentum for reform and modernization. New people have moved into the sector, bringing with them a number of important business ideas and principles, and, at the same time, the environment in which charities operate has been changing dramatically.

Probably the most important development of all has been the beginnings of a new awareness among companies of the merits of giving, and the prospect this offers of the arrival, in what Robin Guthrie calls the Public Benefit Sector, of a new partner to contribute to the work traditionally carried out by the state and the charity sector.

Tax

When comparing the philanthropic traditions and practices in different countries it is important to recognize the crucial role played by the tax system. In the UK, charity is defined in the 1970 Income and Corporation Taxes Act as 'any body of persons or trust established for charitable purposes only'. As we have seen, charitable purposes are 'classified' rather than defined, in common law (notably in Lord MacNaghten's judgement in the Pemsel case). Generally speaking, UK charities are treated equally for tax purposes, although there is some variation in VAT.

Tax concessions for corporate giving have been extended over the years, particularly during the 1980s. Michael Fogarty and Ian Christie, in their book *Companies & Communities*, gave a list of the main landmarks:

Finance Act 1922: introduced seven-year covenanting, to stop tax avoidance by taxpayers giving to non-taxpayers who could then reclaim tax paid by the donor. The requirement to covenant for six years was designed to limit this abuse, but proved to be a stimulus for giving.

Finance Act 1965: made tax on covenanted giving, previously recoverable against income tax, recoverable against the new corporation tax at the equivalent of the standard rate of income tax.

Finance Act 1972: exempted assets transferred to charities from Capital Gains Tax.

Finance Act 1980: reduced the period required for covenants from over six to over three years, thereby introducing four-year covenanting, and reintroduced relief for donors from higher rate tax on charitable covenants.

Finance Act 1982: made payments to approved Local Enterprise Agencies tax deductible. This concession was extended, in 1990, to Training and Enterprise Councils and to Scotland's Local Enterprise Companies.

Finance Act 1983: made salary cost of temporary secondments a tax deductible business expense.

Finance Act 1986: made tax recoverable on single charitable gifts up to the equivalent of 3 per cent of gross dividends.

Finance Act 1987: made payroll giving (Give As You Earn) tax deductible, initially up to £120 a year, raised, by 1990, to £600 a year.

Finance Act 1990: introduced Gift Aid, making tax recoverable on single gifts by companies and individuals, provided that the gift was at least £600 (reduced to £400 in 1992) and that total gifts in any one accounting period do not exceed £5m.

Since the introductions of Give as You Earn (GAYE) and Gift Aid, there has been pressure from such organizations as the Charities Aid Foundation and the Directory of Social Change, to raise the ceiling on GAYE and reduce the lower limit on Gift Aid, but by and large, companies and the charity sector seem content with the general arrangements.

The voluntary sector's main concern seems to be that the new tax concessions should be marketed more actively. Many firms know so little about the concessions that they regard Gift Aid, if they have heard of it, as too complicated to bother with, whereas it is actually of exemplary simplicity. Far more needs to be done to 'sell' the new concessions, particularly payroll giving (GAYE) which has become much more widespread in America than in Britain.

Appendix

Table 1.1: Business philanthropists

Trust	People	Company (business)
Bernerd Foundation	Elliott Bernerd	(property)
Weinstock Foundation	Lord Weinstock and family	GEC
E. F. Bulmer Benevolent Fund, Howard Bulmer	Fred and Howard Bulmer	H. P. Bulmer (cider)
Charitable Trust Gosling Foundation	Sir Donald Gosling	NCP (car parks)
Alan Sugar Foundation	Alan Sugar	Amstrad
Alliance Family Foundation	Sir David Alliance	Coats Viyella (textiles)
Rudolph Palumbo Charitable Foundation	Lord Palumbo	City Acre Property
Ken and Edna Morrison Charitable Trust	Ken Morrison	W. M. Morrison Supermarkets
Rainford Trust	the Pilkington family	Pilkington (glass)
Healthcare Foundation	Richard Branson	Virgin (Mates)
Pearson plc Charity Trust	Viscount Cowdray	Pearson (holding co.)
Clark Foundation	the Clark family	(shoes)
H. Whitbread First Charitable Trust, Simon Whitbread Charitable Trust	Sam Whitbread and family	Whitbread (brewing)
John Thornton Charitable Trust, Michael Thornton Charitable Trust	the Thornton family	Thorntons (chocolate)
Sangster Charitable Foundation	the Sangster family	Sangster Group (Vernons pools)
Body Shop Foundation	Anita and Gordon Roddick	Body Shop
Forte plc Charitable Trust, Forte Charitable Trust, Lord Forte Foundation	the Forte Family	Forte (hotels etc.)
Hobson Charity	Ronald Hobson	NCP (car parks)
Vestey Foundation	the Vestey family	(meat)
B.G.S. Cayzer Charitable Trust	the Cayzer family	Caledonia Investments
Keswick Trust	Simon and Henry Keswick	Jardine Matheson
Hanson Research Trust	Lord Hanson	Hanson
Inchcape Charitable Trust	Lord Inchcape	Inchcape (trading)
Thompson Family Charitable Trust	David Thompson	Hillsdown (food)

Source: Trust Monitor (June/July 1992)

Table 1.2: Business names in the top 100 grant-giving trusts

	Assets (£m)	Income	Grants
Leverhulme Trust	330.0	10.1	11.2
Wolfson Foundation	54.7	12.4	8.6
Baring Foundation	38.6	7.2	7.3
Rank Foundation	107.5	7.6	7.2
Joseph Rowntree Foundation	131.3	10.1	6.0
Ronson Foundation	—	3.6	5.2
Nuffield Foundation	114.0	5.8	4.8
Bernard Sunley Charitable Foundation	47.1	3.5	3.2
Aga Khan Foundation (UK)	13.9	4.5	2.8
J. W. Laing Trust	24.6	2.7	2.6
Wolfson Family Charitable Trust	35.9	3.7	2.5
Philip & Pauline Harris Charitable Trust	4.9	0.7	2.4
Joseph Rowntree Charitable Trust	70.1	5.3	2.1
Sir Jules Thorn Charitable Trust	39.6	3.6	1.9
Joseph Rank Benevolent Trust	37.4	2.7	1.7
Rayne Foundation	16.1	1.9	1.6
Clore Foundation	26.5	1.9	1.5
J. Paul Getty Jnr. General Charitable Trust	23.0	1.7	1.5
Lord Ashdown Charitable Trust 1968	19.1	1.2	1.3
William Leech Foundation	14.6	1.1	1.1
Maurice Laing Foundation	11.5	1.2	1.0
Ernest Kleinwort Charitable Trust	13.2	1.0	1.0
Laing's Charitable Trust	3.3	0.9	0.9
Jane Hodge Foundation	18.4	1.2	0.8
Hedley Foundation	19.6	1.1	0.8
Djanogly Foundation	12.0	1.3	0.8
Harold Hyam Wingate Foundation	28.8	0.9	0.7
Great Britain – Sasakawa Foundation	11.3	1.0	0.7
Sir John Eastwood Foundation	9.1	0.5	0.7
Archie Sherman Charitable Trust	6.5	0.8	0.7
Milly Apthorp Charitable Trust	9.0	0.8	0.6
Dellal Foundation	4.0	0.5	0.6
Paul Balint Charitable Trust	1.1	0.1	0.6
Paul Hamlyn Foundation	50.0	3.8	0.6

Source: Charity Trends, 14th edition.

The following table shows how the total voluntary income of the UK's 200 largest charities shifted, during the six years to 1990.

Table 3.1: Proportion of voluntary income by charity segment (%)

	1984	1985	1986	1987	1988	1989	1990
Medicine and health	31.7	25.6	28.9	31.4	33.0	30.4	32.3
General welfare	23.2	19.0	20.4	21.3	20.3	20.9	21.2
International aid	20.7	34.4	25.8	21.3	19.8	21.4	20.5
Others	24.4	21.0	24.9	26.6	26.9	27.3	26.0

Source: Charity Trends, 14th edition.

This table indicates how poorly the British public rates the honesty of business people.

Table 4.1: The UK public's perception of business honesty

	Standards of honesty (%)		
	High	Low	No view
Doctors	83	2	15
Police	62	7	31
TV and radio	47	10	43
The City	22	24	54
Members of Parliament	18	23	59
Top businessmen	17	29	54
National newspapers	12	41	47

Source: 1988 Market Research Society survey

Americans feel much the same way about the ethics of their business people.

Table 4.2: The US public's perception of business ethics

	% who think business would do this
Harm the environment	47
Endanger public health	38
Sell unsafe products	37
Knowingly sell inferior goods	44
Deliberately charge inflated prices	42
Put its workers' health and safety at risk	42

A quarter of respondents said business would do all these.

Source: 1989 Harris Poll.

This table shows how eight major retail banks compare in charitable giving. The ranking criterion is the amount given per head.

Table 5.1 Generosity per head among UK banks

	Year end	Giving £'000	UK staff	Per head (£)
TSB	10.90	6,360	40,015	158.94
NatWest	12.90	13,712	95,000	144.34
Barclays	12.90	9,959	85,300	116.75
Royal Bank of Scotland	9.90	2,400	23,350	102.78
Lloyds	12.90	4,966	67,000	74.12
Midland	12.90	3,869	53,964	71.70
Bank of Scotland	2.91	955	16,100	59.32
Abbey National	12.90	830	16,500	50.30

Source: Charity Trends, 1991

Appendix

This table summarizes the involvement of the above UK banks in arts sponsorship. The ranking is by the number of involvements, not by the money involved. The columns on the far right show the actual number of involvements (A) and the total adjusted for the number of employees (Adj).

Table 5.2: Arts patronage per head among UK banks

	O	M	Da	E	Dr	Art	Fest	Lit	A	Adj
Bank of Scotland	1	11	2	–	7	2	2	–	25	69.3
Royal Bank of Scotland	3	18	1	–	–	5	1	–	28	53.4
NatWest	7	52	7	4	12	4	22	–	108	50.7
Barclays	7	14	2	1	11	12	17	2	66	34.5
Lloyds	1	16	–	1	1	4	11	1	35	23.3
Midland	2	8	2	1	5	3	3	1	25	20.7
TSB	3	2	–	–	–	8	1	1	15	16.7
Abbey National	1	–	–	–	–	–	–	–	1	2.7
Totals	25	121	14	7	36	38	57	5	303	

Key: O=Opera; Dr=Drama; M=Music; Art=Visual arts; Da=Dance; Fest=Festivals; E=Education; Lit=Literature

Source: Association for Business Sponsorship of the Arts, Annual Report, 1991. (The presentation has been modified a little, to aid comparison)

This table summarizes the pattern of giving in 1990/1 by the UK foods group United Biscuits plc

Table 5.3: United Biscuits plc's giving in 1990/1

	Amount £'000s	% of total
Seconded managers	500	34.0
Charitable donations	260	17.7
Education	240	16.3
Agencies/Trusts	140	9.5
Training	110	7.5
Liverpool Fund	100	6.8
Community organizations	60	4.1
Miscellaneous	60	4.1
Total	1,470	

Source: Community Link (United Biscuits staff journal)

This table gives figures for thirty selected charities to indicate the wide range of dependence on voluntary income, from 100 per cent to 1 per cent. It suggests the sector cannot be fully understood without an appreciation of the significance of the three other sources of income: fees and grants from central and local government; trading; and, in the case of foundations, investment income.

Table 7.1: Dependence on voluntary income

	Total income	Voluntary income	per cent
War on Want	£8.77m	£8.71m	99.3
Charity Projects	£27.82m	£27.56m	99.0
World Wide Fund for Nature	£20.78m	£18.90m	91.0
Prince's Trust	£2.38m	£2.13m	89.3
Help the Aged	£24.51m	£21.67m	88.4
Royal National Lifeboat Institution	£47.44m	£40.49m	85.3
Imperial Cancer Research Fund	£48.64m	£40.30m	82.8
Action Aid	£17.88m	£14.23m	79.6
NSPCC	£28.83m	£22.87m	79.3
RSPCA	£27.24m	£20.46m	75.1
Oxfam	£66.72m	£49.27m	73.8
Save the Children Fund	£51.94m	£36.50m	70.3
Christian Aid	£28.12m	£18.46m	65.6
Shelter	£3.46m	£2.25m	65.0
Royal British Legion	£17.65m	£11.43m	64.4
Guide Dogs for the Blind	£36.27m	£21.54m	59.4
Salvation Army	£56.57m	£29.66m	52.4
National Trust	£89.12m	£43.42m	48.7
British Red Cross	£40.89m	£19.42m	47.5
Spastics Society	£51.32m	£22.35m	43.5
Barnardos	£61.35m	£25.78m	42.0
Order of St John	£7.39m	£2.60m	35.1
Age Concern England	£11.69m	£3.78m	32.3
St Dunstan's	£10.47m	£2.98m	28.5
Mencap	£14.46m	£2.63m	18.2
Royal Opera House	£35.06m	£5.31m	15.1
Scout Association	£4.86m	£0.51m	10.5
Voluntary Service Overseas	£10.88m	£0.98m	9.0
Community Service Volunteers	£8.97m	£0.58m	6.5
Nuffield Nursing Homes	£78.97m	£0.72m	0.9

Source: Charity Trends, 13th edition

This table indicates the similarly wide range in the extent to which charities rely on income from government.

Table 7.2: Dependence on government support

	Government support	Per cent total income
Leonard Cheshire Foundation	£25.9m	72.3
Spastics Society	£24.2m	47.2
Barnardos	£23.9m	39.0
Salvation Army	£19.6m	34.6
National Children's Home	£17.7m	60.4
Royal Opera House	£14.2m	40.6
Save the Children	£11.4m	22.0
Mencap	£10.2m	70.7
Royal National Institute for the Blind	£10.0m	27.3
UNICEF	£9.1m	72.8
Voluntary Service Overseas	£9.0m	82.5
English National Opera	£8.3m	56.2
Oxfam	£8.0m	12.0
National Trust	£7.6m	8.5
British Trust for Conservation	£7.4m	85.8
British Red Cross	£6.6m	16.2
Age Concern England	£6.6m	56.3
Christian Aid	£5.8m	20.5
Welsh National Opera	£4.7m	60.7
Project Fullemploy	£3.5m	74.6
Tidy Britain Group	£1.4m	67.6
Centrepoint Soho	£0.5m	41.2
CBI Education Foundation	£0.3m	42.8
Help the Aged	£0.2m	0.8

Source: Charity Trends, 13th edition

This shows the extent to which selected charities are self-financing. 'All trading' is company-like income, including trading profit, rent, and investments. Charity shops sell donated goods so sales could be classed as voluntary income.

Table 7.3: The top twenty trading charities

£'000s Charity	Trading & sales	Rent & invest.	Charity shops	All trading	Total income	Trading per cent
Oxfam	3,648	2,985	17,800	24,469	62,078	39.4
National Trust	13,829	27,265	–	41,094	104,278	39.4
British Red Cross	9,374	3,367	883	13,624	43,873	31.1
ICRF	326	5,149	7,161	12,636	52,927	23.9
Guide Dogs	296	7,502	–	7,798	32,785	23.8
British Heart Foundation	250	5,043	–36	5,257	29,045	18.1
Spastics Society	3,470	1,272	3,297	8,039	49,150	16.4
RSPCA	–202	4,242	–	4,040	27,879	14.5
Barnardos	1,055	6,100	2,415	9,570	69,553	13.8
WW Fund for Nature	2,144	875	–	3,019	22,139	13.6
Help the Aged	1,845	829	401	3,075	28,253	10.9
Save the Children	419	3,258	1,393	5,070	52,196	9.7
Salvation Army	1,637	5,055	–	6,692	70,207	9.5
RNLI	272	4,701	–	4,973	52,720	9.4
NSPCC	501	1,690	–	2,191	28,575	7.7
Cancer Research	278	2,944	–88	3,134	49,276	6.4
RNIB	152	2,671	28	2,851	46,894	6.1
Christian Aid	–	1,582	–	1,582	31,248	5.1
Marie Curie	–	972	–	972	24,823	3.9
Action Aid	10	584	–	594	21,873	2.7

Source: Charity Trends, 14th edition.

Table 7.4: The top ten grant-making trusts

	Year	Grants £m	Income £m	Assets £m
Wellcome Trust	'90	58.4	63.0	3,250.0
Tudor Trust	'90	15.8	21.0	117.2
Gatsby Charitable Foundation	'90	11.8	7.7	198.7
Leverhulme Trust	'89	11.2	10.1	330.0
Royal Society	'87	10.1	10.1	28.9
Wolfson Foundation	'90	8.6	12.4	54.7
Henry Smith (Estates Charities)	'89	7.5	8.0	100.0
Baring Foundation	'90	7.3	7.2	38.6
Rank Foundation	'90	7.2	7.6	107.5
Monument Trust	'90	7.1	3.2	74.6

Source: Charity Trends, 14th edition.

How salaries compare in the voluntary and corporate sectors. The 'ethos discount' is a measure of how much less people of comparable rank are paid in the voluntary sector compared to the corporate sector. For instance, the chief executive of a charity with a turnover of £25–70m a year is paid on average about 62 per cent of what the chief executive of a company with much the same turnover would be paid.

Table 7.5: 'Ethos discounts' in charity pay rates

Turnover	Chief exec. (%)	Head of function (%)	Functional manager (%)	Average (%)
£1–3m	42.5	43.4	–	43.0
£3–10m	25.3	36.2	29.0	30.2
10–25m	29.1	25.1	10.0	21.4
£25–70m	38.1	16.3	18.1	24.2
Averages	33.8	30.3	19.0	27.7

Source: Charity Recruitment (1991 salary survey)

This table shows how the patterns of giving in America, by individuals, companies and foundations, and through legacies, have changed over the past decade.

In 1990 donations totalled $122.6 billion, against $115.9 billion in 1989 – an increase of 5.8 per cent, barely outpacing inflation. Giving rose by 12.1 per cent in 1988 and 10.8 per cent in 1989.

Table 10.1: USA – a decade of giving

$bn	'81	'82	'83	'84	'85	'86	'87	'88	'89	'90
Individuals	46.4	48.5	53.5	58.6	65.9	74.6	75.9	86.5	96.8	101.8
per cent growth		4.5	10.3	9.5	12.5	13.2	1.7	14.0	11.9	5.2
per cent total	83.5	81.1	82.7	82.9	82.3	82.1	81.3	82.7	83.5	83.0
Corporations	2.5	2.9	3.6	4.1	4.5	5.2	5.0	5.4	5.6	5.9
per cent growth		16.0	24.1	13.9	9.8	15.6	−3.8	8.0	3.7	5.4
per cent total	4.5	4.8	5.6	5.8	5.6	5.7	5.4	5.2	4.8	4.8
Foundations	3.1	3.2	3.6	4.0	4.9	5.4	5.9	6.2	6.6	7.1
per cent growth		3.2	12.5	11.1	22.5	10.2	9.3	5.1	6.5	7.6
per cent total	5.6	5.4	5.6	5.7	6.1	5.9	6.3	5.9	5.7	5.8
Bequests	3.6	5.2	4.0	4.0	4.8	5.7	6.6	6.5	6.9	7.8
per cent growth		44.4	−23.1	0.0	20.0	18.8	15.8	−1.5	6.2	13.0
per cent total	6.5	8.7	6.2	5.7	6.0	6.3	7.1	6.2	6.0	6.4
Total	55.6	59.8	64.7	70.7	80.1	90.9	93.4	104.6	115.9	122.6
per cent growth		7.6	8.2	9.3	13.3	13.5	2.8	12.0	10.8	5.8

Source: Giving USA

This table shows how total American giving is distributed between causes and how this pattern changed in 1990.

Table 10.2: USA – how recipients changed, 1989–90

	1989	per cent total	1990	per cent total	per cent change
Religion	62.5	54.0	65.8	53.7	5.2
Education	10.9	9.4	12.4	10.1	13.3
Human Services	11.4	9.8	11.8	9.6	3.8
Health	9.9	8.6	9.9	8.1	−0.2
Arts	7.5	6.5	7.9	6.4	5.2
Public and Social (*)	3.8	3.3	4.9	4.0	28.2
Environment	1.8	1.5	2.3	1.9	31.0
International	1.7	1.5	2.2	1.8	30.4
Others	6.3	5.4	5.4	4.4	−18.5
Total	115.9		122.6		5.8

(*)Public research and advocacy organizations, including, for example, civil liberties, abortion, traffic safety and rural development.

Source: Giving USA

This shows the pattern of Australian giving, classified by donor.

Table 10.3: Australian donors, 1988–9 (A$m)

	Donations	per cent
Individuals	838.6	49.7
Small businesses	294.6	17.5
Bequests	256.0	15.2
Large businesses	176.1	10.4
Foundations	122.0	7.2
Total	1,687.3	

Source: Australian Association of Philanthropy

This shows the pattern of Australian giving, classified by recipient.

Table 10.4: Australian recipients, 1988–9 (A$m)

	Donations	per cent
Special human services	423.6	25.1
Health	397.7	23.6
Religion	384.4	22.8
Education	189.4	11.2
General social benefit	124.4	7.4
Arts/Culture	87.8	5.2
Other	79.9	4.7
Total	1,687.2	

This illustrates the importance of company foundations in giving in Japan.

Table 10.5: Japan's big corporate givers

	Annual grants ¥m	Assets ¥m	Year Established
National Horse Racing Welfare	2,382	1,931	1969
Vehicle Commemorative	1,425	12,755	1975
Sasakawa Memorial Health	1,015	4,485	1974
Nippon Life Insurance	565	11,945	1979
Uehara Memorial	508	4,099	1985
Toyota Foundation	503	11,679	1974
Japan Foundation for Shipbuilding	491	38,526	1975
Sasakawa Peace	449	34,298	1986
Mitsubishi	348	8,955	1969
Hoso-Bunka (Broadcast Culture)	337	13,377	1974

Source: Japan Association of Charitable Corporations

This shows the breakdown of French associations. These are charity-like organizations, but they also include numerous small clubs and societies.

Table 10.6: French associations, estimated in 1989

	Numbers	per cent total
Sports, hunting, fishing	170,000	25.0
Culture/tourism and recreation	160,000	23.5
Health/social welfare	115,000	17.0
Civic/humanitarian	65,000	9.5
Economic activity	60,000	9.0
Housing/environment	55,000	8.0
Education/training	55,000	8.0
Total	680,000	

Source: Fondation de France

A better indication of the French pattern of giving is the breakdown of different types of association, according to how many salaried staff they employ.

Table 10.7: Salaried employees of French associations, 1989

	Percentage of total salaried staff in French associations
Social services	29.0
Other services	21.0
Education/research	16.0
Health	15.0
Culture/sports/recreation	8.0
'Tourism social'	7.0
Counselling/personal aid	4.0

Source: Fondation de France

At the time of writing, results of an international survey of giving, commissioned by the Charities Aid Foundation, were about to be published. The aim, according to Peter Halfpenny of the Centre for Applied Social Research at the University of Manchester, was 'to present a snapshot of the level of donations and volunteering over the same period across five countries in Europe and North America'.

This indicates the pattern of UK giving, according to how much individuals give.

Table 10.8: Levels of individual giving

	1987	1988/9	1989/90
Proportion donating	80%	78%	74%
Per cent giving £1 or less	47%	40%	49%
Per cent giving £20 or more	5%	8%	8%
Mean giving/month	£6.10	£6.92	£7.73
Median giving/month	£1.40	£1.97	£1.28
Overall giving	£3.3bn	£3.8bn	£4.2bn
Per cent mean giving of average earnings	0.72%	0.75%	0.76%

Source: Charity Household Survey

The Charities Aid Foundation, which publishes the Charity Household Survey, says mean giving is misleading because it is skewed by a very few large donations and it argues that median giving is more 'typical'. It also warns that changes in the way survey information has been collected have affected the results and that the true picture is probably somewhat less healthy than the figures suggest.

This shows how the level of giving by large UK companies has changed in recent years.

Table 10.9: Changes in giving by top corporate donors

	1988/89	1989/90	1990/91
Per cent change in real terms	–	+6	–3
as percentage of profit	0.65	0.54	0.61
Giving per employee	£52.17	£60.57	£71.57

Based on a CAF study of a sample of 100 firms.

This shows how the welfare partnership between the state and the voluntary sector has been developing in recent years.

Table 10.10: Government grants (£m) to voluntary bodies, 1984–90

	1984	1985	1986	1987	1988	1989	1990
Housing	–	–	1,090	1,049	1,138	1,075	1,681
Training	313	444	537	647	632	557	262
Others	164	213	295	322	428	396	417
Total	477	657	1,922	2,018	2,198	2,028	2,360

Source: Charity Trends, 14th edition

Bibliography

Robert Axelrod, *The Evolution of Cooperation*, Basic Books, 1984

Lord Beveridge, *Voluntary Action*, 1948

Richard Gutch, *Contracting lessons from the US*, NCVO, 1992

Bob Geldof, *Is that it?*, Sidgwick & Jackson, 1986

Pauline Graham, *Integrative Management*, Basil Blackwell, 1991

Michael Fogarty & Ian Christie, *Companies & Communities*, Policy Studies Institute, 1991

Charles Handy, *Understanding Voluntary Organizations*, 1988

H.M. Government, *Charities: A Framework for the Future*, White Paper, Cmnd. 694, 1989

Martin Knapp, *Time is Money: The Costs of Volunteering in Britain Today*, the Volunteer Centre UK, 1990

Diana Leat, *Fundraising & Grant Making: A Case Study of ITV Telethon '88*, Charities Aid Foundation, 1989

—— *Trusts in Transition*, Joseph Rowntree Foundation, 1992

Tom Lloyd, *The 'nice' company*, Bloomsbury, 1990

John Stuart Mill, *Principles of Political Economy*, 1848

Michael de la Noy, *Acting as Friends: The Story of the Samaritans*, Constable, 1987

Michael Porter, *The Competitive Advantage of Nations*, Macmillan, 1990

John Swanda, 'Goodwill, Going Concern, Stocks and Flows: A Prescription for Moral Analysis', *The Journal of Business Strategy*, Autumn 1989

Sir Peter Thompson, *Sharing the Success*, Collins, 1990

Edward Wallis, *Explaining Christian Stewardship*, Church Information Office, 1962

Professor Ken Young, *Meeting the Needs of Strangers*, Gresham College, 1991

Index

Main references are denoted by bold figures